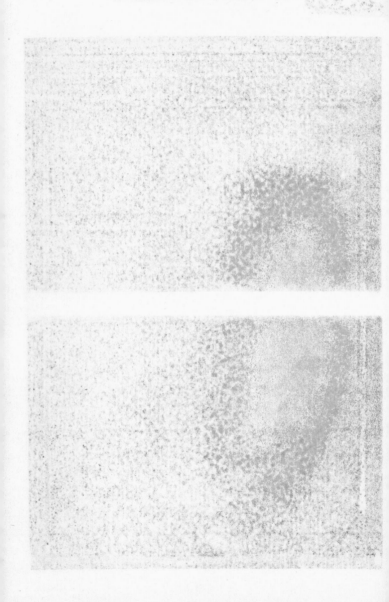

# ENGLISH RECUSANT LITERATURE
## 1558–1640

*Selected and Edited by*
**D. M. ROGERS**

## Volume 148

## THOMAS DORMAN

*A Request
to M. Jewell
1567*

## JOHN FRASER

*An Offer
Made to a Gentleman
of Qualitie
1605*

## JEAN PIERRE CAMUS

*A Discours
1630*

# THOMAS DORMAN

*A Request*
*To M. Jewell*
*1567*

The Scolar Press
1973

ISBN 0 85417 963 1

*Published and Printed in Great Britain by*
*The Scolar Press Limited, 20 Main Street,*
*Menston, Yorkshire, England*

## NOTE

The following works are reproduced (original size), with permission:

1) Thomas Dorman, *A request to M. Jewell*, 1567, from a copy in Lincoln Cathedral Library, by permission of the Dean and Chapter.

*References*: Allison and Rogers 276; STC 7063.

2) John Fraser, *An offer made to a gentleman of qualitie*, 1605, from a copy in the library of St. Mary's Seminary, Oscott, by permission of the President.

*References*: Allison and Rogers 348; STC 11337.

3) Jean Pierre Camus, *A discours hapned betwene an hermite called Nicephorus & a yong lover called Tristan*, 1630, from the unique copy in Cambridge University Library, by permission of the Syndics.

*References*: Allison and Rogers 194; STC 4551.

# A REQVEST

## To M. Iewell.

*That he kepe his promise, made by so-*
lemne protestation in his late sermon at *Pauls Crosse* the. 15. of *Iune.*
Anno. 1567.

*By Thomas Dorman, Bacheler of*
*Diuinitie.*

*LOVANII,*
*Apud Ioannem Foulerum.*
*Anno D. 1567.*

Regiæ Maiestatis Priuilegio concessum est Thomæ Dormáno sacræ Theologiæ Baccalaureo, vt libellũ inscriptum, *A Request to M. Iewell &c.* per Typographum aliquem iuratum imprimere, ac impunè distrahere liceat.

*Datum Bruxellis die 1. Sept. an. 1567.*

*Subsig.*

*De la Torre.*

# A REQVEST TO M.

Iewel that he kepe his promiſe,
*made by ſolemne Proteſtation in his*
late ſermõ at Paules croſſe.
the 15.of Iune, 1567.

*OVR late Sermon pro-*
*nounced at Poules Croſſe*
*the 15 s of Iune laſt, hath*
*miniſtred( M.Iewel )much*
*matter to diuerſe men di-*
*uerſely to diſcourſe thereupon.*

*Some there are with whome as you*
*are in ſuch credite, that they beleue ve-*
*rely eche worde that proceedeth from*
*youre mouthe , to beare for truthe the*
*weight of the Ghoſpell: ſo they thinke*
*it aſſuredlie impoſſible , that that holie*
*mouthe of youres , that perfumed your*
*whole Auditorie at the beginning with*
*this moſt ſweete and fragrant ſauour,*
Humiliamini ſub potenti manu Dei ,
*Humble your ſelues vnder the mightie*
*power of God : could in any wiſe breath*
*vpon them any ſtinking blaſt of vaine*
*glorie .*

A ij Some

Some other more wise, and yet your frindes to no lesse then those, wish that either you had chosen (to preach vpon) some other Theme, or had left the same to be handled by some other man, whose person it might haue becommed better than yours, or at the lest had not applied the same so particularly to your own perso as you haue. For they see (which I trust anon to make all men see) that the more you stirre this mater, of iustifieing your selfe, and accusing of others, the worse it sauoureth: the more you struggle and striue to get out of this gogmire, where-into you are falle, the deeper you sinke in.

Other some (for I can hide nothing from you) saie and mainteine stoutely, that your humiliamini to your audiece, is no better then was the foxes pax vobis, when he preached (as the tale goeth) to the geese: and that you meane most ear-nestly with this hypocrites cloke of dis-sembled humility, to betraie to the diuel the soules of your hearers. This latter

opinion

*opinion pincheth you sore , and it stan-*
*deth you vpon not to contemne it , but to*
*haue an eye thereunto .The which that*
*you may the better doe , remember whose*
*wordes these are:*Nowe here I protest
before God: my consciéce is free and
clene frō al falshod that euer I vttred:
yet I am a mā, ād may be deceiued, ād
if there be any such (error)this mouth
shal cōfesse it, ād this hand shal retract
it:they would be loth to cōfesse their
errours: they seeke to glory in theyr
fleashe.

M.Ievvll
in his ser
men at
Paules
crosse.
an 1567.
.15. Iunij.

    *Is your conscience , say you , free and*
*cleane from all falsehoode that euer you*
*vttred ? Nowe surely then haue you as*
*strange and as large a conscience, as euer*
*I hearde of , or rather no conscience at*
*all. For of so manie hundres of vntru-*
*thes, wherewith by diuerse men you re-*
*main charged in printe, to chose one , the*
*rather because your selfe haue choosen*
*it in this Sermon of yours , I praie you*
*Syr tell vs , howe youre Protestation,*

M. D.
Harding
225.
M.D.
Sander
218.
M.Sta-
pletō.561
M.Rastel

*A iij    and*

and the euident corruption of the Councel of Carthage agree together.

You knowe you haue alleaged it, aswell
in your sermon and Replie pag. 153. a. pri-
uately, as in your Apologie together with
others to proue, that nothing may be
read in the Churche but Scriptures.
And yet you coulde not be ignorant, if
euer you sawe the place in the Original,
that there foloweth, immediatly, sub nomine diuinarum Scripturarum, vnder
the name of diuine scriptures: whiche
wordes you cut of cleane, as you concea-
led also the latter parte of the Canon,
where is an other exception, directlie
making against that for the which you
alleaged it, that is, that besides the scriptures, the Legendes or Passions of
Martyrs may also be read, when their
yearely Feastes are kept: which thing
you denie.

Howe say you nowe once againe? Is
your conscience free from this false-
hode, when in your last Sermon you tell
onely

*onely your Audiēce, that M.D.Harding*
*chargeth you with the omitting of these*
*last wordes of the Canon* : Legi etiam
possunt vitæ Martyrum, *and make no*
*mentiō, howe he also burdened you with*
*the cutting of, of those wordes that fo-*
*lowed nexte, and made perfite the sen-*
*tence*, Sub nomine Diuinarum Scripturarum ? *Is your conscience free and*
*cleane from this false tricke also ?*

*Ye say that it is*. For M.D. Harding
is deceiued. For we alleage not this
place out of the Coūcel of Carthage,
but out of the Councell of Hippo,
being an extracte of that Councel of
Carthage.

M.Iewlls
foule
shifte,

*Marie sir, nowe you saie somewhat in*
*deede, if this be true. For then is M.D.*
*Harding fowly deceiued, and I to before*
*him, who firste charged you with this*
*foule plaie of all other in writing. But*
*what if M. Harding be not deceiued?*
*What if in your challeng at Poules Crosse*
*committed afterward to the printe, as*

The de-
tection
of it.

A iiij *in your*

## A REQVEST

in your late Replie, there be no mention
of the Councell Hyppo, but onelie of the
third Councel of Carthage? What if your
Apology haue these words: Vetus Con-
cilium Carthaginense iubet, ne quid
in Sacro cœtu legatur præter Scriptu-
ras Canonicas. The olde Councell of
Carthage commaundeth, that nothing be
readen in the holie assemblie, beside the
canonicall Scriptures? What if your booke
be thus quoted in the Margent to direct
the Reader to the place, Tert.Carthag.
cap. 47? What if the Council of Hyppo
were before that of Carthage, as it was,
and so could be no extract of that which
folowed after it? What if Hyppo be not
Carthage, nor Carthage, Hyppo.
but be two diuerse Cities in Africa, as
London and Yorcke are in England?
Is your conscience for all this free and
cleane from this falsehoode, thus by you
at the firste vttered, and nowe at the
laste moste grosselie and impudentelie
excused? Surelie if it bee, then may
a man

See the
Apology
both in
latine ãd
english.

*a man boldelie saie, that you are vtterly
geuen ouer of God.*

*You pretende and proteste in Pul-
pite, that if you haue vttred anie falsehoode*, your mouthe shall confesse it,
and your hande shall retracte it . *But
what hope there is of suche promise,
when to defende this false and vntrue
dealing of yours, you labour to make
men beleue, that your bookes which are
to bee seene and readen of all men haue*
Hyppo , *whereas they haue* Carthage:
*I report me to the iudgement of the ho-
nest and learned.*

An ex-
ample of
M. Iewels
humility
in retra-
cting his
errours.

*Howe is it credible , that you will
euer yealde to the Scriptures , Coun-
celles , or Doctours brought againste
you, when your owne woordes be not
hable to conuince you? For if your bookes haue ,* Carthage , *as they haue,
howe is then ᴄMaister Doctour Harding deceiued, who chargeth you with
the place, euen as your selfe haue alleaged it?*

This must
nedes be
correc-
ted, and
for M.
Harding
your
mouthe
must cō-
fesse that
M. Ieuell
vvas de-
ceiued.

*But*

But yet if your boke had Hippo, and not
Carthage, if this taken out of the councel of Hippo were an extracte of that
of Carthage, as I haue shewed it coulde
not be, this Councell of Hippo being
holden before that Coūcel of Carthage:
yet could not your conscience, if it were
like to other mennes, be free and cleane
from falsehoode in the iudgement of the
learned and wise: Who woulde easelie
perceiue, that your shoonning of the ori-
ginall copie, where the decree is to be
sene at large, and claiming by an vnper-
fect extracte, where is nothing but a
collection of the sommes of the chapitres
and decrees whiche the Fathers of that
Coūcel made, not the decrees thēselues,
could not procede of good meaning.

Thus are you euerie waie taken, and
proued to haue wittingly vttred falshod.
Let your mouthe then confesse it, and
your hand retracte it. Let your tongue
tel the truth, that your mouthe made an
execrable lye, when you protested before
Go d

*God*, that your conscience was free
and cleane frō al falshod that euer you
vttred. *God saue all good men from suche*
*a conscience. If you had as good a sto-*
*macke to digest your meate that you re-*
*ceiue, as you haue a liberal and large cō-*
*science in vttring of falsehod, you might*
*eate horseshewes and take no harme.*

   *You knowe with howe manie vntrue*
*pointes M.D. Harding chargeth you. You*
*knawe, that M. D. Sander, M. Rastel, and*
*M. Stapletòn (who hath traced you fur-*
*der then anie other )haue done the lyke.*
*You knowe your vntruthes amounte to*
*the number of at housande and moe. And*
*yet in all these is your consciēce free and*
*cleane? Loe what it is to lacke a spiced*
*and a superstitiouse conscience. Hold you*
*then here M Iewel, and you are safe. For*
*no man can (well you wote)looke into*
*your conscience to comptroll you.*

   *But in case your cōscience were cleane*
*and free in this one false tricke , yet is it*
*in all the rest laied to your charge loked*
                    *for*

*for at your handes, that you discharge*
*your promise in confessing, and retra-*
*cting . For whereas you saie, that your*
mouthe shall confesse, and your hand
shal retracte it, *if there be any suche*
falsehod vttered, *as men woulde that*
*you answered directly, whether you haue*
*vttered any suche or no : so would they*
*without al Shalls, that you discharged*
*your promise presently. For your shals are*
*not, I tell you so good payment, as Vlpi-*
*ans copper monie, that you speake of in*
*your Sermon. And yet you, dissimbling* The pas-
*so manie hundreds of vntruthes, as are* sing ims
*noted in your writtinges, as though no* of M.
*one had bene yet proued against you, say* Ievvell.
*to your audience,* and if there be anie
suche, this mouth, shal confesse it &c.
*adding:*that we would be loth to confesse our errours, that we seke to glorie in our fleshe. *And thus al men are*
*paied at once in one grosse summe.*

*O M. Iewel, this pharisaical iustifiyng of*
*your selfe, and accusing of vs as sinful, and*
*proude*

*proud Publicās, might haue bene spared, til you had cōfessed at the least one of your so many vntruthes hūbly and penitently. It commeth now altogether out of season: especially, whē for any that you haue yet cōfessed, al the world seeth, we are as farr forward in this kinde of humility, as you. Neither is there any hope, that you wil hūble yourself furder, then you haue, cōsidering the foule shifties that you vse to defende your corrupting of the Councell of Carthage by.*

*But to be shorte, if you mind good faith, if you meane not to deceiue the world with shalls, if you wil at the length geue vs the swete kernel of humilitie to fede vpon, by cōfessing your errours and false trickes, then out of hand Confesse.*

*First, that you haue corrupted moste shamfully the third councel of Carthage.*

*Then, that you haue committed a fouler faulte in the impudēt defendig thereof ( against your own alleaging of it ) at Poules crosse, in so honorable an audiēce.*

*Thirdly*

13
The. 3.
Coūc. of
Carthage
mangled
by M.
Ievvel.

2.
He be-
lieth him
selfe.

3.

In the Replie pag. 9.

Thirdly, that in your Reply to the first Article, you haue most miserablie belied that auncient father and learned doctor S. Augustine. For it can not be gathered by him in his 11. booke contra Faustum, that anie parte of Abdias should be written by the Manichees : whiche yet you father vpon him.

4.

S. Aug. 4. times belied by M. leuvel in lesse then a quarter of one side of a leafe.

Confesse, that he accounteth not the storie of S. Thomas (quoted by you lib. 22. cap. 80. but indeede . 79. contra F. Manich.) to be a fable, as you haue reported him to saie: but contrarywise that he suspendeth his iudgement thereof in the verie same chapiter.

5.

Also that he maketh not so much as once mention in the booke and chapiter by you quoted, of S. Mathewe, or S. Andrewe, muche lesse reporteth there of the anie fables, as you saie he doth.

6.

Acknowledge your faulte in mangling these true woordes of S. Augustine. Cõsidre in the acts of Leucius which he writeth vnder the name of the Apostles

poſtles, what thinges they be that are written of Maximilla &c. *Hewing thē after this ſorte*: Beholde what thinges they be, that be writtē of Maximilla: *Leuing out cleane the name of Leucius, wherby it might haue appeared, that not* Abdias , *(whom in theſe woordes you would make S. Auguſtine to note ) but* Leucius *was the authour of this fable.*

Cōfeſſe, which by no colour can be ex-cuſed, that you haue moſt impudently be-lyed Abdias, *in ſaying* that he hath re-ported in greate ſooth the bawdry of Maximilla, *of whom in all his ſtorie he hath no one word ſounding that waies: but contrariewiſe geueth her the praiſe* of a vertuouſe and godly matrone.

7.
Abdias
belied.

*Confeſſe, that to proue your purpoſe, that the daily ſacrifice of the Church is not the holy Maſſe, but onlie praier and thanckes geuing, you haue corrupted that auncient Father Ireneus , by tur-ning the worde* quoque, *alſo, into* quo-tidie, *daily.* Lib. 4. cap. 34. in fine.

8.
Ireneus
falſified.

Replie
pag. 24.
Lin. 32.

*Confeſſe*

Replie.
pag.36.
Lin.30.
9.
Cyprian
falselie
alleaged.
10.

*Confesse, that you alleage out of S.Cyprian,* De cœna Domini, *a saying which he hath not. Confesse, that labouring to proue by Chrysostome, that the Musse is called a sacrifice, because it is a samplar of that bloudy sacrifice offred vpõ the crosse which we denie not, you alleaging for*

Chryso-
stome
mangled

*that purpose,* hoc autem sacrificium exemplar est illius : *this sacrifice is a samplar of that, haue quilefullie nipped away the next words folowing,* id ipsum sem-

Replie.
pag 65.

per offerimus. Nec nunc quidē aliuṁ agnum, craſtina aliū, sed semper eundem ipsum. proinde vnuṁ eſt hoc sacrificium hac ratione. *We offer alwaies the same Sacrifice ( he meaneth, that was offered vppon the Crosse)neither do we offer nowe one Lambe, and to morow an other, but alwaies the same.Therfore for this reason is this sacrifice one.*

*Confesse ( notwithſtanding your Proteſtation before God , that your conscience is free and cleane from all falschoode that euer you vttred) that*

yes

*yet here notwithstanding you foresawe,*
*that if you should haue alleaged Chryso-*
*stome wholly, it would haue appeared,* Id ipsum
*that the sacrifice which we offer, is both* semper of
*a sampler of the sacrifice offred vpon the* ferimus.
*crosse, and the same sacrifice it selfe: and*
*that your foule lie that you made vppon* pag. 65.
*Chrysostom, surmising him to say, that the* lin. 16.
*sacrifice of the church is but one, because*
*it hath relatiō to that one sacrifice of*
*Christ, would haue bene discouered by* Proinde
*the true reason that Chrysostome geueth* vnum est
*him selfe, which is, because we offer al-* hoc sacri-
*waies the same sacrifice, not one lābe* ficiũ hac
*now, an other to morow, ād that ther-* ratione.
*fore you thought it good policy, to preuēt*
*the mater somewhat before.*

    *Confesse, that you haue belyed the same* Chryso-
*Chrysostō by imagining him to say (which* stome
*he neuer said) of Masses, that they please* beelied.
*not God, that they prouoke his angre,* Replie
*that they are all in vaine.* pag. 92.

    *Confesse, that like a false make bate, to* 12.
*make strife where none is, betwē Scotus* Scotus
             B     and

## A REQVEST

Replie.
pag. 34.
and M.D.Harding, you misreport Scotus in leauing out the word simpliciter, simplie or absolutly, which word set in maketh theyr sayinges to agree.

13.
S. Paule
falsified.
pag. 194.
1, Cor, 14
Confesse, that in your Replie to the 3. article, you haue falsified euen S. Paule him selfe. Whose words being: Qui supplet locum idiotæ, quomodo respõdebit Amen, he that occupieth the rome of the ignorant, how shal he answer amē: you turne it, how shal the ignorant say Amen? As though S. Paule had spoken of the ignorāt him self, and not of him that supplieth the rome of the ignorant, or as though ther were no difference in those two phrases at all.

14.
The laste
vvord of
S. Ambr.
cut of.
pag. 176.
15.
Liberat'
mangled
Confesse, that in S. Ambrose brought by you to proue, that the Hebrewes and Syrians vsed the publike seruice of theyr Church in the vulgar tongue, you haue cut awaie the laste word of the sentence ad commendationē for a vaine glorie: In Liberatus also you haue nipped of the last word Quodammodo, after a sorte.

The

*The whiche woordes of what weight they are in both those places, I refer you to M. Stapletõ to know. Although by your self it semeth they weighed heauy: for al the sentéce before you were able to beare awaie, but those two poore woordes you were not able to stirre.*

Replie? pag. 287.
In the Returne of vn= truthes. Art. 3. pa .95. a. Art. 4. pa. 155. a.

*Confesse, that you haue plaied the like part with Innocentius the thirde, omit=ting in your englishe these words which are in the latine, to minister the Sacra=ments of the Church. Whereupon all=though you knew the answer to the place to depéde, yet before God your cõsciéce is free and cleane of this falsehod, if a man may belieue you.*

id. Innocen= tius. 3. mãgled. Replie. pag. 177. See the Returne Art. 3. pag. 98.

*Confesse, that you haue vntruly fathe=red vpon Theodoret, that S. Paule prea=ched in England immediatly after his first deliuery in Rome. For Theodoret, in the place by you alleagéd, saieth no such thing.*

29. Theoret belyed.

*Confesse, that you haue most wickedly slãdered our blessed Apostle S. Austine,*

Replie pag. 190. 191

B ij   calling

Our Apostle hainously slaûdred. Returne of vntruthes Art. 3. fo. 130. b

19.
S. Basile falûfied. Replie. pag. 279.

calling him, an hypocrit, a superstitious man, cruel, bloudy, and proud aboue measure, *fathering al those words vpon Geffrie of Monmouth* , *wheras the saied Geffry hath no one such word.*

Confesse, that you haue falsified S. Basile alleging his 48. epistle. Where *you say he* hath, that the state and saufetie of the church of Antioch depédeth of Athanasius the B. of Alexandria, and not of the B. of Rome. *Where these later wordes,* and not of the B. of Rome, *are not to be sene, nor els where in his workes.*

20.
Bonifac. slaûdred. Replie. pag. 311. Lin. 1. Epist. 87. ad ep. Viē nens. prouinc.
So reade the copies prited at Paris

Confesse, that you haue moste shamefully sclaundered Bonifacius, the Pope, to whose charge you laie that he should say, God tooke Peter in consortium indiuiduæ Trinitatis, *into the felowship* euē *of the indiuisible Trinitie: whereas* both Leo the first, of whō Bonifacius borowed this sentēce, and the Canon texte which you allege, reade vnitatis, *not* trinitatis, *vnity, not trinity, without any word that signifieth* euē, *which you* euē *according*

*according to your malicious nature haue*
*here shuffled in. Retract this foule corru-*
*ptiō for shame, or shew what strāge copy*
*you haue more thē your neighbours, that*
*answereth so iustly to your spiders nature.*

Cōfesse *that in the place that you allege*
*out of Leo his. 24. epistle to Theodosius*
*the Emperour, you steale out of the whole*
*sentence these wordes :* Et quia nostri
fideliter reclamârūt. *Because you would*
*not, that your Reader shoulde vnder-*
*stand, that Flauianus offered vp his bille*
*of Appeale to the Popes Legates . For*
*the better vnderstanding wherof I re-*
*ferre you to the Returne.*

Confesse, *howe you haue mangled and*
*martyred the woordes of Alexander*
*that blessed Pope and Martyr, his wordes*
*being:* In Sacramentorum quoque ob-
lationibus &c. *With the oblations also*
*which are offred to our Lord in the so-*
*lemnities of the Masse, the Passion of*
*Christ must be mingled: you leauing out*
*quite* the solemnities of the Masse, *say,*

B iij      *the*

by Ker-
uer. anno
1505. at
Lyons
1519. by
Franc.
Frad. and
at Parys
by Gul.
Merlin.
an. 1561.

21.
Leo cor-
rupted.
Replie.
289.
Returne.
Art. 4.
fol. 163. b

22.
Alexāder
corrup-
ted.
Replie.
pag. 342.

*the Passion of Christe muste be mingled with the oblations of the Sacramentes.*

23.
S. Hilar.
charged
by M.
Ievvel.
vntruely
vvith
heretical
vvordes.
Replie.
pag. 34 4.

*Confesse the wrong that you haue done to Hilarius, whom you hurde vntruly to haue saied in his .8. booke* De Trinitate, *that we are one with God the father, and the Sonne, not only by adoptio or consent of mind, but also by nature. Which words are not to be found in him. And if they were, they should cōteine a blasphemous heresy. For they import that a Christiā man is cōsubstantial with God, and a very God by nature. Confesse, that wheras S. Austen saieth of Idolles:* Ft Idola quidē omni sensu carere, quis dubitet? Verūtamē cū his locātur sedibus, &c And as for idolles who doubteth, that they are without all sense ? But whē they be set vp in these places in honorable heigth, that they that pray or sacrifice mai loke vpō thē, although they haue neither sense nor soule, yet euē with the very proportiō of liuing mēbres they moue weake minds, that

24.
S. Aug.
miseras
bly cor-
rupted.
Replie.
pag. 514.

they

they seme to haue life ād draw breath,
especially the worshiping of the multitude, wherby so great godly honour
is geuen to them, being ioyned there-
withal. *Confesse, I say, seing that S. Austen so plainely speaketh of idolles, and of
godly honor don to thē by the multitude,
that you haue falsified this place, first by
putting Images in the place of Idols: thē
for the more cleanly conueyance by crop-
ping away the first part of the sentence,
leaste by the worde, Idola, being the
nominatiue case to the verbe locantur,
your iuggling might haue bene espied:
thirdely by leauing out the latter parte
of the sentence for the like cause, whereby might haue appeared, that, whether
they where Images or Idolles, that S.
Augustine spake of, they had godly honor geuen to them, which we allow not.*

*Confesse also, that in the same place you*     25.
*haue again falsified S. Aust. in turnīg his
words,* simulacra gētiū, *the idols of the
gētils, into,* these images *of the christiās.*

B iiĳ     Nowe

# A REQVEST

*Nowe M. Iewell by that great humility of yours I requier you, seing the mater is plaine without al ifs or ands, that you haue falsified the holy scriptures, māgled and corrupted the Councells, belied the Fathers and Doctours of Christes Church: let your mouth confesse (your Protestation alwaies reserued: for it may be, that these thinges slipped from your penne, and leapte into your booke, in which case your conscience must needes be cleane and free from al falsehod, whē you were asleepe and thought no harme) Let your hand retracte these scapes and ouersightes, as you haue promised they should, and that (if you disdeine not to folowe a poore mans conuceil,) before your booke that is vnder the presse, come into the light to shewe it self. Otherwise your merchandize will be more then halfe marred. For men will iudge your wares to bee like your other, and wilbe loth to deale with such a banckrout marchant. When you haue done with these,*

*you*

*you shall haue more, that you may haue more occasiō to merite, by exercising such workes of humility.*

*As for my selfe, whome you burden with alleaging the 7. booke of Theodoret whereas he wrote but .5. and for calling OZa king: beig but a Prophete, as the last I cōfesse to be a scape, so the first is on my parte none. For I must discharge my selfe of that, and charge the Prīter, who for a figure of .5. placed a figure of .7. which I reporte me to the margent of the .9. side of your Reply, whether it be a thing that may easely happē or no. Where your prin-ter, or you, haue for the .79. chap. of the 22. booke of S. Austē against Faustus, the .80. chap. for the 17. against Adimātus the .16. for the .38. chap.* de fide contra Mani-chæos, *the .30. three times in one poore side. Yet no man crieth it in open sermon, that our late brother Iewel hath alleaged one chapter for an other. Our late brother* Iewel hath alleged Athanasius, for Libe rius, the Arrians, for the Eutichiās, both*

Replie pag. 129.

*in*

*in one side of a leafe also. When yet all his*
*authours haue the contrarie, as greate a*
*faulte I trowe, as the calling of Oza king,*
*who was but a Prophet: especially seing*
Liberius *could not be* Athanasius *, but a*
*Prophet might be a king. Well you muste*
*take such pety faultes, or els none: and yet*
*these you borowed of* M. Nowel, *to whō al*
*though you had holdē your peace, by Gods*
*grace I wuld haue made answer in time.*

The fal-
shod of
M. leuell
in char-
ging of
D. Har-
ding.

But in *M. D.* Harding *you haue*
*noted other maner of faultes.* He saieth
the coūcel of Nice was holdē in Pope
Syluesters time wheras Athanaſ. that
was present at it, sayth it was in Iulius
time. *What if it wer ī both their times as*
*the late coūcel of Trent was holdē in Pau*
*lus the. 3. Iul. the. 3. ād Pius the 4. times?*
*And so Cōtarenus thinketh that this coū*
*cel was somoned by Syluester, and ended*
*by Iulius. How euer it be,* D. Harding *is*
*not the firſt author of this opiniō.* Euseb.
in Chrō. Damaſus in Pōt. Platina, Rhegi-
no in Chron. Iſidorus Hyſpalēſis, Sabellic.
Gaſpar

*GaſparCõtarenus,your own brother Pãta*
*leõ,ãd the words of the ſubſcriptiõ of the* Iſid.in
*coũcel,yea the whole ſixt general coũcel* praſat.
*alſo,haue vttred thꝭ before D.Harding.* Nic. Cõc.
*And ſhal it be then any vntruthe in D.* Syn.6.
*Hardꝭng to ſay ſo,after ſo many and ſo au-* Act.18.
*thentike witneſſes? Againe,you ſay very*
*fiercely.* Harding allegeth the Decades
of Sabellicus,and yet Sabellicus neuer
made Decades , but Aeneades. *The*
*more fiercely,the more foliſhly.Be not ſo*
*haſty mã vpõ your game. What ſhall I cal*
*thꝭ: Raſheneſſe,Ignorãce,or Impudẽcy?*
*Loke again inSabellicus,ãd you ſhal find,*
*that he wrote both* Decades, *and* Aeneades. *Of hꝭ* Rapſodia *he made* En-
neades , *of the ſtorie of the Venetians*
*Actes, he made* Decades : *and out of*
*thatſtorie ꝭ D. Hardꝭngs allegation ta-*
*ken. He hath noted truly the booke ,the*
*Decade ,the Page. Conferre hꝭ booke*
*with Sabellicus printed at Baſile , and*
*you ſhall finde hꝭ doeinges in that be-*
*halfe to be true , and your ſelfe to be*
*a ſaucy*

a saucy finder of a faulte where none is, and an impudent lyer, who in the seat of truthe, in the presence of honorable and learned, at that time when you reproue falsehood in other, haue made so lowde and impudent a lye your selfe.

These be the great errours and foule faulties, that you haue noted in M.D. Harding and me. Which if you had not first proclaimed at Poules Crosse, you could neuer haue ben deliuered of that faire babe of yours, that you are nowe in trouaile of. But I trust by that time you haue pfour med your promise in cõfessing and retra-cting these fewe false trickes, that I haue here laied before you: it shal appere to the wiser, whether a figure of s. for. 7. by the Printers fault, or the calling of a prophet King: or the saying that Sabellicus wrote Decades, when he neuer wrote any, or that the Coũcel of Nice was holdẽ vnder Siluesier, not vnder Iulius: if al this wer true, it shal, I saie, appeare, whether such errours and those other that you in your

Sermon

*Sermō laie to the charge of the Fathers,
Clemēt, Ireneⁿ and Chryſoſtom, thinking
you may ſalue one ſore ʋvith an other, be
like to the falſiſyng, māgling and hewing
of Scriptures, Coūcels and Doctors, ſo cō-
mōly and cōtinualiy vſed by you: and that
alwaies to ſuch aduantage, that ʋvithout
ſuch lewd ordering of thē, they ʋvould in
plaine ʋvordes, not only not relieue your
cauſe, but ſlatly and roūdly ouerthrow the
ſame. If they be not: then may al mē ſee,
that you are far from that humility that
you brag ſo much of, ād that you mind no-
thīg leſſe, then once to retract any thing.*

*You charge M.D. Harding ʋvith the
defenſe of the Stewes, his booke from the
.160. leaſe. b. ʋvhere he beginneth to en-
treate of the courtiſanes of Rome, to the
leaſe.164. ʋvhere he endeth that matter,
anſwereth ſufficiently for him . I neede
not to ſay thereof any more . Onely I ſay,
you ſhamefully belye him. For he defen-
deth not the Stewes, but partly ſheweth
the neceſſity of ſuch a miſchief, to auoyde
a further*

Confutation of the apoſlogic.

# A REQVEST

a furder inconuenience euen by the doctrin of holy S. Austen, partly detecteth
your great lying therein, who reporte it
worse then it is in dede.

As for Purgatory and Pardōs, reason
me thinketh would you should first answer the bokes therof learnedly writtē,
of purpose in our englishtonge, beforeyou
foūd faulte with D. Hardig for defending
them. I maruell not though you cal Purgatory fire, cold: considering that you are
a scholer of his schoole, that sticketh not
to call helfire, colde: or rather saieth,
and saieth in dede, that there is there nō
fire at al. Which persuasion, I seare me,
maketh you and others, such marchant
venturers as you are. You maie saie, as
please you, but S. Austen saieth contrary
to you: that Purgatory, which he calleth
the correcting or purging fier, is more
grieuouse, then any paine that a man
can suffer in this life: and condemneth
your maisters doctrine of helfier to. And
therefore if S. Austens credite be grea-

ter

By M.
Allen.

Caluin in
10.cap.
ad Hebr.

Tom.8.
In psal..
37.prope
initium.
Ignis emē
datorius.

ter then yours, this is an other errour to
be retracted.

    Now to conclude M. Iewel, according
to your promise once againe I requier you
that your mouthe maie confesse, and
your hand retracte these foule errours
of yours, the which to that respect I present here vnto you, that men may see you
first practise in your selfe, that which you
comende to other. Otherwise you are like
to heare, that Diabolus nunquam se
prodit aperta facie, the diuel neuer sheweth him selfe in his owne likenesse, that
Diabolus cogitauit nouã fraudẽ, vt sub
nomine Christi fallat simplices, the
diuell hath inuẽted a newe deceyte, vnder the name of Christe to entangle the
simple. That you praise humilitie, as Nero
did his mother, when after he had slaine
her, and embrewed his handes in her
bowelles, he wrote yet of her in all the
windowes of his house: optimã matrẽ, a
very good mother. I trust these thinges
considered, you will at the lenght crie:

donne

De ciuit.
Dei li.21
cap. 9.
& .10.

Hieron.

Cyprian.

doune great harte, and humble your selfe
vnfeinedlie, to the mightie hand of God,
Which lieth so heauie vpon you, by afflicting you for your insolent and blasphemouse challenge, by that lyeing sprite,
Whom once he permitted to deceiue the
*3.reg.22.* Prophets of King Achab, that of al those
that are straied from the vnitie of the
Church, and haue written againste the
same, ther is no one mã that is more grieuously pressed therewith, then you. The
Which that you may earneftly and speedely do, I beseche him, that saieth, discite à me, quia mitis sum & humilis corde, *Learne of me: for I am meeke and
humble of harte,* to geue you the grace.

*Math.11.*

*Amen.*

*Tho. Dorman.*

Libellus iste lectus & approbatus est à
viris Sacræ Theologiæ, & Anglici idiomatis peritissimis: quare tutò imprimendum esse iudico.
Cunerus Petri, P.S. Petri
Louanij 30, Auguft.

# JOHN FRASER

*An Offer
Made to a Gentleman
of Qualitie
1605*

AN
# OFFER MADE TO A
## GENTLEMAN OF QVA-
litie by M. Iohn Fraser, to subcribe and
embrace the Ministers of Scotlands religion, if they can sufficientlie proue, that
they haue the true kirk and lawful calling.

*VVHERETO AR ADIOYNED CER-*
*taine reasons and considerations concerning theis*
*tvvo heades and foundations, vvithout the*
*light of vvhich others can not be cleared,*
*nor assured ground in religion in*
*these dayes established.*

*Nevvlie corrected and set forth, vvith the*
*aduise of the author.*

Ad ipsam salutem ac vitam æternam nemo per-
uenit, nisi qui habet caput Christum Habe-
re autem caput Christum nemo poterit, nisi qui in eius corpore
fuerit, quod est Ecclesia.
*D. Augustinus.*

## Permissu Superiorum.

### M. DC. V.

Munus beatæ vitæ non nisi intra Ecclesiam reperitur, quæ super petram
etiam fundata est, quæ ligandi & sol-
uendi claues accepit. Hæc est vna quæ
tenet & possidet omnem sui sponsi &
Domini potestatem, perquam coniu-
galem potestatem etiam de ancillulis
filios parere potest: qui si non superbiant, in sortem hæreditatis vocabuntur:
si autem superbiant, extrà remanebunt.

*D. Augustinus. Tract. 27. in Ioan.*

Quisquis ille est, & qualiscunque ille
est, Christianus non est, qui in Christi
Ecclesia non est.                         *Idem.*

# TO THE MINISTERS
## OF SCOTLAND, HIS
### DEARE CONTRY MEN,
IOHN FRASER wisheth
the Knowledge of the ve-
rity and eternal lyf in
IESVS CHRIST
our Lord.

*S my offer is reasonable , so hope I that ye vvil accept the same , and cleare your selues vvith reason, both for your ovvne cause, and for the contentment of sic as are in doubt, if ye haue the true Church and lauful calling, or else beleue assuredlie that ye haue nather of them. ¶ am in deed but à particulare and single man , Vvho maketh the offer , yet assure your selfs that there is no Catholique aliue being*

A 2                          *of*

of diſcretion & knovvledge, but vvil
ſay and promiſe, yea muſt accompliſh
the ſame, as being obliged to acknovv-
ledge the true Church ynder no leſſe
paine then eternal condemnation.
VVherfore J pray you to arſvver
yvith à commune accord, or, if anie
particular man amonge you ether taketh the burden on him ſelf, or receueth
that charge of you : to approue his labours by your publique conſent. Morouer becauſe ſundry in place of good
and ſolide reaſons, giue iniurious
yvords, reaſon yvold ye abſteine the-
refro, examining my argumentes &
anſvvering thereto ſolidelie, and to
yveygh yvell my proofes and mynd,
rather then to pikat yvords. For ſo
I think to do, if anie anſvver be made
to me, yvilling nether to giue nor receaue fals or light money, for good pai-
ment, meikle leſſe the droſſe & ſcumme
of iniu-

of iniurious talke for good gold of sufficient proofes. The question is of a most precious ieuuel, let vs touch it vvith an innocent and cleane hand, mouth, and hart. He shalbe victorious, vvho hath or findeth the trueth, vvhich can not be had except in the true Church amongst the lauful pastors, to vvhome vve owe duetiful obedience: vvhich moueth me at this tyme to submit all that I haue vvrittin here, or shal vvrit herafter in matters of religion, to the iudgement of the Catholique Apostoque and Romaine Church and pastours of the same: (as in matters of estait, to his M. his honorable counsel, &) other vvhatsoeuer his magistrats or officers, if I haue spoken in any thing vnreuerently: for my intention is vpright to both) becaufe at this present I am assuredlie persuaded that shee is only the true Church guyded by lauful pastors.

A 3      VVhen

When ye proue me that this honour appertaineth onlie to your companie, and sic other as agreeth vvith you in vnitie of doctrine, I shal behaue my self vvith lyke submission and reuerence tovvards you in al respectes. J haue told you my opinion & ioyned reasons therto, vvhereby ye may see me reddie to receaue yours & to knovv therby vvhat assurāce ye haue of your Church and calling vvithouth the vvhich assurāce nether can vve enter in vvith you, nor they vvho ar alreddie vvith you remaine vvith safe conscience: for vvho can be in quyetnes of mynd, not being assured if he be in Gods house, out of the vvhich there is no saluatiō? I protest before him, to vvhom no thing is hid that my offer procedeth of à sincere mynd tovvardes his honour vvith earnest desyr of your vveal, & al Christians & principallie of my contrymen; & nether of

contempt of you, nor presumption of my
ovvne strength. As to anie of your personnes, the euil arriue to me, that I
vvold vvish to you. I am affectionat
to the religion that J professe, true it is
( vvhich as J beleeue, can not iustlie
offend you, seing that if ye make me
yours, ye may haue me as forvvard for
you ) yet I haue vsed as litlil offensiue
language as I could. But if any thing
hath escapped out of my penne, that
may be interpreted other vvayes then I
vvold vvish, I pray you pardon me;
and think that oftentymes the bitter-
nes commeth rather of the matter it self
then of myne ovvne nature. If anie be
so hard and difficil that he vvil not accept my excuse, nor pardon that
vvhich in his opinion is offenciue : the
best vvay to reuenge him self on me, is
to be more modest then he thinketh me
to haue bene : for he vvil beare avvay

A 4          by that

by that meanes the honour of Christian
modestie, vvhich J vvold gladlie haue.
The armes of chyding ar vnpropre in
this field, vvherin those of solide reason
may onlie obteine the victorie. Jf ye
proue your Church to be good & your
calling lauful, J vvil esteme vvorse of al
other côpanies diuided frome you in doctrine, then ye can saie, write, or thinke.
God of his infinit mercie by vertue of
his truth ioyne vs altogether here by
vertu of his Church militant, that vve
may be partakers of eternal blisse in his
Church triumphant, to the vvhich
bringe vs the father, sonne & holie
spirit.                    AMEN.

### 1. To Timothee. 3.

Theis thing I write to thee, hoping that I shal
come to thee shortlie. But if I tary long, that
thou mayest know how thou oughtest to
conuerse in the house of God, which is the
Kirk of the liuing God, the piller and ground
of truth.

# AN OFFER MADE

## TO A GENTILMAN OF
### QVALITIE BY M. IOHN
Fraſer Priour of S. Nicolas, to ſubſcribe & embrace the Miniſters
of Scotlands religion, if they
can ſufficientlie prooue
that they haue the
true kirk, and lau-
ful calling.

*VVHERTO AR ADIOYNED CER-
tain reaſons and conſideration concerning thes tvvo
heades and foundations, vvithout the light of
vvhich, others can not be cleared, nor aſſured ground
in religion in theſe dayes eſtabliſhed.*

 EI ENG now in the fielde
(where ſolitude giueth me lea-
ſure) & wel myndful of the offer
and promiſe I made you at viſi-
ting, I thought it not out of purpoſe to affirme now by writinge, what I ſpake
then by word vnto you.

*If the Miniſters may ſhevv by good and ſolide rea-
ſons, that they haue the true kirk, and are lauful paſtours therof, I ſhal vvithout any farther inquiſition,
examination, or tryal of their doctrine, ſubſcrybe
th ir confeſſion of faith, obey to their commande and
vvil, yea accept that charge.*

Which promiſe and offer I make for no

vaine

vaine oftentation of my felfe nor to prouoke
any man by fic braging, but that an neceffarie
dutie obligeth me to follow this courfe,
whereof my grounds are thefe. No man can
be faued except by IESVS CHRIST: and
no man can be faued by him, except he be a
membre of his myftical bodie, which is his
kirk, where vnto can be no entrie but by the
doore (if we would not be efteemed as theeues
and robbers) that doore can not be opened
but by them who haue the keyes, that is, by
the lawful paftours Our Lord hath obtayned
al power in heauen and in earth: he hath fent
his Apoftles with like power and charge: and
that they fhold exercife this power truelie, &
in al holynes, perpetual affiftence of the holy
fpirit in al veritie was promifed and giuen
vnto them: and in them and by them to their
fucceffours in the kirk vnto the confumma-
tion of the world. So I am forced to haue
recourfe to the Kirk our Sauiours fpoufe:
which I find in vaine and to no effect, if I be
not receaued by the true officers in that holy
tabernacle and houfe of God. Now in this
great nombre of pretended kirks (for there
be more then an hondreth of diuerfe companies who haue vfurped that honorable and
foueraigne name where as there can be but
one true, except we would gif many bodyes
to one head, which fort of monfter hath hith-
erto furpaffed al poëtical fiction) we fhould
vfe al care & diligence to find out the true kirk

gouer

*Act. 4.*
*12.*

*Ioa. 10. 1.*

*Matth. 28*
*18.*

*Matth. 28*
*20.*

gouerned by lawful paftours: for whofoeuer
goeth wrong in this mater, entring into the
fynagog of Satan in fteede of Gods kirk, he
ftrayeth from eternal faluation, howfoeuer
he perfuade him felfe to be in the true way.

I think the reward or danger might make
anie man careful in feeking; and circumfpect
in election and choofing, not giuing rashlie
credite to euery man, who shal promife or
vndertake to lead him to Gods houfe. We ar
aduertiffed by our bleffed Sauiour to be ware,
and not to beleeue them, who shal fay, *lo heer is*  Matt. 24.
*Chrift, lo there.* We are fallen in a dangeroufe      23.
tyme, where the diuerfitie and multitude of  Mar. 13.
opinions and fectes purteth many men in   21 Luc.
doubt whome to flee, whome to follow.  21. 8.
Only this is confeffed and granted by al men,
that there is a kirk, and but one only (I meane
Catholique and vniuerfal) efpoufe and myftical body of IESVS CHRIST, houfe of God,
piller of veritie, mother of all faithful, out of
the which there is no faluation, nor lyfe. For
no man can haue our Lord for head, who is
not à member of his body. And feing no man
gaine fayeth this, of neceffitie it muft but true,
as a thing printed in al mens harts by God him
felfe, who wil no man to haue excufe where
he willeth no man to refufe.

And for that caufe in the fymbole of faith
immediatly after the articles perteining to the
holy Trinitie and myfterie of our Redemp-
tion, is adioyned: I beleeue the holy Catholique

lique kirk, or as it is in the symbole of Nice,
I beleeue, one, holy, Catholique, and Apostolique Kirk. we must acknowlege hir for our
mother; for by hir meanes the lawful sonne
must knowe his genealogie, birth, & kindred
in this spiritual familie. By hir the child knew
God his father: IESVS CHRIST apperteineth to hir only: and no man can claime
right but by hir only, in whose fauour the
contract of mariage was made: he must be
auouched by hir who wold iustly pretend any
part in Christs eternal inheritance. S. Cyprian.
sayeth very well. *Illius ( Ecclesiæ ) fœtu nascimur*
*Illius lacte nutrimur, spiritu eius animamur: adulte-*
*rari non potest sponsa Christi, incorrupta est & pudica;*
*vnam domum nouit, vnius cubiculi sanctitatem casto*
*pudore custodit: hæc nos Deo seruat: hæc filios regno,*
*quos generauit, assignat. Quisquis ab Ecclesia segrega-*
*tus adulteræ iungitur: à promissis Ecclesiæ separatur.*
*Nec perueniet ad Christi præmia, qui relinquit Eccle-*
*siam Christi, alienus est, profanus est, hostis est: ha-*
*bere iã non potest Deum patrem, qui Ecclesiã non habet*
*matrem Si potuit euadere quisquam, qui extra Ar-*
*cam Noe fuit, & qui extra Ecclesiam foris fuerit, eua-*
*det. &c.* Vve ar borne of hir birth and generation:
vve ar nourished vvith hir milke: vve ar quickned and
take lyf by hir spirite. The spouse of Christ cannot be
defiled vvith adulterie: shee is vncorrupt and chast :
shee knovveth but one house : shee keepeth vvith a chast
shamfastnes the holynesse of one bedchamber: shee doth
keepe vs to God. shee doth appoint to th· kingdome
the sonnes vvhich shee hath begotten. Vhosoeuer being
                                                    separated

*De Vni-*
*tate.*
*Eccle. cap.*
*5.*

*separated from the kirk ioyneth him selfe to the adul-
teresse, he is separated from the promisses of the Kirk:
nether shal he come to the revvards of Christ, vvho
leaueth Christs kirk: he is a mere stranger, a profane
man, an enimie: he can not novv haue God to his father vvho hath not the kirk to his mother: If any
man could escape vvho vvas vvithout the Ark of Noë he
also shal escape vvho shalbe vvithout the Kirk* Sic lyk
S. Augustin sayeth: *Si quis absque Ecclesia inuentus
fuerit, alienus erit à numero filiorum. If any man
shalbe found vvithout the kirk, he shalbe as a stranger
and not accounted in the nomber of the lauful sonnes.*
Out of Adams syde sleeping in Paradise was
formed Eua, of whose mariage came al mankynd; out of Christs syde sleeping on the
crosse was formed the kirk, the only lawful
mother of al the faithful.

*lib. 4. e. 10
de symbolo
To. 9.*

Knowing once this kirk I wil make no difficultie to enter therein, to follow and obey
hir voice; because I am sure shee can not erre,
fail, nor be deceaued, nor deceaue anie man:
And this I beleeue without any doubt, I say
beleeue, for many good and weaghty reasons.
yea and it must be so: for others wayes how
shal shee preserue & keepe me from errour &
heresie, not being hir self exempt & free there
fro, vnles perchance ye wold haue me more
skilful nor my guyd, in which case it were
more seemly that I should guyd hir, nor shee
me: for certainely a doutbful leader can not
make an assured companie. If the wisdome
and authoritie of the Kirk be not sufficient
to help

to help our infirmitie & ignorāce in maters of faith, wher shal we haue a sure guyd knowē to the wordle, to whome men of euery estate and condition, may haue recourse in their doubtes and controuersies *qui dubitat in fide, infidelis est : Who doubtes in faith is an infidelle* ; at least if he remaine stil in doubt.

I doubt not but some wil send me to the scriptures with certaine rules; the which may resolue al questions and cleare al sort of controuersies arrysing in matters of religion. I wil accept their counsel, and serue me with their inuention, prouyding I can see good reason. I wil say only at this time, that they who vaunte them selues to haue inuented and kept ( according to their iudgment ) these rules, cannot agree amonges them selues (as I shalbe habil to proue, God willing, if anie man cal my saying in doubt ) so that I can not hope to accord with anie of them, except, without anie farther rule, I say as he sayes, wherein I must disagree with many, seing he agrees with so few. But to the matter. I know there is no errour teached, nor can be teached in the scriptures : they were dytted by the holy spirite to holy men, who, as good & true instruments of the veritie, did write as it was dytted to them by God. So I worshipe the scriptures for their authors cause, I embrace them for the veritie conteined in them : yet by reason of the high mysteries hid therin, I dare not be so bold as to decyd

al questi-

al questions thereby, knowing assuredly that
no prophecie of the scripture is of priuat interpretation, but must be interpreted by the
same holie spirit by which it was written,
that is by holie men, remaining within the
bosome of the kirk, and authorised by hir, as
they were who receaued it from God: that is,
the true interpretation must be taken of the
kirk, to whome God hath committed
al veritie for our instruction. For if we shal
with some men make doubt of the kirks authoritie and firmitie in al veritie, as not being
euery where certaine, thinking and plainly
affirming, or rather as a ground of religion,
surelie beleeuing, that shee may erre and fail:
to whome shal we haue refuge? what remedie
shal we haue for the woundes of a doubtful
conscience? who shal without iuste reproche
apply thes rules to the scriptures and giue vs
the true senses? Who shal pronunce the sentence, and decree, where to al parties must
stand; there must be one, *ne circumferamur omni* Eph. 4.14.
*vento doctrinæ*: *That vve be not carried about vvith*
*euery vvinde of doctrine.* There wilbe an euil
ordered house if euerie man be left to his
owne fantasie. We are not put here nather to
pleade nor play, but with the honour of God
to seek our owen saluation in humilitie, veritie, and charitie. I must haue better and more
sure guyd nor my self, before I leaue the kirk:
he must be better nor shee also, or else I shal
change in vaine. If ther be anie such-like I

4 A      wold

wold gladly heare his name, his qualitie, wher he dwelleth, how I might know him. I wold willinglie take the paine, and beftow the expenfes to feek him out. The loue and defyre of veritie with hope of a moft ample reward wil make the labour light.

But ye wil fay, it is the fcriptures. But it is not the fcriptures I feek, for I haue found them. I feek that which I could not find, wher I found the fcriptures, to wit the true fenfe of the fcriptures; for other wayes anie librarie might haue fatisfied my iuft curiofitie: for what curiofitie can be more iuft, nor to feek eternal lyf? The heretiks and fchifmatiks, yea fome Iewes and Turks haue the Bible, and alleageth them felues to haue the true fenfe of the fame: but how far they be from it their moft pernicious incredulitie doth declare. But it may be faid, that they take not the fcriptures, as they should be taken. I doubt not but they fail, becaufe they goe wrong not hauing affiftance & help of the holie fpirit: that is as meikel as who wold fay, as long yee goe right ye goe not wronge. that is true: but how shal I goe right? that is my queftion: I defire a guyd (for he who is vnlearned and ignorant of the tounges can not ferue him felf with thes rules, which learned men cannot at al practife) who not onlie knoweth the true way and continueth the fame, but alfo wil shew me it, and in cafe I vnderstand him not at the firft or fecond time, wil tel me it ouer

againe

againe in more plaine language: and if I yet mistake him, wil shew me my fault and teach me the true meaning: And such like, if my nighbour & I, be in contrarie opinion, wil shew vs in plain termes whose meaning is good, and whose meaning is not good: or if there be any other sense better nor them both, will produce it for our good instruction.

The scriptures doe tell me the trueth, I doubt not, but they suffer me to take a wrong sense, and aduertise me not that I am deceaued: as we may see to our great sorrowe now by experience of so manie diuerse sectes bred of sinistrouse interpretation taken out of the scriptures. Think not that al these men do willinglie deceaue them selfs. *decipimur specie recti. VVe ar deceaued by the outward shew of the right.* If they wold haue heard & obeyed the voice of the kirk (who cried high & lowd that they vnderstode not the true meaning of the scriptures) they had not gone wrong, as they haue done now, following their owne iudgement. Ye wil say perchance they lackd the holie spirit, for whosoeuer hath his assistance must goe well. I grant you that ( & conclude thereon, that the kirk must goe wel ) but seing that euerie man hath not the holie spirit; how shal I know who hath him, and who not? Amongst this infinit nombre of them, who pretendeth to haue that priuiledge (notwithstanding of their contrarietie, a manifest mark of their vntruth, and that *Satan oftenty-*

B mes

2. Corynt.
11. 14.
de subsidio
Eucharist.
To. 2.

*mes doth transfigure and change him self in an An-gel of light)* it s al be verie hard to anie man to know whither his spirit be *albus an ater,* Black or *whyte,* as sayeth Zuinglius of his spirit Mo-reouer this can be but a spirit particular, and à spirit of discorde, except he agree with the general: for in matters of religion *priuata Ve-ritas opinio est, non Veritas. A priuat Veritie is but an opinion, and not a Veritie.* It can not be proper to one only which was giuen for al I seek a common guyde of al Christians. I wil not credit my owen priuat spirit, an other should not look for anie farther at my hand. The veritie is but one, the guyd & iudge must be of that same nature. If I find out the true guyd and rule, al men, who wold be safe must follow that guyd and rule. So if myne, or anie other particular mans spirit, be that sure and true guyde, whosouer goeth there to, must goe wrong: yea all other rules without him serueth for nought. Where as the holie spirit can do wel although he haue no rule prescri-bed to him: he who made the Asse of Balaam to speak, may cause any man he pleaseth to tel the veritie, he nedeth no help of rules: his onlie assistance was sufficient for the A-postles to speake, and vnderstand all tounges and know all veritie for mans saluation. If anie particular personne hath gotten the spi-rit in this sort, let him speak boldlie, we must be all his disciples. There ar sundrie who wold willingly take vpon them that name as
their

their straite style in writting may euidentlie declare, yet for feare of mockerie they dare not say it : But let vs retourne to the scriptures examined & interpreted by these rules,

The scriptures (say they) be as the touche-stone, wherwith the gold and siluer of Christian religion be tryed and knowne, from the false and conterfaict gold and base money of erroniouse and hereticall doctrine . Now at euery such tryal ther should be three thinges, the touchstone, the gold or metall to be tried, & the goldsmith : we haue the touchstone, to wit the scriptures, the gold to be tried, ar the heads of religion called in doubt, to know if they be of good and fyne metal of veritie or nor. The debate is for the glodsmith, who should trye the gold. This apperteineth not to euerie man, seing that euerie man hath not learned the craft. Vntil we find a better, I think it best we receaue the kirk, or rather suffer the kirk to stand with that charge, seing no other presenting him self is worthie of that place, as in deed it apperteineth to no other but to the kirk. Yet seing that many doe otherwayes at this time, we may iustlie say with Sainct Hierom *sola scripturarum ars est, Epistola ad quam sibi passim omnes vendicant; hanc garrula anus, Paulinum. hanc delirus senex, hanc sophista verbosus, hanc vniuersi praesumunt, lacerant, docent antequam discunt. There is only the raf of the scriptures, that all men challenge and vendicat to them selfs euerie wherie eue-rie old babbling wyf, euerie rauing old fellowe, euery*

A 2                    *sophist*

sophist ful of vvords, yea euerie one in general doe take this scripture, d smember, and teach it, before that they haue learned it. We at not now in question of the scriptures, but of the interpretation of them, which should not be drawen to our iudgement, but our iudgment drawen to them, *Bringing in captiuitie all ynderstanding ynto the obedience of Christ and hauing in readines to reuenge all disobodience, when our obedience shalbe fulfilled.* IESVS CHRISTS house is the schoolle of faith, and not of science: he knoweth sufficientlie, who beleeueth as he should doe. God hath at all time serued him self with the kirk to teach men, to declare & shewe his will publishing his veritie to the world. He wilbe credited on his onlie word *quoniam ipse dixit & fact a sunt, ipse mandauit & creata sunt.* His saying is more sure, then anie mathematical demoustration, he may make an instrument of anie thing, who made all thinges without anie instrument. So our maister and Lord made clay with his spittle to heal the blind man: in the hand of anie other that had bene sufficient to make a seeing man blind. May he not the with the clay of mortall men heall our blindnes in the truth? The riuer of Iordan had only common water without anie extraordinarie vertue, yet Naaman being sent there, by the prophet, it receaueth the power to heal him of his leprosie. The prophete of all prophetes, or rather the maker of all prophets hath sent vs to the kirk: why shall since

*2.Cor.10.5.*

*Ion. 9. 6.*

*4 Reg. 5.*

shee not haue the vertue to heall vs of our le-
profie of ignorance by him , who fent vs to
hit? S. Peter faid in his name to the crippel
man *furge & ambula. Ryfe and walke.* the natu-   *Act. 3.6.*
rall ficknes from the birth could not refift his
command: his fhaddow healed infirmities:his   *Act.5.15.*
worde flayed: his prayers raifed vp the dead:
And fhall Chrifts owe worde haue no ftregth? *ib.* 8. 8.
there is vertue in all aboundance`, wher euer 9. 4.
he will: our weacknes can not ftoppe him. I
muft fay with Orofius : *Hoc fi quifquam homi-*   *Aduer.*
*num ita dicendum putet, Vt fub infirmitate hominis* *Pelagium*
*Deum non poffe affirmet, & omnipotentiæ Dei ali-* *de arbit.*
*quid impoffibile fufpicetur in omni creatura Cœle-* *liber.*
*ftium, terreftrium, & infernorum : hunc non tan-*
*tùm fententia mea dixerim blafphemum, anathema*
*detestandum, fed etiam vel in exemplum Nadab &*   *Leu* 10. 2.
*Abiu Diuino igne damnandum, vel iuxta perdi-*
*tionem Dathan & Abiron hiatu terræ receptum* *Deut.* 11.
*viuum ad inferna mergndum.* If anie man thin- 6.
*keth that it may fo be faid, that by reafon of mans*
*infirmitie and weaknes he will fay God cannot, and*
*thinketh any thing impoffible to the omnipotencie*
*and almightie power of God in all creatures of hea-*
*uen, of earth, and of hell. I wold efteem according to*
*my iudgment this man not only blafphemoufe, &*
*detestable but alfo either to the exemple of Nadab*
*& Aoiu worthie to be condemned by the fire com-*
*ming from God, or according to the perdition and*
*destruction of Dathan & Abiron being receaued*
*by the opening of the earth, worthie to be quicke*
*thruft doune to hell.* Shal our Maifter and Lord
       B 3          haue

haue no ſtrẽgth except that which he receaus
from the inſtruments he imployeth? ſhal the
weaknes of the inſtrument hold back his will?
*Quàm potens in faciendo de nihilo ; tam facilis in*
*perficiendo de facto. He is as facile and eaſie in per-*
*fecting anie thing made, as he is mightie in making*
*any thing of nought.* There can be no weak inſtrument in ſo mightie a hand. *Poteſt ergo om-*
*nia* (ſayeth the ſame Oroſius) *in homine qui vti-*
*que poteſt omnia He may then do all thing in man,*
*who may do all things.* I wil therefor follow the
kirk with ful confidence: I ſhal haue a good
guyd, ſeing God hath commanded me ſo to
d o. It wil be hard to perſuade me that the
contrarie ſhould be donne, except they may
ſhow that ether they ar more wiſe then God,
in taking an other guyd, or that he hath giuen
vs that command to deceaue vs; wherof neither can be true. He is a God of wiſdome and
truth, he hath promiſed to gouerne his kirk
in all truth. If ſhee erre the ſhame redoundeth
to hir head & ſpouſe I ES VS CHRIST, who
is hir guyd, redeemer, groundſton, & maſon,
who promiſt to build hir vpon a rock, and
that the gates of hel ſhould not preuail againſt
hir. What reproche ſhould it be to his wiſdome or power, if he could not, or wold not
keep hir from errour, according to his promiſe? But he knew not perchance, when he made this promiſe, what power he had: theſe
new Lords had not as yet limited the marches
of his might: their breif of perambulation
was

Idem.

was not put, as yet, in executiô, or shal we say:
*Immensa est finémque potentia cæli non habet, quic-*
*quid superi voluere peractum est: Promisit quia vo-*
*luit, seruauit quia potuit.* He promised; *because he*
*wold, he keeped it, because he might.* And in trueth
if this sure ancre of the kirk were lost, how
shal we be assured of the veritie? Wher shall
we seek it? at their hands perchance, who as-
sures vs that the wholl Catholique kirk may
erre, because they ar but men. If they be Gods,
or may shew vs any special priuiledge, wherby they ar exempted from the generall rule of
errour, to the which al men without exception (according to their iudgment, notwithstanding Gods promise) ar subiect, it is reason
we should hear them, obey, and follow them,
because of their special prerogatiue aboue all
others. But whosoeuer sayeth that al men ar
subiect to errour and fals opinions, looseth
his credit in all other things, hauing obteined
credit in that: yea being a man as others, why
may he not be deceaued in that, as wel as in
the rest? And doubtles he is deceaued, if he
think his maxime of errour to haue place in
the kirk of God, wher he is ruler and gouernour him self. Who can keep anie thing wel,
if it be so vnsure which he hath taken into his
owen keeping? Farther the certaine and in-
fallible constancie of the kirk in matters of
faith may best be seene in the grounds & meanes shee vseth in teaching and guyding vs. It
is most certaine that the work dependeth on

B 4                    the

the worker, the effect on the cause, and the
end, on the cheife beginning. Where the authour, worker, cause, fondament, & original
beginning ar necessarie alltogither and vn-
changable, the work, effect, and end must be
of the same nature and condition : Now seing
the kirk hath for hir internal author, mouer,
cause, and beginning, the Father, the Sonne,
and Holie Ghost spirite of veritie and truth,
who hath assisted, assisteth, and will assist hir
to the end of the world, why shal not hir doctrine, and shee hir self be without errour or
fault because of hir good guyd ? For faith
which surpasseth al naturall and humain reason can haue no sure ground but by the reuelation of God in his kirk. This assurance may
be easelie seen in the scriptures, because wher
it is spoken of the mission and power which
our Lord geueth to the officers and magistrates of his house; here also is made mention of
the promises of his perpetuall assistance and
presence to his kirk. *All povver is giuen to me in*
*heauen and in earth : going therefor, teach, ye all*
*nations, baptizing them in the name of the Father*
*and of the Sonne & of the Holie Ghost, teaching thē*
*to obserue all things vvhatsoeuer I haue commanded*
*you : and behold I am vvith you alwayes euen to the*
*consummation of the vvorld : As my father hath*
*sent me, so I send you* &c. *And I vvil ask the fa-*
*ther and he vvil giue you an other paraclete, that he*
*may abyd vvith you for euer.* Item. *but the para-*
*clete the holie spirite, Vvhom the Father vvil send in*
*my name,*

Matt. 28
18.

Io.20.21.
Ion. 1..
16.

*my name, he vil teach you al things, Vvhatsoeuer I say vnto you.* And in an other place he prayeth for his kirk. *For them do I pray &c. Sanctifie them in trueth &c. as thou did send me in the vvorld, I haue also sent them in the vvorld.* The whole place is to be readd for it maketh to the purpose. Now if nether his promises doeth oblige him, nor his prayer hath anie place for the stabilitie of the veritie in his kirk, how can it be true that S. Paul sayeth. *And he gaue some Apostles and some prophetes, and other some Euangelists, and other some pastours, and doctours to the consummation of the sainctes vnto the vvork of the ministerie, vnto the edification of the bodie of Christ vntill vve meet all into the vnitie of faith.* Wher it is plainlie said that our Lord hath established Ecclesiastical personnes for the perfection of his elect in coseruing thē from the maliciouse craft of sata̅, that they be not deceaued by errour, not caried away with euerie wind of doctrine; which cannot be eschewed, vnlesse the doctrine of the kirk be without errour. We see the people of euerie country do embrace the religion of their true or fals pastours: so except the pastours haue some certaine rule & guyd more then humaine, without doubt their inconstant doctrine shal make à flock inconstant. *Ye ar the salt of the earth, ye ar the light of the vvorld &c. Ye haue not chosen me, but I haue chosen you, and appointed you that ye go and bring forth fruict and that your fruict, remaine:* Which things were said to the Apostles as re-

presen-

*Ion.16 13.*
*4: 26.*

*Eph.4.11.*

*Matt.5.*
*13.*
*Io. 15. 16.*

preſenting the kirk, becauſe they were the firſt
ſondaments therof, laide by IESVS CHRIST
him ſelf oeing yet on earth.

Gen. 2. : 8.    The words of God haue yet their force:
*creſcite & multiplicamini, bring forth fruict aud mul-*
*tiplie* the words apperteineth to the poſteritie,
and yet doe keep their ſtrength, which they
receaued in the begining. If ſo be in the temporall and corporal propagation, what ſhal it
be in the ſpirituall?or ſhal his liberalitie be leſſe
towards his kirk? ſhal ſhee be *vnius æui*, of on
lib. 1. dec.  age: as ſayeth Liuius of Rome new begonne?
1.    Shal we think that ſo great priuiledge & ſo
deere boughte apparteineth onlie to the Apoſtles? there is no apparance of reaſon, ſeing the
promiſes conteine à perpetual & continual
Ion. 15. 16.  aſſiſtance: *I haue appointed you, that ye goe, and*
*bring forth fruict, & that your fruict remaine. that*
*what ſoeuer ye aske of my father in my name he may*
*giue it you.* Who can doubt but they haue deſired that according to his owen ſaying, the
fruict brought out by them ſhould remaine in
the kirk: that is, that the veritie ſhould remaine for euer in the kirk? Should not the
ſpirit of conſolation & veritie eternallie abyde
in the kirk, wher as none of the Apoſtles did
liue an hondreth years? When they paſt vp to
heauen by their glorrouſe martyrdome as our
eldeſt brethren to enter in to the land of eternal lyfe, which our Lord had bought to them
with his pretiouſe blood, they drew not vp the
ladder after thē. The aſſiſtāce in al veritie was
giuen

giuen to thē, as being neceſſarie for mans ſal-
ua ion:the necesſitie remaineth,why ſhal not
the gift remaine? It was not giuen to the kirk
for the Apoſtles ſake,as apparteining to them
onlie, but to the Apoſtles for the kirks ſake
they being hir principal membres:ſo the principall motiue remaining, whyſhal not the priuiledge ſo neceſſarie remaine? They receaued
it but as membres neareſt to the head, to be
continued and conuayed by them to the reſt       *Pſal.* 1,3:2
of the body, *ſicut vnguentum in capite, quod de-*
*ſcendit in barbam, barbam Aaron, quod deſcendit in*
*oram veſtimenti eius.* This ſweet oyle of veritie
which is in the head I E S V S-C H R I S T, why
ſhal it not deſcend vnto the beard of Aaron
& to the border of his garment, that is to the
Apoſtles & their ſucceſſours, to the extreme
border of Chriſts kirk ſignified by his garment?And reaſon wold,or rather Gods infinit
mercie, that the ſucceſſours of the Apoſtles
ſhould haue that ſame aſſiſtance of the holy
ſpirit, becauſe they haue the ſame place and
charge for the perfitting of Chriſts body,whi-
ch is his kirk. And therefor they ar called his
officers & ſeruants. And doutbles it were a-
gainſt all good reaſon to think, that the holie
ſpirit had gotten onlie charge to guyde the
Apoſtles, as though our Sauiour had ſufferred
death for them onlie, & not for the kirk in all
ages About the yeare of our Lord 1525.(ſundry ſectes being riſen vp vnder the colour,
that the true kirk had failled, all the paſtou-
                                              res

res hauing erred, & at laft hauing decayed, and
therefor alledging that they were fent by God
to teach the verity fo many yeares vnknowen
to the world) Dauid Georgius a cheif of the
Anabaptifts taking occafion of that alledged
& imaginarie falle of the Catholik kirk, gaue
him felf out for the true Meffias: Amongeft
the reafons he vfed againft the Lutheriens &
other fectes, the principal was taken from
their newnes, & from the defectió of the kirk,
which they preached for that fame occafió of
their nouueltie; for other wayes they could not
haue reached, nor yet bin minifters, Doctours
or Paftours. *If the doctrine of Chrift* ( fayeth this
peftilét Dauid Georgius) *and of his Apoftles was
true and perfect, certainlie the kirk that they planted and
formed by their doctrine shold haue remained, and du-
red necessairly, and newer haue decayed, feing that Iefus faid, that the gates of hell shold neuer preuaill againft
hir: but now it is manifest & knowen to the whole
world (according to your owen commone faying) that
the Antichrist hath altogither ouerthrowen the doctrine of Chrift & his Apoftles, & the kirk founded
and builded by them, as may be feene in the Papiftrie:
wherfor the doctrine of Chrift, & of his Apoftles was
falfe and imperfect.* A blafphemoufe conclufion,
yet altogether neceffarie, if the affumption were true, which fundrie now adaves not onlie
admittes to be true, but alfo taketh it for a gro-
und moft certaine, whervpon they haue builded their new kirk. *Abyffus abyffum inuocat.*

But to refute this pernicioufe opinion let
**vs**

vs fee and confider what honorable titles the
kirk hath in the holie fcriptures, & how faire
promifes ar made by God of hir ftabilitie and
infallibilitie : : she is called the *bodie*, the *fulnes,*
the *fpoufe of Iefus Chrift*, the *houfe of our Lord, the
pillar and firmament or ground of truth*, *bought with
his blood,his wealbeloued, his Douue, his winiard, his
inheritance,his kingdome*. &c. ouer faire & beau-
tifull names to vanish fo fone contraire to his
bountiful promifes. *I will marrie thee vnto me for
euer,yea I wil marrie thee vnto me in rightioufnes iudgement & mercie*. &c. May I not fay heer with
S. Aug. *Hæc eft mater vera, pia mater & cafta in-
trinfecus viri fui dignitate ornata, non forinfecus men-
dacio fallente turpiter colorata This is the true mother,
godlie and chaft mother, decked in wardlie with the
dignitie and maieftie of hir husband, not shamefullie
coloured out wardly with à deceauing lie.and in deed
as the fame S. Aug. fayeth, In ventre Ecclefiæ veritas manet:quifquis ab hoc ventre Ecclefiæ feparatus fuerit,neceffe eft vt falfa loquatur, neceffe eft, inquam, vt
falfa loquatur qui aut concipi noluit,aut quem concep-
tum mit:r excufsit. VVithin the belly or bofome of the
kirk the veritie remaineth. VVhofoeuer shalbe feparated
frome this bofome of the kirk,of neceffitie he muft fpeak
lies,of neceffitie,I fay,l.e muft fpeak lies,who either wold
not be coceaued & ingendred,or els being coceaued, the
mother hath caft him out. But if shee hath become
an harlotte & adultreffe,shee hath made diuor-
fe,shee hath violated the law of mariage,which
God hath promift should be kepe in faithful-
nes.I doubt greatlie if they be lauful childré to
　　　　　　　　　　　　　　　　　　　　　　God,

Hofe. 2.
19.

Tom. 6.
cocione ad
Cath. cap.
22.

Tom 8. in
pfal. 57.

God, who calleth their mother à whore, *matris*
*adulterio patrē quærunt*: can any mā say more freelie that he is an heretik, nor to say that the kirk
he followeth may & hath erred: shee who abā-
doneth hir self so easelie to euerie suter, cannot
be a true spouse, shee must be an harlotte. Excuse me if I say, that such men may be bastards,
but the kirk of God wil remaine à virgin for
euer, by the assistance & diligence of hir head
& spouse: he was born of à virgin, he wil haue
his membres & ofspring to haue that same honour, their true and spiritual mother being à
virgin, because shee is his spouse. God must ha-

*Eph 5.27.*  ue some thing out of the deuils power; *He hath*
*made to him self a gloriouse kirk not hauing spot or*
*wrincle or anie such thing: but that shee should be holy*
*& without blame.* to wit in doctrine. If God be
*ourthrowwen in his owne house,* he must be weaker

*Matt. 12.* then the deuill: which can not be granted, yea
*29.* not thought, without execrable blasphmie.
Wherfor I must say with S. Aug. (whom I cite
the more willinglie for that sundry of the pro-
testās alledge that he is theirs, not withstāding
he be their greatest enimie, at lest to their do-

*Tom 9.* ctrine) *Credimus Ecclesiam Catholicam ipsa est Ecclesia*
*de symb.* *Sancta, Ecclesia vna, Ecclesia vera, Ecclesia Catholica,*
*lib. 1. cap.* *contra hæreses omnes pugnans: pugnare potest expugnari*
*5.* *non potest: hæreses omnes de illa exierunt tanquam sar-*
*menta inutilia de vite præcisa: ipsa autem manet in ra-*
*dice sua, portæ inferorum non vincent eam.* *VVe beleeue*
*the Catholik kirk, shee is the holy kirk the true kirk,*
*the Catholik kirk fighting against all heresies, shee may*
*fight*

fight, but shee can not be ouercome, al hereſies ar gone out
of hir, like vnprofitable branches cut of the vynetree.
shee, the kirk, doeth remaine in hir owen roote : the
gittes of hell shal not oue come hir.

Let vs ſee the other promiſes made to hir,
by hir head and maiſter, which ar ſo cleer & in
ſo great noimber, that no man can doubt, except he that wil receaue no thing, but that onlie which hath paſſed by the tryal of his iudgement, to whoſe iudgement to ſtand, were to be
without any iudgement. God promiſed, as I
haue ſaid oftymes, that the gates of hell, that is    *Matt. 16,*
the power of Sathan by errour and hereſie    *18.*
should not preuail againſt hir. Hath not Satan preuailled, if he hath cauſed hir to erre in
teaching & authorizing fals doctrine? S. Aug.
ſayeth paſſing wel. *Non insultant heretici per partes*    *Tom 8 in*
*concisi, non se extollant, qui dicunt Ecce hic eſt Chiſtus,*    *Pſal 47.*
*ecce illic: Qui dicit ecce hic eſt ecce illic ad partes inducit,*    *Matth 4*
*Ynitatem promiſit Deus. Reges in Ynum collecti ſunt,*    *23.*
*non per ſchiſmata diſipati ſunt. Sed forte iſta ciuitas,*
*quæ mundum tenuit, aliquando euertetur? abſit : Deus*
*fundauit eam in æternum: Si ergo Deus fundauit eam*    *pſal. 47.*
*in æternum, quid time: ine cadat firmamentum? Let not*
*the eretikes inſult & triumphe being diuided in ſe-*
*cte, let not thes magnifie & praiſe them ſelf, vvho ſay-*
*eth lo here is Chriſt, lo there. VVho ſayeth lo heer is*
*Chriſt, lo there, be inducetb to factions. God did promi-*
*ſe Ynitie and concorde. The Kings vvere gathered to ge-*
*ther in one; not ſcattered by diuiſion. But perchance i his*
*citie, Vvhich bath comprehended & occupied the*
*Vvorld, at length ſhalbe ouertbro Vven? God for bid:*
God

God hath founded and established hir for euer. If then
he hath founded hir fo euer, VVhat feare ye leaft the

**Matt. 28.** firmamet fhould fall: He promifed alfo he should
**20.** be with hir all wayes cue to the confummatio
of the wold: if he left hir not one day, when

**Ioan. 14.** should errour haue occupied hir? fo should the
**16.** holie fpirit tary with hir for euer, & teach hir
al veritie: al veritie & errour can not confift
togither. The father promifed to his eternal
Sonne, the fame perpetual veritie for his

**Ifa.59.21.** feed. *I vvil make this my conuenant vvith them
fayeth our Lord : My fpirit that is vpon thee, & my
Vvords, Vvhilk I haue put in thy mouth, shal not depart
out of thy mouth, nor out of the mouth of thy feed, fayeth our Lord from henceforth euen for euer.* For his

**Iuc. 1.33** kingdome shal haue no end. So fayeth Daniel
**cap 7.14.** of his domination, which shalbe through al, &
**& 27.** for euer. And Micha fayeth as far. Now behold
**cap. 4. 7.** the amplitude greatnes & authoritie. *I shal giue*
**Pfal. 2. 8.** *thee the heathens for thyn inheritance, and the endes
of the earthe for thy poffeffion.* In another place *al*
**Pfal.85.9.** *nations, vvhome thovv haft made, shall come & vvors-
hipe before the oLord & shal glorifie thy name* Ifaias
**2. 2.** fayeth: *In the laft dayes shalbe prepared the mountaine of the houfe of our Lord in the toppe of the mountaines, and shalbe exalted aboue the hilles, and all nations shal flovv to it* : not onlie Ifaias, but alfo the
other prophets fay the fame. Moreouer the fin-
nes of the children shall not take away his inheritance of veritie amonges the Chriftians:
**Pfal. 88.** King Dauid affureth vs:*his feed Vvil I make indure
**29.** for euer, and his throne as the dayes of the heauen.* But
if his

*if his children leaue my lavv , and vvalk not in my*
*iudgments, if they break my statutes & keepe not my*
*commandements; then wil i visit their iniquities vvith*
*a rodde & their sinnes vvith strokes; yet my mercy*
*vvill i not take from h m; nor offend in my ruieth my*
*conuenant vvill i not break. &c.* Ye see that God
wil keep his Sonnes heritage notwithstading
of mans iniquitie.

But they who approue not this stabilitie
and coustancie of the kirk, answers that shee
failleth not, as longe as shee heareth the voice
& obeyeth the commandement of hir spouse
I E S V S  C H R I S T, & is guyded by the holie
spirit, following the word of God , which is
perpetuallie ioyned with the holie spirit : but
if shee leaue the word & obey not hir spouse,
shee may fail and erre. What is this other to
say, then that the kirk cannot fail nor erre at
all? For we haue shewen alreddie that there
can be no such separation, nor disobedience:
where vpon we haue concluded the certaine
and perpetual veritie of the kirk, in respect of
the perpetual and assured assistance of I E S V S
C H R I S T and of his holy spirit in al veritie: for if shee were without hir head and
gouernour , shee could no more be a kirk.
In which case they might rather say shee
were decayed and dead , not erred and failled. But nether of these can be true as we
haue shewen by euident places of the scriptures . We must think that our Lord hath
builded hir vpon a rock, as it becommeth his
C       wisdo-

*Matth.* 7.
24.

wisdome, and not vpon the sandes, as fooles doo, whose howses can not stand because the ground is not sure.

As touching the promises, which some men pretendes to be conditionallie made to the kirk, because some promises are of that nature: they must vnderstand that such promises toucheth onlie the particular, if they remaine in the kirk, if they follow our Lords commande-

*Exod.* 33.
21.

ment. God sayeth to Moses *Ecce est locus apud me & stabis supra petram* Behold there is a place by me, and thow shalt stand vpon the rock : On this rock the kirk is builded, shee must be stabell: Shee is our Lords inheritance giue to him by God his Father without anie condition: which may be shewen by great number of places of the scriptures . It dependeth not vpon mens vertue or vice, strength or weaknes, folie or wisdome:

*Matt.* 11.
29.
*Mar.* 3.
27.

he hath taken the keeping of his owen right in to his owen hand: he wil not be spoiled by a mightier, because there is none mightier: if it had depended vpon our worthines, I doubt if Christ Iesus should haue had anie kirk at all; we must lay clayme to his infinit mercie, goodnes, & exceedinge loue by the which he hath promised not to abandonne his kirk, nor to suffer hir to go wronge: his grace is a sufficient shrowd againest al stormes, and a sure ancre in al dager: he wil care for nothing in this world,

*Can.* 2. 7.
6. 8.

if he be careles of his wealbeloued spouse, who is his doue, perfite and vndefiled.

The ark of Noë was not surmonted by the floods

flood;it was euer higher thē the water of the
flood,which notwhitstāding was higher then
all the rest of the things vpon earth. Men,
townes,hilles,mountaines were lower thē the
water,which yet acknowledged the Ark to be
aboue thē: for they drouned the rest,but lifted
vp the Arke. *quia dominus supposuit manum : Be-* **Psal. 37.**
*cause our Lord did put his hand vnder it:*and what **23.**
could surmount it, which was susteined by
the mightie hād of our Lord? This was without anie condition: but who were to be saued,it behoued them to be therin:for to them
the promise was conditionall. The Ark , if it
had not had the special assistance of God, had
bene ouerthrowen as the rest , who wanted
that safegarde and protection.

The veritie of that figure is giuen to Christ
our Sauiour without anie limitatiō or condition: but to the particulars, if they be therein.
The water which out of the ark was mortall
and deadlie,within it, serueth for lyf. So may
we say of the kirk, *sola est, quæ intra se positos* **Aug. to.**
*validæ caritatis compage custodit; vnde & aqua* **10. de tēp.**
*diluuij arcam quidem ad sublimiora sustulit,omnes* **serui 181.**
*autem quos extra arcam inuenit, extinxit. It is shee*
*onlie who keepeth with a mightie band those who*
*ar within hir: where by the water of the deluge car-*
*ried vp the ark on high , but whosoeuer it found*
*with out the ark, it destroyed.* Why shal not *Arca*
*Ecclesiæ superior esse omnibus vndis & fluctibus*
*erroris?* No thing can be in danger that con-
stantlie remaineth in our Lords keeping, how

weake foeuer it be of it felf, hauing ftrength
of tne keper.

But they wil fay petchance that all thefe
promifes and perrogatiues ar ether to the kirk
inuifible, or for the reuelation of the holie
fpirit made to euerie man in particular, where
by they ar gouerned and called his. Let vs fee,
or rather let vs confider (feing it can not be
feen) this inuifible kirk. I pray you read the
places cited before, & ye shall fee that the promifes ar made to a vifible companie. The falt
of the earth: the light of the world: as a ci ie
fet vpon à mountaine: à candle fette vpon a
candleftick: who heareth the kirk, heareth
God, who contemneth hir, contemneth God:
Who wil not here, nor obey the kirk should
be to vs as an excommunicat perfonne. Shee
is fignified by the Ark of Noë: By the children
of Ifraël in the defert: by the vyniard : by S.
Peters shippe: by a mountaine : by the nettes
cafte in the fea: by à piller &c. w' at is here inuifible, or rather what can be vifible to him
who feeth not thefe things? he hath need of à
Phifician, and not of reafons, who cannot fee
à shippe & nettes, an Arke of three hondreth
cubites long, à vyniard, a citie, a candle vpon
an candelftik, à mountaine, à pillar, fyue or fix
hondreth thoufand perfonnes to gither. what
remedie for fo defperate a blindnes, in fo woe-
ful à ficknes ? *Iubeas miferum eße libenter.* He
muft perish in his owen blindnes, who wil
not opé his eyes. How can we acknowledge or
obey

obey this inuifible Iudge? Wher shal we find
hir? *nufquam est si nufquam videtur, cùm non sit
incorporea*: how can we be ioyned with hir? &
out of hir bofom there is no faluatiõ. The kirk
had charg to teach al nations & baptize them.
I think it shalbe as difficil to hear as to fee inuifible doctours, except we wil receaue the
olde hob goblins for paftours. Shal we beleeue that the kirk of God hath neuer bene feene, becaufe the doctrine teached now in fundrie places was neuer heard before, the doctours therof not being as yet borne? If the
kirk was euer vifible, it was that shee might
be knowen & fo followed. Vntill thefe men
came shee was hid, now shee is knowen. why
hath she changed hir nature? is it to deceaue
vs? God forbid: shall we giue the caufe wonne
to the Anabaptifts, with their foolish & new
inuented fynagoge? Which doubtles muft be
receaued according to this opinion: or if it be
receaued in others, why shall it not be receaued in them? If they had yet remained inuifible, they had bene more worthie of credit.
But what, anie thing is good enough to theis
fantafticall fpirits. *Notus in Iudæa Deus*, God is *Pfal*.75.1.
not knowen but in his kirk, and by his kirk,
feing shee is the pillar of veritie and trompet
of his holie name. It is shee who hath difcou-
uered, affaulted, and condemned, yea and at
laft deftroyed all herefies in euerie age, not by
iuuifibilitie, but by vifible prefence, in general councels, by dayly preaching and teaching
C 3                    o. hir

of hir doctours and paftours , and foueraigne decrees of hir minifterial head. If ther be none of thefe things true , the kirk muft be onlie a vaine phantafticall imagination forged to abufe men , lyke to the philofophical ftone, where foolish men imploye their lyfe, mynd, and fubftance to find right nought at laft. *Quid*

Tom. 9. in *amplius* (fayeth S. Auguftin) *dicturus fum quàm*
Epift. Ion. *cæcos qui tam magnum montem non vident? qui*
tract. 2. *contra lucernam in candelabro pofitam oculos clau-*
Ibid. tra- *dunt. VVhat shal I fay farther but that they ar blind*
ct. 1. *who fee not fo great à mountaine? who cloffeth their eyes against the candle put on the candleftik.*

Daniel. 2. And in an other place. *Ecce mons implens vni-*
35. *uerfam faciem terræ. Ecce ciuitas de qua dictum eft:*
Matt. 5. *non poteft ciuitas abfcondi fuper montem conftituta.*
14. *Illi autem offendunt in montem, & cùm eis dicitur, afcendite, non eft mons, dicunt: facilius illuc faciem impingunt; quàm illic habitaculum quærunt. Be-hold the moûtaine filling the face of the whole earth. behold the citie of which it is faid: à citie fette one an hil can not be hid. They* (to wit the heretikes) *do ftrik them felfs against the hil. & when it is faid to them, go vp, they fayi, it is not the hill. They do more willinglie dash their face against that hill, nor*

To. 8. *feek any dwelling there.* I muft fay with the fame
pfal. 56. S. Auguftin. *O hæretica infania, quod non vides, credis mecum: quod vides, negas. credis mecum Chri-ftum exaltatum fuper cœlos, quod non vidimus; & negas gloriam eius fuper omnem terram, quod vi-demus. O heretical frowardnes, and obftinate mad-dneffe, thou beleeueft with me that thou feeft not; thou*

*thou denyes that which thou seest, Thou beleuest with*
*me that Christ is exalted aboue the heauens, which we*
*haue not seene; & thou denyest his glorie to be vpō all*
*the earth, which we see.* And if I be not abused, the
persecutions (which continued almost from
Christs dayes to Cōstantin the greate, although
not in al place & with lyke crueltie, wher many thousand martyrs did bestow their lyues)
were against the visible kirk of that age: for if
this new inuisible kirk had bene in those dayes
shee had conserued al hir membres from danger, by meanes of hir inuisibilitie: And in deed
al such men escaped the tyrannie of the most
cruel Emperoures by that ring Gyges. or ra- *Plato 10.*
ther because none of these inuisible men as *de repub.*
yet were forged. Shall the kirk of God haue
no other refuge in persecutions (whither they
come of tyranntes, or of heretiks oppugning
the veritie) but to flee to the darknes of inuisibilitie (more fitte for the membres of Satan
prince of darknes, then for the membres of
IESVS CHRIST author of light) as Sepia *The con-*
to hir black blood or inke? God forbid. If they *fession of*
answer that they vnderstand by the inuisible *faith art.*
kirk, the elect, who because they ar knowen *17. insered*
onlie to God ar called inuisible. I answer that *in the act*
the same argument maketh the condemned *of parlia-*
personnes as well to be inuisible, seing they ar *ment hol-*
knowen to God onlie in that qualitie, so all *den the*
the world shalbe inuisible. Secondly seing *1567. prin*
that I am obliged to ioyne my self with the *ted 1568.*
true kirk onlie: how shal I know hir being *& 1597.*
knowen

knowẽ only to God? I say onlie that we found
as long as they did reigne, a visioel, at leaſt
senſible, and moſt cruel perſecution, againſt
ſuch as could not come out of the country:
for they were conſtrained to ſubſcribe and
ſweare that the preſent religion was good, albeit in their conſcience they knew and were
perſuaded to t'ie contrarie: which perſecution
was ſo cruel that the death it ſelf had bin more tolerable: yea I perſuade my ſelf that if the
Miniſters wold haue proceeded by way of
death againſt the Catholiks, that they should
not haue wonne ſo meikil againſt them as
they did then, by an extreme neceſſitie to
which they put them. But to retourne to their
inuiſibilitie: we ar ſeeking à kirk to guyd vs,
shee was inuiſible before our dayes (and now
we haue ſo manie kirks viſible that we know
not which to chooſe) why ſo longe inuiſible, and why now ſeene? inuiſible when
shee might haue bin knowen, becauſe ther
was but few, and now viſible when the
great nomber maketh hir vncertaine to vs.
Theſe dark queſtions requireth a new Oedi-
pus to ſolue them. I ſay that abſolutlie shee
muſt be knowen to vs, & not to God only:
God of his infinit mercie, and goodnes, hath &
wil communicate to vs his knowledge ſo far
as it is neceſſarie for our ſaluation: but it is altogither neceſſarie for vs) to knowe the true
kirk. ſeing shee is the only houſe wher God is
ſurelie to be found, truelie ſerued, duelie obey-
**ed and**

ed and eternal lyf mercifullie ob-eined, as is
suffi:ientlie proued before. If I should promise
à thousand pound to any mã, & after send him
to an inuisiole Tresourer to be payed, should
he not haue iust occasion to think me an abu-
ser? God hath promist truelie to his Sonne by
the mouth of Dauid that *his seed shal remaine for*   Psal. 88.
*euer, & his throne shalbe as the Sunne before him, &*   36.
*lyke to the Moone perfect for euer*: if the Sunne and
the Mone, when they ar in their great clear-
nes be inuisible, I vnderstand no thing. The
kirk neuer hath bene obscured so far by persecutions, but shee might be knowen, besy-
des the miserable blindnes of the Iewes &
Gentils, & maliciouse obstinacie of hereriks,
or factiouse separation of schismatiks. What?
Wil they make the enimies of God to be easse-
lie seene & found, wher is seruants & frends
dare not shew thē selues? Then God man hyde
and keep close his freinds for feare that Satan
spoille him: he shall haue onlie such as he may
steale without the deuils knowledge by meanes of the inuisibilitie, changed now in to à
visibilitie, by vertue of an act o parliamēt holden at Edenbrugh without approbatiõ, in the
Quenes M. absence the year of God 1560 ratified by a parliament of lyk force in his Maie-
sties minoritie 1567. But I passe this *nec veterum*
*memini, latorue malorum*. The deuil should fight
against the members of the kirk, but should
nor preuail, because the victorie should be theirs, and they for their victorie should be crouned,

ned, which can not be without battail. *Nam*

*qui cærtat in agone,non coronatur nisi legitimè cer-*
*tauerit. And if anie man stryue for a maistrie, he is*
*not crouned except he stryue as he ought to doo.* And

Sainct Paul sayeth of him self , *Bonum certamen*
*certaui,cursum consummaui, fidem seruaui : in reli-*
*quo reposita est mihi corona iustitiæ , quam reddet*
*mihi Dominus in die illa iustus index* &c. *I haue*
*fought à good fight,I haue consumate my course,I ha-*
*ue kept the faith. Concerning the rest,there is laid* Vp
*for me à cro* Vne *of iustice, wbich our Lord wil ren-*
*der to me in the last day,à iust iudge.*

If any think hir inuisible becauſe ſhee can
not be ſeene all at one tyme , but only in hir
partes:by that ſame reaſon they may think hilles & mountaines inuiſible,or rather no thing
in the world tobe viſible, nether man nor be-
aſt,nor other thing,great nor ſmal;becauſe no
thing can be ſeene al at one inſtant , one part
cutting away the ſight of an other , as may be
ſeene by daylie experience.

As to them who thinketh that all Gods promiſes apperti eneth to the particulares, whome he aſſiſts by a ſecret and particular inſpira-
tion , & fortifieth by an internall and inward
conſolation; whereof the holy ſpirit is called
the ſpirit of conſolation:we haue refuted them
before , and if this opinion were true, as it is
not , it wold confirme & ſtrengthen our ſen-
tence:For if the ſpirit of veritie be geuen to e-
uerie man in particular, meikil more to all togither. So the kirk hauing the ſpirit in ſo greae
                                        abon-

abondance could not erre. And doubtles naturall reason wil constraine vs to think that if
the particular can not erre (which must be if
euerie man be assisted with the holy spirit according to Gods soléne promises (the pastours
of the kirk shoul lesse be subiect to errour, because of their office , seing that the charge is
geuen to them to teach and & guyd the faith-  *Eph. 4.14.*
full that they be not caried away with euerie
wind of doctrine, except they wil say that pastours be altogither vnneedful , seing that the
holie spirit hath taken the office vpon him to
guyd euerie one in particular , or that the particular men hath the holie spirit in all abondance, which is denyed to the pastours , who
for that cause may erre , wheras the particular
is assured, an opinion ridiculouse and pernici-
ouse, although it be embraced by manie now
adayes. But this opinion of priuat inspiration
is false, because our Lord (to whom all apparteineth by the gift of his Father) made theis
promises to the Apostles when hesent them as
maisters, gouernours, and pastours of his kirk,
to preach and teach throughout the whole
world, and therfor it was for the publik char-
ge, duetie, and vtilitie of the kirk vniuersall. *In*  *Psal. 18.5.*
*omnem terram exiuit sonus eorum, & in fines orbis ter-*  *Rom. 10.*
*ræ verba eorum* . Moreouer this opinion is ab-  *18.*
surd, for if euery man hath the holy spirit , in
such abondance, no man could erre, but wold
say the truth in al thinges ( I mean in maters
of faith) yea no man could haue need of à master

ster or paſtour,(as is ſaid)euerie one being moſt
ſufficientlie inſtructed by the holie ſpirit, who
can not erre: vpon theis vaine imaginatiõs the
Anabaptiſts haue builded their folies. Neuer-
theles it muſt not be thought that we deny
that the holie ſpirit doeth aſſiſt the particulares: For he aſſiſteth them indeed with his grace, wherby they ar moued to obey, conſent, &
beleue the doctrine of the kirk, & to keep the
vnitie required therin, but not to command,
guyd, and gouerne, which appatteineth onlie
to the paſtours, as is ſaid·

　There reſteth yet two obiectiõs againſt the
ſtabilitie of the kirk in all veritie. The firſt is,
that the particular kirk may erre, which may
be ſhewẽ by manie exãples:& therfor the kirk
Catholik and vniuerſal may erre. The ſecond
is, that the kirk Catholik is repreſented by a
general Councel: but the general Coũcel may
erre, and hath erred: then the Catholik and
vniuerſal kirk may erre. To confirme the firſt
obiection they collect againſt the Iewes kirk
the faultes committed frome the beginning of
the world to our Lords tyme:to the which albeit it be eaſie to anſwer, yet becauſe it is not
our queſtion, who ar ſpeaking of the Chriſtian
kirk, I wil paſſe it for the preſent, as making no
thing againſt vs. I ſay only that they ſhal not
be abil to ſhew anie errour in the Iewes kirk
approued by publik conſent. For the ſentence of death pronounced by Caiphas againſt
our Lord was no wayes erroniouſe of it ſelf,
(if we

(if we wold lay afyd the wicked mynd from whence it proceded) feing it was according to our Maifters will (*qui paffus eft, quia voluit*) and Gods owen decree of his infinit mercy & loue towards mankind. And S. Iohn approueth it as comming of the holy fpirit, who prophecied by the mouth of a wicked man. The words of the Euangelift ar thefe: *But one of them named* Io. II. 49. *Caiphas, being the high prieft of that year, faid to them, you know nothing, neither doo you confider that it is expedient for vs that one man die for the people, and the wholl nation perish not. And this he faid not of him felf, but being high prieft of that year, he prophecied that Iefus fhould die for the nation, and not only for the nation, but gather into one the children of God, that were defperfed.* VVherby we may vnderftand the qualitie of the decree, not withftanding the wickednes of the inftrument. God bliffed his people by Balaams mouth: but this is Nom. 23. more folemne, feing that IESVS CHRIST is put in poffeffion of his inheritance by the fentence and decree of the fynagoge, pronounced by Caiphas at that time high prieft, Chrift being declared to be he, who was to redeeme the world with his death, by the which the facrifice of Aaron was to take end, the fynagoge hauing refigned ouer al right to the true heire, and that by a general confent, to the Iewes greatter and inexcufable condemnation.

As to the reft of the argument it followeth not. The particular may erre, ergo the general
may

may erre: For the partes (which ar as it were particulars (of the elements do perish euerie day, the elements notwithstanding doe remaine, yea and recouer at one syd, what they loose at the other: for it is impossible that the whole elements can perish all at one tyme, I meane naturalle.

So we see men die euerie day and that in great nóbers at some times, yet becaufe there commeth others in their place, man can not perish altogether, becaufe God hath blissed him, and al liuing things by these words *Crescite & multiplicamini.* Arist. wold haue answered *homo non morietur, fed hic homo.* And which is more, as man in particular remaining man, that is, reteining the nature and proprieties of man, cannot die (for if he die he ceasseth to be man) so the particular kirk remaining a kirk, that is remaining in the doctrine, vnion, and communion of the Catholique kirk, cannot erre: for if she fal in errour of doctrine generally receaued and approued, withdrawing hir self from the holie Catholique kirk, shee is no more a kirk, but as a dead body possessed by schisme and heresie. But if shee remaine in obedience and vnion with the Catholique kirk, albeit shee be assaulted with anie sicknes, or troubled with any wound of errour, yet by the lyf, strength, and health of the whole body of the Catholik kirk, shee may recouer hir health. Euen as we see the finger being cut from the body,

the

the interne and inward forme being loft, it loosseth the nature of à finger, although the material part remaineth as before; But remaining ioyned and vnited with the body, notwithstanding any infirmitie or wound, it may be cured and healed, by reason of the lyfe and health of the rest of the body with the which it is conioyned. A greene tree by violence of stormie wind, frost, or season of year, may loose the leaues or branches some tyme, which the spring or space of tyme will bring againe: but if the stock be rotten or drawen out of the ground, there is no hope of leaues, meikel lesse of branches, he must plant an other tree, who wold see leaues or branches there againe: which experience can not be sought in the kirk: FOR IESVS CHRIST wil plant no other; and I know not who could take the charge in his place, for it behoued him to do better then our Lord hath donne before him, wherby the promises made to the perpetual kirk might once be accomplished, seing that Chrifts kirk hath failed by interuption, as they say: which can not be, notwithstanding the saillinge of some partes, prouyding the noble partes doe keep their integritie: but they being loft, there is no meanes to set vp againe that kirk; they may perchance sett vp an other, if they haue receaued that power. And thus far for the first obiection.

As to the second we receaue the proposition as good and true, if they vnderstand à gene-

general Councel laufully called, holden, concluded, & confirmed: for doubtles sic à councel reprefenteth the Catholique and vniuerfal
kirk, which we beleeue can not erre : but that
sic councels hath erred or could erre, we deny
plainlie Yet to proue their faying, they alledge
that the councels ar contrarie one to an other,
which can not be but errour of one, or both
the parties. And farther, councels haue corrected councels, as fayeth S. Aug. but correction ( say they ) prefuppofeth errour : For
the proofe of the firft they bring examples ether of particular & prouincial fynods againft
general councels : or conuenticles of heretiks againft à general, or els councels fufpect
and difallowed againft à lauful and general :
Wherfor that proueth nothing againft vs, no
more, then maketh againft the authoritie of à
lauful parliament ( *si parua licet componere mag-
nis* ) the conuentions holden in diuers shyres,
being one againft an other, or anie of them
againft a iuft and lauful parliament : or yet à
feditiouse affemblie of rebelliouse perfonnes
ryfing againft their lauful Prince : or againft
a parliament of the whole eftates called, holden, concluded, and confirmed by the free authoritie of a iuft & lawful Prince in his maioritie. There can not be anie contradiction in
a Kings or commune Wealth edicts, or actes,
for correcting, or agreing together, the opinions of particular townes or shyres, or for
condemning of rebelles, and their famouse li-
                                    belles:

belles : or by improuing of actes neuer approued by his forfathers; yea nor for changing of any thing of policie in a better forme
being admonished by good experience, although it had bin otherwayes ordained by a
parliament before; prouyding the matters of
them selues were indifferēt. Where it is to be
noted firſt, thaṭ we ſpeak here of general
Councels, and nor of particulare, which as
they may erre, ſo ought they to be corrected
by the general(as meaneth S. Auguſtin againſt
the Donatiſts) if there be anie thing wrong.
Secondlie it is to be noted, that this diſpute
should be taken of thinges apperteining and
concerning the ſubſtance of faith, wher there
can be no changing or varietie, meikel les
contrarietie: for that which is once veritie remaineth euer veritie, becauſe the veritie is but
one, which may be made cleare and plaine,
not changed in the contrarie. But things apperteining to maners, ciuil diſcipline, commone policie, and ceremonies, becauſe they
touch oftentimes but ſingular mens actions,
or certaine countryes and perſonnes, or els ar
made by reaſon of the tyme; not onlie may
they be changed, the circumſtances being
taken away, but ſome tyme of neceſſitie muſt
be changed, except men wilfullie wold looſe
all: of which things. S. Aug. may be vnderſtood : for it is certaine he could not vnder-
ſtand of matters of faith, ſeing in his dayes
there was but two general Councels holden
                              D            (except

(except ye wil compt the Councel holden by
the Apostles at Ierusalem for one) the first of
Nice, and the first of Constantinople, which
with one consent are estemed to be without
errour, and so could not receaue correction
the one, from the other. Thirdlie it is to be
noted that we vnderstand the only Conclu-
sions, which ar taken in the general councels,
& not al things which ar done or said during
the tyme the councels holde, as in disputes
and conference; which things procedeth of
men, and may therfore be conioyned with errour: and so can serue for no argument against
our sentence. Although the matter requireth
a more ample discourse (if our intention had
bin to expouud this subiect at length) yet this
may serue for the present.

But ere I passe farther I wold pray you not
to mistake me in my former discourse (for I
see many mistaken in the same matter) as if I
wold thrust doune, and tread vnder foot, or
diminish the authoritie of the holie scriptures, by hauing recourse to the kirk in seeking
the true sence of them : we acknowlege them
both in equall dignitie, veritie, and certaintie,
becaufe they ar both of the holie spirit, hauing their vertue & force of him, as the Am-
basfadour and ambasse or commiffion of the
King or Prince who fendeth them. The one
derogateth nothing from the other : for if
there be anie thing obfcure in the cómiffion,
why may we not ask the Ambaffadours iud-
ment

ment without anie preiudice of his commiffion? or rather as apperteining to him, shal
we not ask his iudgement? for the letters oftentimes ar verie shorte conteining brieflie
the matter, whofe more ample declaration is
referred to the Ambaffadour, who for that
caufe is fent with letters of credit, he otherwayes not being neceffarie, becaufe the letters might do all, except they might not authorize them felues.

The kirk is Gods Ambaffadour fent to declare his will, hauing the fcriptures for letters of Commiffion and credit, & that in moft
ample forme; as we haue shewen before: why
shal not hir voice be heard before al others in
declaring the true meaning of hir commiffion? shal I ask of anie other why shee was
fent? The kirk and the fcriptures ar two lawful fifters of one father, none of them should
be cafte out, *Alterius fic pofcit opem res & con-* To 9.con.
*iurat amicè.* Therefor Sainct Auguftin fayeth, *Crefc. lib.*
that we keep the veritie of the fcriptures, 1.c 33.
when we do that which is approued by the
whole kirk, whome we fee fo wel recom-
mended to vs by the authoritie of the fame
fcriptures, as that which can not deceaue vs,
becaufe it is the holie writ. So without anie
preference we proue the fcriptures by the
kirk, and by hir alfo the true fence of them, as
the commiffion and the intelligence therof,
is authorized by the Ambaffadour.

IESVS-CHRIST proued him felf to be
D 2                      the

the true Meſſias promiſſed to the Iewes, and
that by the prophetes and law : becauſe all
things were compleat in him, that were fore-
ſpoken by them to be in the true Meſſias. The
ſame was donne by the Apoſtles and is donne
now euerie day againſt the Iewes : yet it is not
to be concluded that the prophetes and law ar
preferred before our Lord. It is inough that
the witnes be of ſufficient credit and authoritie with the parties. If any man denie this
dignitie to the kirk, I wil pray him to pardon
me, if I ſay he doeth that which Satan deſy-
reth moſt : for he laboreth to take away the
three thinges which onlie doe aſſure vs of
our Maiſter and Lord IESVS CHRIST, to
wit, the kirk, ſcriptures, and miracles, which
may be eaſelie ſeene : for the kirk being eſtee-
med a liar, and worthie of no credit, what can
be thought of the ſcriptures and miracles,
which we know by the kirk only : but if the
kirk be (as ſhee ſhould) of ſufficient authoritie with al true Chriſtians, thoſe thinges can
not be called in doubt. And why ſhould not
hir depoſition be heard, or rather hir iudgement receaued, in whatſoeuer mater of religion, as a thing apperteining iuſtlie to hir,
and which ſhee may better know then any
other, by reaſon of the ſtrait alliance betwixt
hir head and ſpouſe IESVS CHRIST, and
hir ? Shal euerie man know the will of the
Lord, and ſenſe of his commandements, and
his deare ſpouſe onlie ſhalbe ignorant ? Then
in vaine

in vaine hath he kiſſed hir with the kiſſe of his
mouth : in vaine hath he put his left hand vnder hir head, and with his right hand in vaine
hath he embraced hir, in vain hath he brought
hir into his chambers, if any man hath greatter priuiledge then ſhee; which muſt be, if
euerie man ſhould take that, which he thinkes
good and true, and not that which the kirk
thinketh and declareth good and true. And in
very deed, none of theſe new factious ſectes
can haue credit till they haue perſuaded their
auditours that the ſpouſe of our Lord is an
vnworthy liar. O blaſphemous tounges, and
foolish heares, who ſo raſhlie geue credit, to
a thing of it ſelf ſo incredible, & ſo pernicious
when it is receaued. Chriſt commandeth vs
to hear the kirk, Knox, and Caluin forbiddeth
vs, and wil, we follow only the ſcriptures,
that is their, or our owen iudgemér. Should it
be doubted to whom we ſhould here obey? I
muſt of force receaue the iudge ordained by
the Prince, and not to conſtitute my ſelf, or
anie other in that place, for that were a cryme
of læſmaieſtie, and worthie of a moſt ſeuere
punition, to ſerue for example to all other pre-
ſumptious perſonnes.

Now if we ſhould preferre the kirk before
the ſcriptures (which we do not, although we
preferre hir before priuat mens interpretation
forged now of new, which when we contemne and reiect, they deceptfully alledge vs to
deſpiſe the ſcriptures) who could iuſtlie be offended

fended with vs, seing shee is the spouse of our Lord and Maister, and the scriptures the contract of mariage betwixt them? who doubteth but the spouse is to be preferred before the contract of mariage? Moreouer the scriptures are made for the kirk, and not the kirk for the scriptures: *The sabboth was made for man, and not man for the sabboth,* sayeth our Lord. And also the kirk was before the scriptures, & shalbe after them. For the kirk triumphant shal haue no need of theis memories and directions, hauing the plenitude of al knowledge & veritie in the contemplation of him, in whom can be no ignorance, *in cuius lumine videbimus lumen : satiabimur enim cùm apparuerit eius gloria.* And last of al, our Maister & Lord died for the kirk, & not for the scriptures: the pryce should make the matter more precious. VVherfor shee must haue some prerogatiue, seing shee lacketh nothing that the scriptures haue, and hath manie things which nowayes can be attributed to the scriptures? here I may say with S. Augustin. *Me piget eam* (Ecclesiam) *commendare verbis meis, & hæreticos nõ pudet eam oppugnare verbis suis, I am in paine to praise hir* (to wit the kirk) *by my words: and heretiks ar not ashamed to assault hir with their words.* But it may be asked seing it is so, to what end serueth the scriptures ? (suffer me to vse à familiare example to declare, & expound à difficill and obscure matter: we see by daylie experience the blind ( notwithstanding he haue a guyd, on whom he dependeth and in

Marc. 2. 27.

To. de vnitate Eccle. c. 10.

whome

whome he trusteth) seek for à staff by meanes
of his guyd, wherby he may be more habill to
follow him ouer high mountaines and rockes,
riuers and myres, saue him self from stockes &
stonnes in the way, and precepices or down ne-
falles besides the way, and defend him self
from bytting of dogges wher he shal passe.
The kirk (who often in the scriptures is compared to the moune, and to a body) of hir self
blind, hauing the light and sight of hir Sunne
and head I E S V S C H R I S T, hath for hir guyd
the holy spirit, by whose meanes shee hath
the staff of the scriptures, wherby shee in following hir guyd & leader surmounteth more
easelie the high mountaines of spiritual & su-
pernatural difficulties, and rockes of naturall
subtilities, passeth ouer the deepe riuers of tri-
bulation and persecution, and myres of vyce,
saueth hir self frome stumbling stockes and
stonnes of this present lyf, and precipices of
schisme and heresie, not standing to goe the
straght way for the sclandrous tounges of the
one or the other. This is donne to hold vs in
exercise of al vertuous humilitie and good
actions: God doth nothing without good and
iust reason: *sed qui scrutator est maiestat is opprime-*
*tur à gloria.* This staffe which our mother hath
receaued of hir guyd should nether be violen-
tlie nor craftelie taken from hir, to abuse or
beat hir; it is good in hir hand, to whose vse it
was prepared; It is violence and spoliation, if
it be found any other where: It apperteineth
D 4                          onlie

onlie to hir and hirs: as geuen for hir seruice.
Other men haue no part by iust tytle.

And to conclude this dispute of perpetual
veritie in the kirk (for that is my principal
motiue to seek to the kirk) it can not be
thought with good reason that God hath suffered his kirk & welbeloued spouse, to whom
he hath made so many great and notable promises, geuen so high titels, and honored with
the mariage & death of his onlie Sonne, hath
suffered (I say) his kirk to perish in hir chyld-
hood and first age, for lack to haue continued
in hir the lyf of veritie, which hath bene lost
euer since the Apostles dayes, if we wil beleue
some men. Shal we not rather think that God
is merciful without repentinge him, & constât
in his liberal promises; and that sic pestilent
opinions ar inuented onlie by presumptious
braines, whose vaine imaginations could haue
no place if the kirk keepe hir authoritie, which
they wold gladie ouerthrow to establish and
authorize their nouelties, by the which, they
whold haue vs beleue that God is à liar: For
what is it other to cal and think God a liar,
then to say that nether is it, not can it be true,
which he hath said and promised. S. Augustin
disputinge against the Donatists of the greatnes and amplitude of the kirk, maketh almost
*de vnitate* the lyke conclusion. *Quasi aliud sit prophetiam*
*Ecclesiæ c.* *crimine falsitatis arguere, quàm dicere quæ prænun-*
*9. To. 7.* *ciauit non posse compleri: hoc est enim dicere, non esse*
*prophetiam, sed pseudoprophetiam.* As if it vvere any
other

*other thing to accuse the prophecie of falshood then to say that, vvhich it had forespoken could not be compleit: for that vvere as meikel as to say that it vvere not à prophecie, but à fals prophecie, or lie.*

Becaufe I haue made mention now fundry tymes of S. Auguftin, and fome other ancient writers, and should be ouer prolix, if I should cite al the places which may be proper here, I will pray the learned reader to take the paines to fee and read diligentlie. S. Auguftin *de vtilitate credendi ad Honoratum*, and *de vnitate Ecclefia contra Petiliani Donatifta epiftolam*. & Tertulian *de prafcriptionibus aduerfus bareticos* To thofe may be adioyned S. Cyprian *de vnitate Ecclefia*, & Vincentius Lirinenfis *aduerfus prophanas nouitates*.

I know fundry wold be glad to read thefe bookes, who cannot haue them; to whofe iuft defyre I wold willinglie fatisfie, if I had the meanes. In the meane tyme, if I shal gather out fome proprieties, which the ancients haue noted in the true kirk and, paftours, and alfo fals kirk and fals paftours, no man iuftlie can be offended

| | |
|---|---|
| 1 Antiquitas. | 1 Nouitas. |
| 2 Vnitas | 2 Schifmata. |
| 3 Confenfus & concordia. | 3 Diffenfio ac difcordia. |
| 4 Multitudo idem fentientium | 4 Paucitas idem fentientium |
| 5 Amplitudo per orbem terrarum. | 5 Auguftia in angulis. |
| 6 Maiorum reuentia | 6 Maiorum, etiam fuorum contemptus. |
| 7 Maieftas etiam regibus ipfis veneranda & culta. | 7 Obfcuritas, vicinis vix cognita, fuis neglecta. |
| 8 Paftorum fucceffio. | 8 Sibi fuccedere & in fe definere. |
| 9 Perpetuitas. | 9 Nupera origo. |
| 10 Vifibilitas. | 10 Inuifibilitas. |

11 Error.

| | |
|---|---|
| 11 Veritas. | 11 Error. |
| 12 Conſtantia in eadem patrumque doctrina. | 12 Inconſtantia in ſua patrumque doctrina. |
| 13 Firmitas contra omnes omnium hoſtium incurſus | 13 Infirmitas, æui breuitate cognita. |
| 14 In iis quæ ad nominis Chriſtiani propagationem pertinent, diligentia. | 14 In ijſdem vel propagandis inertia, vel euertendis peruerſitas, quia deijcit, non erigit. |
| 15 Doctrinæ vniuerſitas. | 15 Priuata opinion. |
| 16 Victoriæ contra hoſtes hæreticos & ſchiſmaticos. | 16. Inſœlices, etiã contra ſuos pugnæ. |
| 17 Authoritas ſecure audienda quia, ſine errore. | 17 Nullum ad firmandos animos pondus, quia agnoſcit ſe errori obnoxiam |
| 18 Humanitas & modeſtia | 18 Superbia & iactantia pluſquam Thraſonica. |
| 19 Ordo & diſciplina. | 19 Ataxia & futilis conuerſatio. |
| 20 Certa fides & minime dubia. | 20 Perpetuo inquiſitio, aut verius fluctuatio. |
| 21 Fidei regula Chriſtianis Eccleſia, quia Dei tabernaculum in ſole poſitum & vitis frugifera Domini manu plantata. | 21 Apud hæreticos ſibi quiſque regula eſt, quia in ſenſu ſuo latebras quærunt, vt ſarmenta inutilia a vite reſecta facile agnoſcas. |

I haue put theſe two rancks the one oppoſite to the other, to know what the Miniſters will approue, or improue in anie of them: as to vs, we firmly beleue that the qualities mētioned in the firſt doe apperteine to the true kirk onlie; and ar found in the Catholik, Apoſtolik, Romaine kirk onlie; which we conſtantlie beleue to be the true & onlie kirk, becauſe we find none but hir, to whome ſic notable promiſes hath bene made; or in whome they haue bene accompliſhed, but in hir onlie. Wherfore if the Miniſters wil haue vs to leaue the place where we are, as being vnfytte for our ſaluation, becauſe the qualities which we alledge ar not to be found in hir, they muſt

shew

shew vs an other, wher we shal find them,
seeing they are altogether necessarie to be
found in the spouse of IESVS CHRIST:
for otherwayes ether will they trauell in vaine, or we change lyk fooles, changing for the
worse, and leauing à kirk, which (as we ar surelie persuaded) is sure & can not erre, to follow à companie that they them selues, who
inuiteth vs, assureth vs to be vnsure, affirming
that it is subiect to errour so far, that God
him self can not keep it therfro, at least hath
not kept it, notwithstanding of his manyfold promises. Doubtles whosoeuer persuadeth vs that the house, where he wold haue
vs enter, is not sure, consequentlie persuadeth
vs (by presenting vs the danger which may
arryue) not to enter therein, except he be a
foole, or think vs fooles. It shal not be need-
ful here that the Ministers accuse, or speek
euill of any other man: but rather speak good
of them selues, prouyding they proue it well,
shewing that they haue the kirk *Dominam &
matrem gentium* indued with the notable and
excellēt qualities required in the true kirk, &
can not be found but amonge them, & theirs.
It will not content vs (if we be carefull, as we
should be, of our saluatiō) to say that our kirk
is euil, they must proue that their owē is good.
I say this because in place to proue thē selues
to haue the kirk, they raill aganist the vyce of
the Catholiks, as if our sinnes made thē à good
right, or they them selues were without sinne.

Many

Many haue left the Catholik kirk, and yet
haue not followed them, but haue taken an
other partie. Many alfo haue fled frome vicious Catholiks, & haue entered amonges more
vicious Proteftats: for I heare of none, as yet,
who ar become better men, for the leauing of
vs, or being out of our kirk. I call their confcience and our whole country to be witnes.
Iam fure that Luther and Caluin firft inuen-
ters or renewers of this religion, acknowledgeth that the world is become worfe fince the
comming of their new Euangell. I doubt not
but they know what is Cal_ins opinion here
aboute feing the eftimation they haue of him.
Luther fpeeketh plainlie. *Mundus indies ex hac
doctrina fit peior: homines vno antea, nunc septem dia-
bolis obsidentur, diabolus nunc plena cohorte homines
inuadit, vt sub clara Euangelij luce multò sint quàm
antea sub Papatu auariores, astutiores, fraudulentiores,
libidinosiores, procaciores ac peiores. The wordle becommeth daylie more wicked by this doctrine: before men
were befieged by one deuill, now they ar befeiged by
feuen. The deuill now doeth affaile men with a whole
bad of deuils, so that vnder the cleare light of the Euangell men ar become meakel more couuetous, more craf-
tie, more deceptfull, more cruell, more lecherous, more
shamleffe and more wicked, then before vnder the Pa-
pistrie.* An other of theis good brethrine fayeth
almoft the fame, *Vt totus mundus agnoscat eos non
effe Papiftas, nec bonis operibus quicquam fidere, illorum
operum nullum exercent penitus; ieiunij loco comeffati-
onibus & perpotationibus nocte diéque vacant; vbi
paupe-*

Smideli-
us.

*pauperibus benignè facere oportebat, eos deglutiunt &*
*excoriant:precationes vertunt in iuramenta, blasphemias*
*& diuini nominis execrationes, idque tam perditè, vt*
*Christus ne ab ipsis quidem Turcis hodie tantopere blas-*
*phemetur. Demum pro humilitate regnat passim super-*
*bia,fastus,elatio;atque hoc vniuersum vitæ genus,ab illis*
*Euangelicū dicitur institutum.* That all the world may
kno̅w̅ them not to be Papists, nor trust in good works,
they exercise none at al of theis works ; in place of
fasting they imploy their tyme night & day in extraordinarie eating and drinking. where they should haue
behaued them selues liberallie and bountefullie to wards
the poore,they deuoore them , & as it were pluckes of
the skinne of them:they change their prayers in to oothes,
blasphemies,and execrations of Gods name,and that so
desperatlie,that Christ is not this day so greatlie blas-
phemed amonges the Turkes them selues. finallie in
place of humilitie doeth reigne through all,pryd,disdai-
ne,presumption and they cal al this sort and maner of
lyf, à trade euangelik. If these men saye true, the
matter is euill mended, and we haue lytill occasion to change . I may truely say that they
haue made our men worse,and haue not mended their owen. That we may say with Tertu-
lian that *stantibus ruinam, non iacentibus eleuatio-* de proscri-
*nem operantur .* If true pastours should be kno- ptionibus
wen by their works , I leaue yow to iudge aduersus
what shal be thought of theis new Ecclesia- hær.
stical order & new kirk, where so few good
fruictes ar to be found by their owin confes-
fion. It is an euil brewing that is not good in
the newing: I think the Ministers of Scotland
                                                    wold

wold say as meikel of their flock, if they wold
lay to their conscience the hand, that they haue laid to so meikell kirk geare so wrongfullie.
At this tyme I will say no more, but (abyding
their answer) pray God grant vs al, for his infinite mercies sake, his trueth and grace that
we may know his veritie & follow his commãd. And this meikell touching the first head,
and reasons which moueth me to seek & cle-
ame to the kirk and offer to acknowledge the
Ministers, if they haue hir: now to the nixt
article.

T H E house of God, that is, the
kirk being found, I must adresse
my self to them, who haue the power & charge to lette me in, who
haue the keyes; who may not on-
lie shew me the infinite treasures of Gods
goodnes towardes vs, with his manyfold mercies and grace, but also will, and may by vertue of their charge make me partaker thereof
being grafted in the tree of lyf by participa-
tion of the holie sacraments and knowledge
of the true faith, & receauing of the same: that
is, I must go to the true and lawful pastours
and prelats, whome I must know, not by the
execution of that charge (albeit that be also
required) but by the power they haue receaued to execute sic a charge. For it is not a certaine

raine and folide proofe, that anie man is a
lawful magiftrat, if it may be shewen that he
hath geuen out fundry fentences and decrees;
or that he hath caufed execution of fundry
men to death ( for thofe thinges ar done oftentymes by wrongfull and tyranicall vfur-
pers ) but the power he hath to pronounce
and execute decrees, is required : otherwayes
the fact should make the magiftrate, and not
the authoritie, which is contrarie to al good
reafon. So I aske not now, who taketh vpon
them the offices & functions of paftours, but
who haue that power, that is, who haue the
lawful power and miffion, which is fo neceffarie in the paftours of the kirk, that although
anie man should haue the doctrine as pure as
the Apoftles them felues, with lyke knowledge; yet should he not be receaued as a pa-
ftour, except he haue the vocation of them,
who haue the power to giue it him, *nemo poteft in alium conferre quod ipfe non habet.* I am affured that the Minifters wil not fuffer within
their iurifdiction anie man to ftart vp at his
owen hand of his particular and priuat authority making affemblies apart , although he
should preach the fame doctrine, and adminifter the facramentes in the fame fafhion
grounded on the confeffion of faith, now receaued by the whole Minifterie of Scotland;
which confeffion they force, or wold force
al men to fubfcribe. The puritie of the doctrine wold not ftoppe them to condemne
him

him as a feditious fchifmatik, feing he had no
authoritie, or (albeit he had the authoritie) if
he lacketh the vnity required in the kirk : for
doubtles although he had the vocation as
lawful, as they can giue him, yet becaufe of his
fchifme, he fhould be efteemed to haue iuftlie
loft it, albeit in other things he keepeth the
fame doctrine in al refpectes; for the nature
of fchifme is fic, that as the diuifion of anie
member from the body, bringeth certaine
death and priuation of lyf (which cannot be
had but in, and with the whole ) fo doeth
fchifme in the kirk, to him, who is deuyded
frome the kirk. The Donatifts may ferue for
example, who in the begining were but fchifmatiks, yet at laft by there diuifion did fall in
corruption of doctrine and become heretikes;
euen as the member which is cut of, being de-
priued of the lyf (which it had in the whole
body) of neceffitie at laft muft rotte. Siclyk
Lucifer Bifhope, before Catholik, by his
fchifme did lofe him felf, although he did approue the Councel of Nice in all poinctes;
how deteftable the cryme of fchifme is before God, may eafelie be iudged by Core Dathan
and Abiron, whofe punition was more fear-
ful and terrible, nor theis, who made and adored the golden calf, notwithftanding of their
idolatrie.

But to retorne to our purpos, it is altogether
required, that the true doctrine and lawful
power be ioyned together in thofe, who wold
com-

command and rule in the houſe of God : the
law maketh vs al ſubiect and equal: the power
and authoritie (which ſhold be giuen by him,
who hath it) maketh the diſtinction and difference betwixt vs, and geueth charge to one
aboue the others : for what domination or
commandement had S. Peter S. Paul and the
reſt of the Apoſtles ouer the kirk of God, till
they receaued that charge and authoritie of
IESVS CHRIST him ſelf, to whome ap-
perteined the ſouueraine domination ? For al
being his, no man could command except he
had receaued power and comiſſion of him:
Nor yet anie man obey to an other, vnles he
were aſſured of the commiſſion. We ſee that
Princes punish ſeuerelie, but iuſtlie and neceſ-
ſarilie, ſic as take on them to command without charge: for of theis vſurpations ( if they
be ſuffered) commeth open rebellion againſt
the prince, oppreſſion of the ſubiects, and
wrack of the whole commone wealth. Al is
not done at the firſt inſtant, piece and piece
men proceede both in vertue and vyce, *nemo
repente fit turpiſſimus*. There be certaine degrees
to that high work of plaine rebellion and out-
caſting of the lauful & ſouueraine magiſtrate :
he who maketh the firſt breache, giueth the
firſt blow to his prince. Wherefor if the be-
ginner ſhould fill vp with his owen dead body
the breach that he had made, he ſhould find
few followers: the prince ſparing the firſt inuiteth others, and at laſt is conſtrained to pu-

E                          niſh

nish many, who wold not, at the beginning
punish one : *Crudelis est humanitas , quæ dum vni
parcit, multos perdit.*

    In this general, I doubt not but the Mini-
sters and I shall agree verie easely: For I see Beza one of their brethrin auoucheth that none
should command, or haue charge in the house
of God except sic as ar sent by God , which
sending he wil haue ruled according to the
order which God him self hath established in
his kirk, and thinketh it no wayes lawful to
anie man to violate this order : yet that our
Lord and Maister is not bound thereto , but
may dispose of the house of his father as he
thinketh best , notwithstanding of this order ;
if in case confusion be entred in the place of
order , that is , if the ordinarie vocation established by him self in the personnes of the
Apostles and their successours , shal faile and
cease ( which, as we haue proued before , can
not be ) for lacke of true pastours; he may send
extraordinarily and immediatly pastours to
guyd, rule, and gouerne his house and feed his
flock. I wil wel it be so (for no man should or
can deny that soueraine power to IESVS
CHRIST, although it be brought in here vpō
an absurd supposition, if true pastours cease )
prouyding there be no interruption in the
gouernement of the kirk , that is , prouyding
the kirk neuer want lauful pastours necessarie
for the edification of Christs mystical body ,
which is but one, & can not suffer so euident
con-

de notis
Ecclesiæ.

renuulfion: for by diuifion it muft be two bodyes: which muft be if the extraordinarie fucceed not incontinent to the ordinarie, when he shall ceafe. For we haue shewed be-fore that Chrifts kingdome muft be perpe-tual: it muft alfo be granted of neceſſity that the true kirk can no more want the lauful paftours, then she may want the trueth it felf. For the true doctrine muft be in the true do-ctours and paftours, or els it can net be had in this world. S. Paul ioyneth thefe two fuccef-fions together, as things which can not be fe-parated the one from the other, to wit, the word, of which commeth faith, and the pa-ftour who is fent with charg to preach the word. *bovv shal they belieue in him of vvhom they haue not hard? and hou shal they hear vvithout a prea-cher? but hovv shal they preach vnles they be fent?* we may fee the band and connection which S. Paul maketh here, the faith by hearing of the word proceeding from the preacher or pa-ftour, who hath gotten lauful power being fent for that effect by him who might fend him. The firft, to wit faith, perteineth to the fucceffion of doctrine which we ar obliged to beleue. The reft apperteineth to the fucceffion of perfonnes: the faith commeth by hearing, which cannot be without fpeaking (I mean ordinarily) & fpeeking requireth a preacher, who can not be lauful without miffion. wher-for as the kirk militant is perpetuall (for God neuer wanteth his kirk) fo hath shee perpe-

*Rom. 10, 14.*

E 2                   tuallie

tuallie true and lawful paſtours to gouerne
hir; becauſe without them, there can be no
kirk, ſeing that faith is required, which commeth by hearing, as is ſaid.

Let vs then ſpeak of this vocation, ſeing it
is ſo neceſſarie that without it the charge can
not be wel donne. I demand therefor who ſent
the Miniſters to preach in the kirk of God?
who hath geuen them that power vpon the
Chriſtian people, to nouriſh the good & obedient by preaching, to puniſh and cut of the
wicked & diſobedient by excommunication?
I haue ſaid already (and it is true) that the
law maketh vs al equal: the commiſſion or
power maketh the difference, in geuing authority to ſome to command, others remaining within the compas of obedience to beleue & do as they ar taughte and cōmanded.

de notis
Eccleſiæ
& epiſt.
Theolog.5.
    This power and vocation, according to Be-
zais diſtinction, is ether ordinarie or extraordinarie. The ordinarie lauful (ſayeth he) con-
ſiſteth in certain rules ordained by God, which
ar three: to wit Examination and tryal of doctrine & maners: Election made by the kirk:
And Impoſition of hands or ordination, Let
vs apply theſe three rules to the vocation of
Knox, Caluin, or Luther: for if it be not found
lauful and iuſt in the firſt authour, in the reſt
it can not be better; Quod ab initio non valuit,
tractu temporis conualeſcere non poteſt. The longer
that vſurpation leſteth, the worſe. Now to
ſay that anie of them had their calling of the
Catho-

Catholique and Romaine kirk ( as some doe say, when they ar pressed to shew their holding) it is nothing to the purpose: for the Ministers, to let the world vnderstand that they will not serue them selues therewith, will haue al men refuse and abiure al righte they may haue by the Pape and kirk of Rome: as may be seene in their confession of faith. And Caluin with the rest of the Ministers of Geneua wold not suffer the Bishopes of Troy and Neuers ( who leuing the Catholik kirk fled to them) in any wayes to preach til they had abiured al power receaued before, and taken of new their commission and authoritie of the Ministers, because in their opinion the former was not lauful. And in veritie the vocation cōming of the kirk of Rome can serue them to no purpose. For ether it was good or not: If it was good, doubtles they haue lost it by their schisme & rebellion, seing they haue left the kirk, of whome they had their vocation. The lyf can not be communicated nor extended to mēbers separated from the whol body. No man giueth power to be abandoned, nor to arme men and rebelles against him self, nor to be cast out of his owen place: Princes giue power to inferiour magistrates, but reteine euer ful power to them selues, to discharge or punish all rebellious personnes, whatsoeuer degree or preheminēce they haue within the realme, the higher place the greater fal, & greuouser paines to follow there vpon.

E 3                    *Poten*

*tentes potenter tormenta patientur*. If it was not
good it was nothinge of it self, of no valour
in the giuer, and so nothinge in the receauer.
Of force they must think so, if they wil abyd
at the first principel of their religion, to wit,
that the Pape is the great Antichrist : which
ground if it were true (as it is most false) their
vocatiō must needes be voide : for what commeth of Antichrist (who shalbe as it were Satans eldest sonne) must come of Saḍā: as whatsoeuer commeth of IESVS CHRIST commeth of God, becaufe he is Gods eldest and
onlie naturall Sonne. Wherfore hauing no
ordinarie calling of the Catholik Romaine
kirk, it followeth that they haue none at al.
For if they had anie of the Catholik kirk ( as
in deed some of them had being priests ) they
lost it by their schisme, and can haue none
from any other, but from them selues. And so
I may say of him whosoeuer shalbe first a-
mong them, that which Optatus Mileuitanus
sayeth of Victor first Bishope of the Donati-
stes: *Erat ibi filius sine patre, tyro sine Principe, disci-*
*pulus sine magistro, sequens sine antecedente, inquili-*
*nus sine domo, hospes sine hospitio, Pastor sine grege,*
*Episcopus sine populo. Ther was there a sonne without*
*a father, a new souldier without a commander or ru-*
*ler, a disciple without a maister, a follower without*
*any to go before, a tenant without an house, an hoste*
*without a lodging, a pastour without a flocke, a Bis-*
*hope without a people.* For the three conditions
required by Beza in a lawful pastour and ordi-
nar ie

narie calling can not be found in any of them,
if they be considered out of the Catholik Romaine kirk. Let vs take anie of them, whatsoeuer he be, and we shal see it to be so: For as to
the examination and tryal of doctrine, who
could examine him, seing he had no man aboue him, nor of higher power. And farther that
proofe could not be made vpon the first, leing
he was the finderout of the doctrine, he preached: wherfor as it was vnknowé to others, so
they could not examine him there vpon. Sure
I am that they wil not ascribe this examination to the people seing the people should be
taughte and examined, not teach and examine: but of this shortlie at more lengeh. As to
their maners, I find not that anie of them were angels, nether any of thes who haue followed after them: I say no farther, I excuse not
the faults & vyce of the cleargie; Iudas might
loose the Apostleship, he could not defyle it,
meekel lesse take it away or make it inutile in
others.

The Second is the franck & free election of
the personne examined, made with consent
& knowledge of the kirk where he should exercise that charge and function. This can not
be found in the first, and ring leaders of this
new kirk: for what kirk could' choose them,
seing they were before their kirk: for they
who liued in those dayes knew no sic doctrine, nor doctours; and so nether could examine
the doctrine nor elect the personnes, whose

opi-

opinions were so new at that tyme, that they
were not yet heard of.

But ye will say that their doctrine was most
ancient of it self, although not knowen so pu-
blikly. I answer that it can not be ancient nor
ould which continueth not frome the begining; for that which dieth as soon as it is borne, meriteth not the name of ould age, *quod
nascens moritur, senectutis nomen non meretur*. Ye
may wel say it is long since it hath bene ( if
perchance it haue bene manie yeares before
our age) but it is not long since it is: for being
doeth include continuation of à thing, which
they acknowledge not to be in their doctrine,
at least publiklie and knowen to the world.
But that which is confirmed with one simple
word, may sufficientlie be refuted with an
other: it was, it was not.

*Inst. lib.
4. cap. 14.
sect. 20.
& cap.
19. sect.
28. & 31.*

*Caluin in
the prefa-
ce of his
instit. and
Beza epist.
Teolog. 5.*

The thrid qualitie to wit Imposition of
hands (which Caluin acknowledgeth for à sacrament) shalbe lesse found in them: for who
could consecrate or ordaine them pastours by
imposition of hands, & geue them power to
command and rule the kirk of God, seing
they were the first them selues? There could
be none before them, the ordinarie succession
(as they alledge) being altogether perished and
lost. Moreouer it is to be considered that in our
country the imposition of hands hath bene
admitted within thes six yeares onlie, to wit,
the year of God 1598. and that not without
great difficultie and contention, and contrarie
                                        to the

to the opinion of sundry of the ministerie:
where I wold gladlie know of whom they
receaued imposition of hands, who that yeare
begane to impose the hands on others. As to
the foolish conceit of these that thinketh the
commone people to haue that power, they ar
more worthy of exemplare punition as trompettes of sedition, subiecting al sort of magistrats to à popular temerity and rage, then
worthie of credit or answer as honest and reasonable men. Out of thes factious shoppes
aganist the authoritie of lauful Princes and
their heritable right ar come *Francorum Galli s,*
*Vindiciæ contra tyrannos*, the pestilent pamphlet
*De iure regni apud Scotos*, th: fi.st blast of the tro-
pette, & other sic lyke vnhappie libelles verie
cutthrottes of al Princes, that hath good and
lauful right to any realme: becaufe sic iurisdi-
ctions ar, as it were, à strang and mightie bry-
dle to conteine within the compas of reafon al
seditious and ambitious spirits, of which our
age (to our great griefe) hath bene ouer plen-
tiful and aboundant, fomtyme vnder one colour fometyme vnder an other, lykwaves
whehaue had againft the Ecclesiastical order
within thefe thousand yeares, good store of
thefe busie writters, and amongft other we
haue found fome lytel touch in *affertionibus*   *affertione*
*theologicis, aut verius, negationibus cacologicis cu-*   2.
*iuflam Britannorum Scoti, qui inconditæ p'ebi ordi-*
*nationem Ecclfiafticam(licet in eo parùm fibi conftet)*
*committit.* The Ministers (if I be not deceaued)
wil

wil not authorize these toyes, yea no more
then Beza doeth approue Ramus dreames
in religion. Wherefor I wil not enter farther
therein, but wil retourn to these who so vn-
reuerentlie doeth traict their princes, as he
doeth prelats. Thes men thé must suffer me to
say that the subiect who wil haue no superiour sauing sic as he finds good and to his gust,
or sic as he may change when he list, should
feare to find the gibbet, to his superiour or hell
to his habitatio, no other place iustlie resting
for him who will not content him self with
his owen place, that is, which he is borne to,
or which his Prince of his proper motiue a-
vanceth him to. Shal the contentement or
miscontentement of rhe vncorstan: multitude, or of anie factious and seditious head, be à
rule in so great and weghtie a matter? shall sic
foolish braines be the square of al good and
lawful gouernement? These maximes set
doune to allure the people, ar to destroy both
the people and Princes, & commeth of them,
who beyond their merite looketh for auance-
ment to honours, to the which otherwayes
they could not atteine; so while they aspire
thereto, they conspyre against their Prince
and Maister. Certainelie as the inferiour magistrate is answerable to his Prince not to his
inferiour, so the Prince is answerable to God,
and not to his subiect. Otherwayes how often soeuer thes trompettes of sedition should
blowe, we should be as often in sollicitude of
Prince

Prince and commone wealth, and in place of
one pretended tyrante , we should haue ten
thowfand, who iuftlie might be called tyran-
tes. Thefe fyrbrands doe rail & cry out againft
the lawful Princes, to put in that place many
tribunes of the people, in hope to haue their
part, as others, who iniuftlie at entred there.
for why may they not fay with the naughtie
woman, *nec mihi nec tibi , fed diuidatur* , feing *3. Reg. 3.*
they haue no iuft part therin? But the iuft pof- *26.*
feſſour cannot approue fo pernicious a diuifion. If we lacke examples of our owen, there
might be found out ouermanie in other real-
mes. But by what right ( I pray you ) fhal the
feditious fubiect (for no other wil vfurpe that
place) be aboue his lawful Prince, to fit as
iudge on his eftate, lyf, and honour? Who is
amongft vs that wold willinglie fuffer to be
commanded ( what fhal I fay iudged? ) by
his owen feruant, by whome he were igno-
miniously accufed? It is not lawful to the partie to fit as iudge, nor to be witnes in a priuat
mans caufe: what fhall it be then in Princes?
We laugh & ieft when we fee anie priuat man
that thinketh him felf monarche of the whol
world, as being ficke of a pleafant imagination
& phantafie, without any mans hurt or dom-
mage. But it is no fport nor bourd to fee the
furious multitude medle it felf with the eftate,
lyf, and honour of their Prince, where many
thoufands ar oppreffed, vnder colour of the
commone wealth and libertie , which doubtles

les ar loft when they fall in the hands of the
multitude. If the Prince wold force vs to do
anie thing againſt God and good reaſon, we
should arme our ſelues with patience, and not
with rebellion, that is we should follow
Gods command; and if the Prince wold be ſo
rigourous as to punish vs therefore, we, after
the example of the Apoſtles and primitiue
kirk should ſuffer it, and not to take armes

Luc. 21.
19.
againſt him : *In patientia veſtra poſsidebitis animas
veſtras. In your patience you shall poſſeſſe your ſoulles*,
ſayeth our Lord. what good Chriſtian wold
not rather chooſe to be for the trueth a martyr before God, then as a traitour for rebellion
executed by men? we may without danger of
conſcience ſuffer a wrong, but not do a wrong
without danger of conſcience : It is but by
M. Foxes new martyrologe that men become
martyres for hereſie and rebellion. In the kirk
that honour is giuen only to them, who dieth
for the trueth ( as in the primitiue kirk) without any ſpot of rebellion : *cauſa martyrem facit,
non pœna.* I wil pas theſe opinions becauſe they
require a more sharpe maner of refutation,
ſeing they bring with them ſo many heapes of
miſeries, if they be not ſpedelie ſmothored in
the beginning. For to lay aſyd the commone
and publik calamities, wherein no man can be
in ſuretie, often tymes chooſing a new King,
we looſſe an ould kingdome. But to retourn
to our purpos : This ordination of paſtours
could not come of the people, becauſe at the
begin-

beginning of this new religion al the people was Catholik , and knew no sic doctrine nor doctours, and so could not make them pastors who were first actors of this tragedie. Moreo- uer Beza in his epistles seemeth no wayes to approue this populare forme of gouernement in the kirk. Wherefore seing the first Mini- ster nether had Examination, Election, nor Ordination , or Imposition of hands , it may be easelie concluded , that they had no lauful ordinarie calling,& so could nor giue any true vocation or calling to others,because they had it not them selues.

*Epistol Theolog* 83.

Let vs goe forward. The Catholik kirk (say they ) hath lost the ordinarie vocation, and they haue found the extraordinarie. We haue lost one thing, and they haue found an other; it is mutuallie mett with our losse. But seeing they haue not found our goodes , we can pre- tend no right therto : So , as we pretend no right to their extraordinarie calling , they can pretend no tytill to our ordinarie , as is said.

They ar called and sent extraordinarily (say they) to gouerne the kirk of God: if their vocation be extraordinarie it passeth the bounds of the order Apostolik: For how can it be Apostolik without continuation since the Apostles, not hauing beginning nor au- thoritie of their vocation. If the race and suc- cession of the Apostles be lost,why vaunt they them selues to follow the Apostles? at least they

they follow them not in their vocation, and
therefore: the tytils and euidents of the Apoftles can ferue them for nothing. They muft
shew their new holding, feing the ancient
tytles ar expyred and rune out; if there refteth
no man hauing the right of the Apoftles, the
Minifters can not haue it. We muft fee their
new charters paffed vnder the great feal of
I E S V S  C H R I S T, marcked with miracles,
wroght by the holy fpirit: if they can shew
anie fic thing, it will put them out of trouble,
and vs out of doubt, and take away al shadow
of excufe, which otherwayes we might iuftlie
pretend for our difobedience.

But in good confcience may we credit
them, who with their fimple word wold
make vs beleue that the ancient fucceffion of
the Apoftles is petished? Shal I not think (if
that be true) that the tribe of Leui was more
deare to God, then the fpiritual pofteritie of
the Apoftles, yea then the pofteritie of I E S V S
C H R I S T him felf, out of whofe feedes
mouth, the veritie should neuer depart? Shal
it ferue for nothing that that vyniard was
planted with our Maifters owé hand, bought
with is death, nurished by his Apoftles, wat-
red with their blood, and with the blood of
fo manie thowfand martyrs, keept by the affiftance of the holie fpirit, in the learned and
Godlie fathers, and in their pofteritie? Shal
the order of Aaron be fo far preferred to the
order of Melchifedech? the body to the fpirit,
the

Ifa. 59, 21.

the figure to the veritie, and man to God? Shal
the ministers haue the honour to haue resto-
red the kirk, which the holie spirit by his ne-
gligence had lost? their onlie hand hath holden our Lord in his right: Wel, geuing and not
granting that our Maister had lost his inheritance in this world for a tyme through negli-
gence of his officers, or rather by their malice
and knauerie: he hath cast them out: he hath
placed in their place and charge others, more
worthie. Yet before I see their letters of commission, I wold gladlie know why they were
geuen: for it could not be a light cause which
moued God to geue a new charge. They wil
say, perchance, to reforme the kirk, and take
away the manifold abuses that were both in
the doctrine and maners. A iust reason truelie
and a charge worthie of eternal memorie and
thankes, and most necessarie (if it be true) to
be put in execution, for the publik good, saluation of many soules, and (which is the principal) for Gods glorie, and he to be praised and
loued who doth his duety in the execution of
the same: But with what sinceritie and Godlie
dealing it hath bin fulfilled & accomplished,
the miserable estate of our country may beare
witnes: Where many haue learned the science
of Adam and Eue in eating of the forbidden
tree, knowing the good they haue lost & euill
they haue found. And I feare that these new
pastours haue vsed as litill discretion in gouer-
ning mens soules, as policie in doune casting
the ma-

the material kirks.

*Intempestiuas sed supprime Musa querelas.*

Put the case that they were sent to reform the
kirk in doctrine and maners. These heauenly
phisitions then found à scik persone before
them but not a dead, to procure whole health
they were sent. Why haue they rent this body
in peaces, and made vp so many others, so different and contrarious euery one to an other,
lyke the Cadmeian brethrin? These agree not
with their letter patent, if they haue any: they
should not haue passed the boundes of their
legatiō. If they were sent to reforme the kirk,
according to my iudgement ( I dare not be
bold to pronunce anie farther for feare of offence) they should haue remained in the kirk
( *fugiendo non curantur ægri, sed medendo* ) and by
vertue of their commission taken away the
causes of hir sicknes and deformitie: he who
gaue them the charg wold haue giuen them
the strength, *qui dat velle, dabit & perficere* : he
wold not haue left them in so notable and
good an enterprise; they could not haue lacked
meanes nor wisdom hauing so mightie a maister. If they feared the plauge or rather the iust
punition, I excuse their flight, yet can not
praise them, that they chose rather to seall
their doctrine with other mens blood then
with their owen. But to passe this extraordinarie stoutnes ( which hath moued them to
rent the kirk in peeces by so many sundrie
sectes, rather then to suffer martyrdome them
                                                    selues

felues & fo paffe to heauen) why did they goe
befides their commiffion ? they difcharged
not them felues in making an other kirk. To
make a kirk, and to reforme or heale a kirk, ar
diuers things. They muſt acknowledge a double fault which they haue committed, the
one in not doing that which they were commanded, which was in reforming the kirk;
the other in doing of that which they were
not commanded, in building a kirk. If there
was no kirk at all, when they came, their
commiffion was in vaine and ferued for nothing: they should haue retourned and taken an other, to make vp and build a kirk of
new, and not to reforme that which was not:
For reformation prefuppofeth a fubiect and
matter lacking fome thing neceffarie to the
perfection: fo their procuration (if there was
no kirk) was nothinge of it felf, and can nether ferue them nor their fucceffours for anie
warrand of this work they haue taken in
hand, how beutiful & glorious a name foeuer they giue it.

*Aspiciunt oculis superi mortalia iustis.*

Think ye it reafonable, that any man should
take vpon him to caft doune the houfe, which
IESVS CHRIST him felfe hath builded,
becaufe it femeth to his vaine imagination to
haue many deformities and vncomlineffes, &
build vp an other at his fantafie, alledging
that the Lord hath fent him? I can not beleue
that any man can be a better painter or maiſ-

F          fon

son then God, wno said *tota pulchra es amica
mea, & macula non est in te*, and who builded
his kirk vpon a rock. wel I know rhat it is
Gods wil that his house stand to the end of
the world. But let this be an errour of the Se-
cretarie, who should haue written formation
of a kirk; or the fault of the messenger, who
spake ouer softlie in our first commissioners
eare, whereby one word was taken for an
other. But whither it should be Formation,
Reformation, or Deformation, for the present I stand not, prouyding the commission of
this extraordinarie calling be good. They were sent (say they) by God extraordinarilie. I
desyre they proue that: for simple and proue-
les sayings, in matters of so great consequence
(as where it is question of eternal lyf & death)
can not be receaued, except by them, who
wold hazard their part of paradise on a simple word: we must see the commission alledged, if it be good and haue the best and assured mark, that it may serue vs for our warrand, when we shalbe called to rendre compt
of our rentes and dueties in commanding or
obeying. It is as dangerous to beleue euery
man, as to beleue no man. I see the Ministers
haue dispossessed those, who were pastours by
iust succession (as hauing receaued that charge from hand to hand since the Apostles) and
haue placed them selues in their roome desy-
ring or rather commanding vs to acknowledge them as true pastours, follow and obey
                                              them,

*Knox ap-
pellation
2.*

them, geuing our foules and confcience to be
nurished by them in trueth and pietie, of the
which they haue the diftribution delyuered
to them by God him felf, as they alledge.

Truelie feing that no man, no not of their
moft zelous brethrin will giue them a thowfand pound on their word without good and
fufficient caution , should we not be great
fooles to giue them our foules not asking of
them any fufficient warrand. but their word?
The matter is fo weightie that they can not
iuftlie be offended with vs, if we defyre to be
affured that we may haue no loffe in beleuing
them. Let vs fee the great Seall and mark of
this extraordinarie calling, that is miracles
and wonderfull works aboue nature , where
by we may know that it is God who fent
them, and that it is his wil we receaue them
with due reuerence and obedience. I know
they wil anfwer me here, that they at not
obliged to bring miracles, feing they teach no
new doctrin. I pray al good and Godlie Chriftians confider if this be a propre anfwer and
to the purpofe: For firft they take that for a
proofe, which is in controuerfie betwixt the
parties, as is ouer euidentlie knowen : for we
fay (as we shalbe able to proue by them felues) that the doctrine they teach now is new,
at the leaft in many heades of controuerfies.
Secondlie the prophetes, who brought miracles , brought no new doctrine, otherwayes they could not haue bin receaued,

F 2                    the

the law being so formall against them.
Thridlie it must be new to vs , seing that nether we, nor anie of our forefathers before Knox euer heard of it in our countrey.
Last of all, we seek miracles for their alledged
extraordinarie and marueilous calling, & not
for their doctrine, which can not be true,
seing it is so new , the veritie being so ould.
Our Maister & Lord commandeth vs in matters of religion to obey his kitk: & to obey &
acknowledge none other. Why shal we now
heare the Ministers without anie assurance of
their charge and commission , ether ordinarie
or extraordinarie ? If anie man wold aske of
the subiectes of a noble man(who were out of
the country) the rentes and dueties, alledging
he had commission of their maister : VVold
they not iustlie answer,that their maister before his parting out of the country , had put
order to all his affaires , giuing charge to certaine men whome he had chosen for that effect and made officers ouer his wholle lands
with ful power to sett and lett,take vp dueties
and rentes , giue quittances, sett and hould
courtes, and al other things necessarie , with
expresse commãd to acknowledge none other
till his retourning : wherefore if he had any
commission from their maister, it behoued to
be communicat and seene, yea assuredlie knowen to be auailable & sufficient? Certainlie it
wold not serue nor moue them (if they were
well aduysed)to say that theis things , which
he re-

he requireth were due & owing to their maister and that he asketh no thing, to which
they were not obliged: Nor yet to say that the
officers had neglected their duetie both in wa-
sting their maisters goods and misgouerning
his house, and also in oppressing his subiectes.
wold they not answer, that they were sorie for
sic mens misbehauiour, yet because their maister had geuen them charge to obey onlie thois
officers whome he had established, they could
not passe the bounds of their maisters command ; and therfor wold in no way acknowledge him, who sheweth no commission, nor
power of their maister? Shall poore men be
more wise & circunspect in a quarter of meal
or 40. shillings , then I in my soule? Shal they
seek for good warrand in paying of their dueties, and shal I giue my soule to the first that
craueth it ? It shall not be needfull to tel me
here, what I owe to my maister, what I should
beleue, what reuerence I should beare to the
scriptures and pastoures of the kirk. I beleue
that more is true, then anie man can tell: I aske
onlie wherefro commeth thes extraordinarie
officers , and what power they haue ? I wold
pray them to cleare me of this subiect. For in
matters of faith , the authoritie maketh all;
which can receaue none other warrand, but
God him self, or else sic as ar sufficiëtly authorized by him. They wil say that sundrie of the
prophetes came without miracles , and therefor it can not be iustly asked of them, which

hath not bin asked of others before them,
comming with lyk calling. I answer, that a
great part of the Prophetes brought miracles
with them to confirme their sending, & principally, when their vocation was, or might be
called in doubt.wherefor Moses shewed miracles not onlie in the beginning, when he was
first receaued, but also against Core Dathan
and Abiron. Elias against the prophetes of
Baal in burning the sacrifice vpon the Alter
before the people. And to passe vnder silence
al other, IESVS CHRIST acknowledgeth
miracles to be necessarie. *If I* (sayeth he)
Io.15.24. *had not come and donne works amonges them, that no*
*other man hath donne, they had not had sinne. But*
*now they both haue sinne, and haue hated both me and*
*my father.* To Sainct Iohn the Baptist asking
by two of his disciples, if it was he who was
Matt. 11. to come, he answereth, *the blind see, the crippel*
5.        *walk, the lepers ar made cleane, the deafe heare, the*
Luc.7.19. *dead ryse againe, to the poore the Euangelle is preached.*
Moreouer the prophetes, who were sent ex-
traordinarilie neuer intermedled them selues
with the office of preesthood and pastours
(except they were of the Tribe of Leui)
nor euer put them out of their place. We
neuer heard that any, becaufe he was sent
extraordinarilie, took the place of the high
preest: or took the Ephod, or censure out of
the preests hands: For the sacrifice was euer
continued by the preestes and by none other.
So that the ancient prophetes howsoeuer they
were

were called extraordinarilie (as is said) did
neuer pretend thereby any charge in the sacrifice as appertening to the priestes only. For
the prophetes came as a new succour & helpe
sent by God to fortifie and comfort the ordinarie officers, to waken them vp from negli-
gence, to aduertise them of their duetie, to
loue honour and serue their God vprightlie.
Lykewise to admonish the Prince and people
of their office, reproue them of their faultes
and sinnes, with threatnings of punition and
vengance there vpon to follow, except they
did preuent the wrath of God with speedy repentance. In which charges miracles were
not verie necessarie, seing they demanded but
amendement of mens lyues, and Godes seruice
to be donne, by sic as had the charge, not med-
ling there with, notwithstanding of their extraordinarie sending by God him self. Euen as
if a Prince or noble mã absét, wold giue charge
to anie man by mouth, to aduetise his seruan-
tes and subiectes to be more diligent in their
office and duetie, shewing them wherein
their maister were offended, and what punition he had deliberate to take of sic as he foũd
culpable and giltie; it should not be necessarie
therefore to bring his maisters great sealle. But
if he wold enter to gouerne and rule, he wold
not be receaued vpon his simple word. Morouer, although there be no mention in the
scriptures of the miracles of sundrie Prophetes, yet it is not to be concluded that they did

no miracles : yea their prophecies were sufficient warrands for their miſſion, they being,
as it were, the ordinarie poſtes & meſſengers
in thoſe dayes betwixt God and his people, to
whom Gods will was to be shewen according to the peoples behauiour and new occur-
rantes. It can not be shewen where that anie
prophete is come to execute anie great enter-
priſe without miracles, ether preſente, precedent, or ſubſequent. In S. Iohn the Baptiſt
there be manie things verie miraculous, his
mothers age, his fathers dumnes before his
conception, and ſpeach reſtored at his birth,
his education commanded by the angel, his
lyf; and laſt of all the teſtimonie of I E S V S
C H R I S T more then all miracles, ſeing he
was the authour of all miracles, which at that
tyme for iuſt reaſon he had kepte to him ſelf:
whereby he might be knowen from others,
Now there came neuer anie prophete for ſo
weightie a matter as this, for which, they ſay,
that they ar come, to wit, to reſtore the ſpouſe
to I E S V S C H R I S T, the body to the head,
to make a new flock to that heauenlie Paſtour,
to reſtore him to his ould & ancient heritage,
to build vp the eternal houſe of God, to deſtroy the reigne of Satan: to bring new light
to the world, to take mankynd out of the
thraot, as it were, of the deuill: to publish
the verity ſo long vnknowen : to shew the
kirk ſo long vnſeene and inuiſible. And to
be ſhort, to do that wherefore our Maiſter
                                                 and

and Lord of his infinite goodnes came in to
earth, and took vpon him our mortall nature, and therein suffered death and passion, that
is, to make vs immortals, and of sonnes of
man, which we were, to make vs sonnes of
God, to be partakers with him of the eternal
inheritance, hauing nurished and brought
vs vp in his owen house: the which to gouerne if Luther, Caluin, or Knox pretendes
any right by new extraordinarie charge, is it
not most reasonable that they shew an au-
thentique commission? Should not the great
sealle be here imployed? Elias for lesse cause
made the fyre come out of heauen. If a simple
alledgeance of reformation be a sufficient
warrand, we shall haue incontinent good
store of reformers and extraordinarie pastours
to correct, or rather to corrupt, the whole
world. The Anabaptistes and Libertines with
manie other siclyke pernicious pestes should
shortlie occupie all places: For their word is
as good as the other is, in matters of religion,
if the word be inough, and the saying a sufficient proofe. But if there be anie other thing
requisite to haue and procure credit, what-
euer is necessarie in one, is necessarie in all,
seing there can be no authoritie and power
but in the ordinarie: because it onlie was sufficientlie authorized by IESVS CHRIST,
and executed by his Apostles (who receaued
it immediatlie of their Maister) and by their
successors to our dayes. Otherwayes the ex-
traordi-

traordinarie muſt haue as good and ſolid
proofe as the ordinarie. If it be ſufficient to
ſay that is was Gods will and pleaſure, that
ſic men ſhould take that worke of gouernement and reformation in hand: when they
cote the place, we ſhal ether anſwer, or agree
thereto. But IESVS CHRIST will diſa-
uow ſick extraordinarie reformers. *The Pro-*
*phetes lyes in my name. I haue not ſent them, neither*
*did I command them: nether ſpake I ʋnto them: but*
*they prophecie ʋnto you, a fals ʋiſion and diuina-*
*tion and ʋanitie and deceatfulnes of their owne*
*hart.* Let them ſhew (if they haue anie charge)
the expreſſe and particular command they
haue of God to come: for the general and ancient commandement without doubt apperteineth to the ordinarie officers of the houſe,
whoſe commiſſion is of long tyme both confirmed and acknowledged: Noueltie ſhould
be ſuſpect of al men ſeing, as is ſaid, the veritie is ſo ould.

    Some anſwere that it is a great miracle and
ſufficient to proue Gods wil and pleaſure, that
in ſo ſhort a tyme they haue drawen ſo manie
to them from the kirk of Rome. If that were
a ſufficient reaſon and great miracle ; then
ſhould Mahomet and Arius be holie men ſent
by God, and his welbeloued; for certaine it
is that the impietie of Mahomet, or hereſie of
Arius was more mightie then al thoſe who
haue ſeperated them ſelues in theſe late dayes
from the Catholique Romaine kirk : yet I am
                  aſſu⸗

*Ierem.* 14.
14.

assured that no man of iudgement wil thinke
that Mahomet, or Arius did miracles by their
seduction, or that sic reuolts were sufficient to proue them to be sent by God with
new commission. Therefore although Luther,
Caluin, Knox and their successours had bran-
gled the whole world ( as they haue not done,
and the Antechrist wil do )with their authoritie and doctrine, it followeth not that it is a
work approued by God & his extraordinarie
sending : For albeit it be contrarie to al ordinarie course, it should not be concluded , that
it is good and procedeth from a power extraordinarie geuen by God : For we see manie
extraordinarie actions, and punished extraor-
dinarelie , as things donne with violence and
contrarie to all order. I can not beleue that
the Ministers them selues wold now receaue
any man, who wold come with an extraordinarie calling to reforme them , notwithstand
of their short possession : wherein there be
manie thinges thought(euen by some of them
selues ) worthie of a good reformation. I
doubt not but they wold alledge their order
alredie receaued , confirmed and established.
And in case he wold not desist , I am assured ,
they wold imploy the force of their excommunication and actes of parliament , as a sou-
ueraine remedie against al rebellious personnes. If it was lawful to a few vnquyet spirites
to ryse against the whole Catholique kirk
being in possession 1500. yeares established ,
                                                      why

why shal it not be laufull to ryse againſt a few new incomes ? might it not be iuſtlie ſaid here *Patere legem quam ipſe tuleris*? The iuriſconſult ſayeth well, *quod quiſque iuris in alterum ſtatuit, ipſe eodem iure vti debet.* Shall it be permitted to them to do what they liſt, againſt whome they pleaſe, in what maner & matter they will, and shal be lauful to no man to gainſay them. *O duram aliorum ſortem ne dicam ſervitutem.* They wil alledge perchance the ſcriptures for their watrād & that they teach the veritie conteined therein. I anſwer, that euerie heretik ſayeth the like, and that al our diſpute, for the preſent, is of their power and calling : and that it is an other debate betwixt vs and them touching the ſcriptures and veritie, as we haue ſaid before. We grant the ſcriptures and the veritie should be receaued and imbraced, and all good reaſon doth teach vs that there should be paſtoures ; but they giue no aſſurance yea no appeerance that Luther, Caluin, or Knox, or anie of their ſucceſſours, can be theſe true paſtours, but rather the contrarie, as we haue proued. Wold they then thus argument ? I haue the bible, I ſay the trueth, I am then a true lauful paſtour and doctour of Godes kirk ? I vnderſtand not this conſequent, except they wold ſay that all (be they men, wemen, or children, learned or ignorant) who hath the bible and ſayeth the verity ar true and lauful paſtours, that is, haue lauful power and authoritie in, the

kirk

kirk of of God to preache, teache, and administer the facramentes, bind and loose,
take in and put out, excommunicate and abfolue, which I am affured, they wil not fay.
What wold be thought of me, if I should argument thus? I haue the actes of parliament,
I fay no thing but according to the Kinges
Maieftie lawes and ordinances, therefor I am
a shiref or lieutenant for his Maieftie: that is,
I haue power to adminifter iuftice, condemne
and abfolue, head and hang, banish and cal
back &c. perchance this vaine imagination
wold be tolerat and laughen at in me, as oftentymes fic phrenetik fpirites ferueth for
other mens recreation: but if there vpon I
should take anie man who had committed a
murther and (keeping the ordinarie forme
of iuftice in all other things, except in the power which I had not) should call in 15. or 20.
honeft men on his Affifes, & by them, for the
flaughter well verified,& confeffed, côdemne
him in the mouth of the doome-giuer, & execute him by the hangman, wold it be a fufficient warrand for me to shew the actes of parliament or lawes of the country & perpetuall
practife in lyke thinges? It wold not be asked
of me what the law ordaineth, but what power and authoritie I had to take that man,
call in a Syes on him, condemne and execute
him: my commiffion wold be fought, and
not the law. Yea for lack of a lawful commiffion I should be found not onlie a manflayer
with

with Syes, Doome=giuer & Hangmā (whom
I had drawen in that cryme with me ) but
alſo an vſurper of the Kinges authoritie, without his knowledge or wil, ſo I and all my
adherentes should be found in that action
more giltie, and to haue offended the Prince
more greuouſlie then the murtherer, whome I had executed: For beſyde the ſlaughter,
in my action should be found vſurpation, oppreſſion and coniunction of ſo manie perſo-
nes therin, which should augment my cryme:
For as in good thinges the more the better,
ſo in euil thinges the more the worſe. Lykwiſe we aske not of the miniſters, if ther
should be any lawful paſtoures who should
preach, teach, adminiſter the ſacramentes,
exhort to vertue, reproue vyce, cut off rotten
and rebellious members : we know theis
things may and should be donne by them
who haue the lawful power: But we demand
who gaue them that power to exerciſe theis
charges & offices to enioye that priuiledge?
Shal not the vſurper here be in greater dāger,
as the matter is greater? Or shal Kinges and
Princes, nobles & gentilmen, commoune we=
althes and burgiſes, priuat and ſimple men
haue order and diſcipline, wereby ſome command and others obey without confuſion, and
God shal haue none in his houſe ? In the kirk
shalbe no thing, but diſorder trouble and
diſcorde?that it may be ſaid of hir, which the
poëte ſayeth of the ſea waues.

*Neſcit*

*Nescit cui domino pareat vnda maris.*

If euerie man wil command (which muſt be
if the bible may make a paſtour) who ſhal not
command ? only they ſurely who wanteth
ether rneanes or wil to haue a bible . It is permitted to euerie man to ſhew the law and
trueth to any man: Yea it is a work of charity,
to teach the ignorant, pincipally in matters
of ſaluation: but to take on him the power &
iuriſdiction to command aboue others as
being à paſtour or magiſtrate , not hauing
charg of them , who hath that power , *num-
quam licuit , numquámque licebit* . It was not , is
not`, nor euer ſhalbe lauful. The kirk is as *Ca-
ſtrorum acies ordinata* : Not lyke to the *Chaos* of
poëtes where.

*Frigida pugnabant calidis, humentia ſiccis,*
*Mollia cum duris, ſine pondere habentia pondus.*

Sic confuſions agrees not with Gods infinite
wiſdome, *quæ attingit à fine vſque ad finem fortiter,*
*& diſponit omnia ſuauiter* . The qualities that S.
Paul requireth in a Biſhope, ſheweth how careful God is to haue his houſe well-gouerned.
Men wil not ſuffer euerie man to medle with
the keeping of their beaſtes,& I think nor that
God hath leſſe regard to his kirk . It may be
that they ſay that there was no paſtours in the
kirk, when theis new Euangeliſtes came, ſeing
they who were in poſſeſſion had loſt their
right, becauſe they had not donne their duetie : and therefor the miniſters *quaſi in vacuam*
*veneruut*,did occupie a place vacan`. Although
it be

it be a thing verie hard to be beleeued, yea altogether not to be beleeued, that God contrarie to his promise hath so abandoned his owen inheritance, that he hath no man; who with lauful authority did his duetie, or might giue power to others to gouerne our Sauiors house, yet I wil passe it at this tyme. I take onlie that pastoures hath not lost their place by reason of non entry, in which case it behoueth them to haue recourse to their maister, all retourning back againe to him. If they haue neglegentlie and vnproperlie donne their office, as the cryme was personal, so should the paine and punition be personal: seing in felonies the heires or successours be not pursued for the cryme of their predecessours, except they be found socy criminis, or else that their predecessours haue committed lesmaiestie. Now seing the successour is nowayes debarred for commoune cryme committed by his predecessours: it resteth the cryme must be of les-maiestie, by rebellion or treason against the Princes personne or estate, counsel taken with the enimie, aspyring to the croune, or other sic poinctes as theis. Now giuing & not gräting (for the Ministers can neuer be able to proue sic thinges, as we haue shewen before) that the pastoures of the Catholique kirk haue lost their place by one of theis crymes : what syn? Followeth it that the ministers haue the iust title? Quo iure? By publique authoritie and forme of iustice the charge, power, and office

of pa-of paſtorrs was geuen to the Apoſtles and their ſucceſſors til the worlds end. Yet if they haue failled ſo greuouſlie, that God hath called back the gift made to his onlie ſonne, let them be accuſed, examined, iudged, and condemned by publique authoritie and forme of iuſtice, and ſo diſcharged, diſpoſſeſſed and caſt out, as men orderlie conuiꞔ and adiudged to forfeit: and let others by lyk forme and authoritie be put in their place, by them who hath the power thereto. The offence maketh men worthie of condemnation, but condemneth no man. The ſentence and decree of the iudge muſt firſt be pronounced. Manie men committe great crymes, yet poſſeſſe their lands til they be forfaulted : and ſundry getteth their remiſſion before they be accuſed: and others, notwithſtanding they be iuſtlie accuſed of treaſon, yet becauſe they ar not condemned and forfault, without anie remiſſion they ſtand ſtil in poſſeſſion & their heires after them.

Seing the Kinges authoritie and publique forme of iuſtice ar required to put anie man in iuſt poſſeſſion of his owne, ſhal it be permitted to euery man at his phantaſy to caſt him out, who is in poſſeſſion ? And when the aꞔ of forfaultrie is paſſed and giuen out in due forme, the landes or offices ar not abandoned to euery one, who wil occupie them: but they returne to the Prince or ouerlord. So whoſoeuer will iuſtlie poſſeſſe and enioye

G                    theis

theis lands or offices, muſt haue a new gift of
the Prince or ouerlord, new charters, euiden-
çes , infeftments , commiſſions well made,
ſubſcribed , and ſealed, with all other circumſtances ( berter knowen to men of law
nor to me) which ar neceſſarie ; whereby he
may be knowen to be the iuſte poſſeſſour or
lawful magiſtrate: for the charters, euidences,
infeftments, commiſſions or liueree, or anie
other tytles which were before , ar anulled,
as apperteining only to the perſone forfault,
and therefor inutile for al other men , except
perchance to his heires , if the Prince wold
haue pittie of them: or if he wold ſuffer the
forfaultrie to be reduced of ſpecial grace and
fauour. Whoſoeuer wold ſtart to at his owen
hand, and occupie the place vacant without
conſent of the ſuperiour, might thinke aſſuredlie that his vſurpation wold be as heauie
a cryme as the others was, who had loſt the
place.

Lykwiſe ( as ſaid is ) if the paſtors haue failled , let them be accuſed before their lawful
iudge: where they ar found giltie, let them be
condemned : thereafter ſic as ſhalbe found
more qualified , and worthie of ſic offices
may be choſen in their place and obtein a new
commiſſion of them, who hath that power
in the kirk vpon earth. If ther be none at al,
who hath iuriſdiction , they muſt take new
holding of God in the ſame forme and maner
as the Apoſtles receaued it from Ieſus Chriſt,
                                                        the

the posteritie and successors hauing failled, as
they alledge, but not proue. Now what forme of iustice hath bene keept ? Who warned
the pastoures? Before what iudge were they
accused? Who condemned them? who gaue
the new title to the Ministers? I see the lawful pastores accused, or rather abused, with
out law, or reason, or iudge: condemned without any forme of iustice; cast out with violo-
lence, and their places occupied by others,
without, yea against al right. I see their contrarie partie make him self iudge, take a commission of him self, and put it in execution on
his priuat authoritie.

--- *Díne hunc ardorē mentibus addunt Euryola?*
   *An sua cuique Deus fit dira cupido?*

If al things must be made new before they
haue good right, it were best they made a new
God to authoriz their new procedinges and
practise of law: for if theis fashions were
good and reasonable, who could be assured, I
say not of his goodes office or landes, but euen
of his verie lyf, euery man making him self
partie, witnes, iudge, and executour of anie
accusation he should forge against anie man
it pleaseth him? I might insist here with manie other reasons, if I feared not to be tedious
in vrging a matter so cleare of it self.

I know some, for defence of the Ministers,
sayeth that their vocation is nether altogether ordinarie, nor altogether extraordinarie,
*partem capiens ab* '*troque*, that is ( when al is

well confidered.) nether the one nor the
other. There is no moungrill religions, as
ther is halflang dogges. They wold ferue them
felues with the authoritie of the Catholik
kirk to enter in Gods houfe with order, and
afterward withour order, which they call extraordinarilie, guyde, or rather mifguyde all
at their phantafie.

But is it poffible that they wil ferue them
with the kirk of Rome, feing they haue taken for a ground of their religion and lawful
caufe of their feparation, that the Pape is the
great Antechrift? They muft on force laying
this ground, acknowledge that they haue
their entry in the kirk frome the Antechrift.
Truelie if they haue no better porter then
Satans eldeft fonne to let them in, I fear they
shal not be wealcome to God, who vfeth in
his merciful workes to imploy better fer-
uantes. If that opinion were true, then
should Satan be halfe maifter, feing that the
half of the charge commeth of him: yea he
muft haue (according to that doctrine) the
moft apparant part, feing that the ordinarie,
which is well authorized commeth of him:
where as the extraordinarie, which they
wold afcribe to God, commeth without anie
a vow, except of their bare faying. I wold be
more ample in the refutation of this branded
vocation, if I thought not that few, or none
wold clayme thereto.

As to them, who ferue them felues with
the

the wordes of our Lord, *vvhere there be tvvo or* Matth.18.
*three assembled in my name, there I am in the middest* 20.
*of them.* I answer shortlie, first, that it is question there, of the assistance of our Lord to the
prelates of the kirk or people, and not of the
calling of pastoures in particular. And who
doubteth but holie and Godlie men hath the
assistance of God whither they be in smal or
great nomber. Nixt, if that should be taken
generallie and for the vocation, wherfoeuer
there be two or three gathered in Christes
name there must be there power to make a
pastour, So where there be two or three in
anie house they must constitute a pastour to
them self, and so change al priuat houses in
kirkes, contrarie to that, which we see now
in Scotland where kirkes ar turned in priuat
houses. Morouer if that were the sense of
Christes wordes, it should apperteine to the
people to cal the pastours, which the Ministers of Scotland verie wyslie, as yet haue neuer approued, And last of al, this could make
no thing for the first Minister, who being a-
lone could not be elected by two or three.

   Notwithstanding of al this, I will giue and
suppose in this matter as far as I can without
preiudice of the veritie. I wil so enter for the
present to receaue the extraordinarie vocation ( which with reason can not be receaued,
except it haue a verie good warrand ) if it can
serue vs to anie vse as I fear it can not do : For
if so many hondreth yeares vnion of the Ca-

tholik doctrine can not serue to maintaine vs
in our ordinarie right, how shal so many hundred daylie confusions iustlie maintaine them
in their extraordinarie vsurpation ? But to
what vse can their extraordinarie calling serue
vs although we wold receaue it ? There be
more then a hundred diuerse religions (at least
opinions vsurping the name of religion ) euerie one condemning one an other , and ascri-
bing to it self that glorious title of true extraordinarie calling vnder pretence of the pure
and true word of God , and administration of
the sacramentes. What shal I do in this great
confused multitude , where none can stand
sure, except al his compagnions be declared
vsurpers and fals prophetes ? Ye wil say perchance that the Ministers of Scotland haue
none of these sectes amongs them , where of
they ar verie glad. I wil not for the present
contest there vpon. But sure I am , that they
who haue not the Ministers of Scotlands religion amongst them, ar as glad , and sundrie,
who haue it , wold be glad to be quyt therof.
I may truelie say with an ancient authour
speaking of the philosophers of his tyme, that
all theis sectes may be false, but sure I am there
can be but one true. If al can not be true,
whome shall I credit ? Whome shall I follow ?
I can not credit nor follow them all, seing they
ar contrarie, euery one condemning an other.
The choise must be difficil, seeinge that euerie
one sayeth stoutlie that he hath the trueth.

                                              Euerie

Euerie man pretendeth the verity, citeth the scriptures, confereth place with place, confirmeth his owen opinion (if ye wil beleeue him) solidlie & refuteth al others sufficientlie. But if ye wil credit all the rest, he sayeth nothing to the prupose, except so far as he agreeth with euery one of them in particular.

So who soeuer wil agree with any of them, must of force disagree with manie. And yet there can be but one trueth : and if we wil beleue the greatest parte of them, none of of them hath the trueth: because for one who affirmeth he hath the trueth, there be an hondred who gainsayeth him. For euery one of them alledgeth that al the rest goeth wrong, which is verie easie to be beleued, because the Catholique kirk sayeth the same of them all, shee being, when they were not to say the lyk of hir. And how can any man of iudgement think other ways of them ? VVe see the scripture taken by them al for an ordinarie proofe of their extraordinarie calling; it speaketh (as they say) in al their fauoures. Yet can we not be of so manie religions: nor acknowledge or obey so many pastours of so extraordinarie and contrary opinions. But ye wil say that he should be receaued, followed and obeyed, who agreeth best with the scriptures. That is most reasonable, if it can be knowen . But whose iudgement shalbe taken in the matter? None wil heare the Catholique kirk, because they haue left hir : and so as rebellious subie-

G 4 &tes

ærs can abyd nothing but iuſt condemnation
of their ſchifme and errour. If we wil credit
the parties, euerie man interpretes the ſcriptures beſt. The crowe thinketh hir owen bird
faireſt:& vaine men eſteeme moſt of the birth
of their owen braine. So ſhal I be in lyk paine
and difficultie, as before, not knowing whome to flee. If they ſay that I muſt read the
ſcripturs and follow thoſe who ſtandeth beſt
by the veritie conteined therein. What? Muſt
I be a profound theologue before I know my
paſtoures? Muſt I be ſo deeplie learned before
I knowe my maiſters ſchool? ſhall I be iudge
extraordinarie to this extraordinarie calling?
Muſt I read al theſe who haue written, before I enter in Gods houſe or acknowledge
anie of his officers, for *Qui ſtatuit aliquid parte
inaudita altera, æquum licet ſtatuerit, haud æquus fuit?*
Muſt I be ſouueraine magiſtrate in this matter
to giue out the final decree? Muſt I be the in-
terpreter of our maiſter and Lords reſtament?
Shall my fooliſh braine be a ſquare of his veritie? Truelie if I ſhould ſtand to that which I
think beſt, I muſt be iudge: and if my iudgement be a rule to me to atteine the veritie, and
conſequentlie eternal lyf, al men ſhould follow my iudgement: For there can be but one
rule ſeing ther is but one veritie, except we
wold think that the trueth ſhould be bowed
to euery mans fantaſie; which we ſee now is
done thorough out al Europe whereſouer this
extraordinarie calling hath anie credit, which
　　　　　　　　　　　　　　　　　　hath

hath brought in this multitude of sectes: For the iudgement being referred to the particular (who for that cause is sent to the bible, which he must haue to consult with all, as if he were some profound doctour in Israël) according as he shal find by his iudgement, he pronounceth the sentence of true and lauful extraordinarie calling in fauour of his Minister. According to this forme, in Scotland the Ministers following the doctrine of Sir Iohn Knox, or frere Iohn Crag ar thought to haue a good calling. In England the Brounistes, Puritaines, and family of Loue, or any hid new inuented fantasy, thinketh their pastors truely called. In France Caluin and Beza whith their adherentes ar thought to haue a lauful vocation amongest the greatest part of our simple Protestants, except perchance Monsieur du Plessis haue drawen anie to a more recent imagination. I say the simple protestants, for they who haue any good opinion of them selues, taketh to them self the free will which they refuse to others

------ *nullius iurant in verba magistri,*
they receaue nothing, but that which agreeth with the scriptures, that is, with their iudgement and opinion, wher these new holy fathers ar oftyms reiected by vertue of their owen rule, that is of euery priuat mans opinion.

In Almanie there be good store of theis new extraordinarie called men. The freedome

of the

of the townes maketh manie free vocations:
For there they haue liberty to think, fay, and
follow what euerie man pleafeth. There is no
acte of parliament to keep their vnion, nor
force them to an accorde, which can not be
had by anie other way amongeft them, who
wil haue the holy fpirit fpeaking no farther
then he whifpereth in their eare. True it is
that where there is a Prince who commandeth, the people muft change their religion
with their maifter: As long as their maifter is
Lutherian, they muft fay with him:if he chan-
geth opinion or dieth, they muft be reddie to
receaue fome other faith. This hath bene
fundrie tymes experimented in that contrye.
But in free townes as euerie man hath receaued of his Minifters preaching,he iudgeth the
fcriptures to fay the fame, where our commone prouerbe may iuftly be imployed:as the
fool thinketh, the bel clinketh. If there were
publick place in Scotland for Minifters of
other fectes, I doubt not but they wold auan-
ce their caufe alfo. For that licence giuen to
euerie man to be iudge on the fcriptures, without anie acte of parliament to tye them to
a certaine confeffion of faith (which in Almanie hath made this multitude of extraordinarie vocations) wold do the lyke amongeft vs.
How miferable is the eftate of Almanie in that
diuerfitie of religions, if not openlie at leaft
priuatlie, I think euery man knoweth, who
hath bene there. It is moft certaine that in
                                        fundry

fundry townes there be publicklie profeſſed ten, twelue, yea twentie, or twentie two fundry faithes, euerie one deteſting an other. As to the priuat opinions, I had an euident experience my ſelfe in our voyage of Italie, retourning to France through Almanie the yeare of God 1600. in the moneth of December. For being in Ausburgh (where publike exercice is granted onlie to Catholiques and Lutherians) we were at the table a good nomber (I think aboue 12.) of honeſt lyke men of diuerſe nations, but meakle more diuerſe of religions, where one of the companie more zelous then the reſt (as it appeared) taking occaſion of our being at the Iubilee, did aske fundry curious queſtions there about. A Frenche gentilman, who was come frome Rome with vs, picked with the matter, merrilie, and yet courteouſlie, did pray the companie, if it might be without their offence to grant him a requeſt, which being accorded, he should anſwer to their queſtions according to his knowledg, if he found it agreable to them: this being propounded ſo diſcreatly and honeſtly (as that nation can do it verie well) it was not onlie accepted and granted of all the companie, but alſo made a great ſilence throughout all the table, euerie man being deſirous to know his requeſt.

Then hauing thanked them all, I am deſirous (ſayeth he) to know what profeſſion of religion now adayes, euery one of yow doeth
moſt

moſt approue, or what man ye think moſt
worthie of credit when it is queſtion of anie
head of religion called in controuerſie. And
that no man may think I deſyr of others
which I wold not do my ſelf, I wil ſpeak for
my compagnions & me (meaning of vs three)
we approue aboue all others the Catholik A-
poſtolik Romaine religiō, & eſteeme the reſolutions geuen by the ſea Apoſtolik in Rome,
pronounced by the Pape, to be preferred to
all other, becauſe we find ſo manie ſolemne
promiſſes made by God to S. Peters ſucceſſors.
As I pray the companie not to be offended at
my demand and iudgement, ſo I promiſe not
to take in euil part when it ſhal pleaſe anie of
you ether to aske at me any queſtion, or freely
to pronunce what he meaneth.

Skarſlie had he ended his purpoſe when an
other (who was a citizen of the towne) anſwered, that doubtles the true religion was
conteined in the confeſſion of Auſburghe,
and that Luther had bene one of the moſt notable men of our age in all his reſolutions,
prouyding he be taken as he ſhould be, becauſe as an other Elias he came to inſtruct the
world in theſe latter dayes. The towne (as it
appeared) gaue him courage to ſpeak ſo far to
the praiſe of Luther, and made him tell his
opinion ſo freelie.

His neighbour (ſo farre as we could con-
ieἀure of his countenance) approued not his
iudgement altogether, which, being required
he did

he did shew by his words, saying that he acknowledgeth Luther for a verie notable man, yet who had not seene al, which was necessarie for the reformation of the kirk of God, and cheeflie touching the Lords supper. His reformed supper made vs beleeue he was ether a Zuinglian or Caluinist. The Lutheran wold haue entred in defence of his maister, but being requested by the companie, desisted, although with difficultie.

Nixt to him was sitting a certaine man verie modestlie clad, who made a great owtward shew of simplicitie of mynd, he with a lowe voice sayeth thus: I think no man should acknowledge anie religion but that, which commeth immediatlie of the holie spirit, who only can be receaued as a true master in that matter, *vnus est magister vester; & Psal. 93. beatus homo quem tu erudieris Domine.* His answer 12. shewed him to be of the Suentfeldien sect, who wil heare nothing but that, which their priuat spirit doeth teach them, hauing euer in their mouth, *audiam quid loquatur in Psal. 84. me Dominus Deus.* 8.

He who was ioyning with him, sayed with a laughing visage, that he had neuer beene to curious, as to examen al other mens religions or deuotion, but was accustomed to take thinges as he found them, leauing euerie man at his freedome, thinking it very reasonable that euerie man should haue the priuiledge which God had geuen him. It was not diffi-

difficill to coniecture that he was one of the
Libertins, who in matters of religion thinketh it lawful to contrefait and diſſemble al
thinges and beleeue, what they liſt, or rather
beleeue nothing at all.

Heer we had ſome lytill ſilence, becauſe
he, who nixt followeth made difficultie to
tell his opinion, which neuer the leſſe he did
vtter, ſaying he did no wayes approue diſcorde amonges Chriſtians, ſeing our Lord & his
Apoſtles had geuen vs ſo notable examples of
vnion in making al thinges commone, which
were propre and priuat before, which might
eaſelie be put in vſe againe, if men wold
take away *meum* and *tuum*, myne, and thyne.
We vnderſtood by his words that he was an
Adamit, who amonges other deteſtable errours, thinke that wemen ſhould be commone as well as other thinges. The whole reſt
of the companie, as it appeared, did abhorre
frome that opinion. Yet one ſayed; at leaſt
ſeing it was lauful to the people of God in ould
tymes to haue manie wifes, why ſhal it now
be forbidden? The Lutherian who ſpak firſt,
hauing anſwered that ſic lawes were neuer in
practiſe amonges the Chriſtians, becauſe they
were improued by IESVS CHRIST. Yet
your Luther (ſayeth he) made no difficultie
to preach, *si non vult vxor, veniat ancilla*. This
anſwer made the companie to laugh, and re-
membred vs that ſome of our contry men,
had good ſtore of wyues by a new forme of
deuor‑

deuorcinge, the partie taking the cryme one him, in hope to haue a new wyfe shortlie after.

He that was nixt wold gladlie(as it seemed) haue holden his peace, yet for feare we should take worse opinion of him, hyding his pernicious errour the best he could, said that it had pleased God in our dayes to shew the light of his verity in Pole, Lithuania, & Transsyluania, although other nations had not as yet, receaued it. These words gaue vs to vnderstand that he was one of the new Arrians whose errours were brought in by Gregorius Pauli Minister of Cracouia, Valentinus Gentilis, Seruetus (who was burnt at Geneua by Caluius pursuite) and some others of lyk stooffe, whose doctrine is ful of blasphemies.

The nixt following with à litill smylling, sayed, that he meruelled not of so many diuerse opinions which were entred in the world, seing that men seeketh rather subtil interpretations, then the veritie. As for my part(sayed he) I bear my warrand about with me (shewing vs his Bible he had in his bosome) which is most easie to be vnderstood of it self, and therefor onlie to be reade, all other bookes ether being false, or inutill, what soeuer estimation other men maketh of their long commentaries ould or new. If it had bene in England I wold haue taken him for a Brounist. Onlie could I iudge for the tyme that he approued no mans sentence that had
                                                    spoken

spoken before him.

To be short there was none at the table (except so manie Catholiques as we were) who agreed with one an other. So euerie one hauing ether openly or couertlie shewen his opinion, we perceaued an honest man (who had dyned with vs, and for some affaires had bene occupied in the towne verie late) sitting at the head of the table: his honest and homelie behauiour made vs al cast our eyes on him, & as it were, with our silence and looking desyre the lyke of him. He being a man of iudgement and doctrine, and who was (as well apeared by his discourse) very weal trauelled, after he had hard the whole matter and what we looked for, sayed in this sort.

Although the tyme and place (good sires) might iustlie excuse my silence, yet that I seeme not to be by my fellowes, or refuse your desyre, I wil some what say to the matter I heare hath bin amongest you, rather to end the dispute vnfite for the table, then to continue it. Which I wil labour to do by the reciting of a notable historie of a most noble and wyse Prince.

Being in France during the reigne of Charles the nynth, his brother Héry the thrid being then our King (whereby we knew him to be a Polonian) I passing through the contry chanced on a noble man of my ould acquaintance at Rome, who (after he had imbrassed me with great affection, and asked of my
other

other voyages fince my parting ) inuited me
to his houfe which was hard by : which I did
willingly, not only becaufe I looued him ten-
derly, but alfo becaufe I had hope by his meanes to knowe the fingularities and cuftomes
of the country (which was my principal arrad
there) by reafon of his quallitie. Amongft many notable thinges. I heard of him, I marked
this hiftorie as he was rehearfing the fingula-
ritie of the court of parliament of Paris,

King Louis the 12 being earneftly requefted
and prayed by one of his fauorits and greateft
courtiers (who had an action of great impor-
tance before the court of parliament) to fpeak
to the prefidentes and chief counfellers in
his fauoure, giuing his M. to vnderftand the
great right he had , and what wrong he receaued of his aduerfe pattie . The King on
this information partly for iuftice caufe ( of
which he was verie zelous , and therefor called the father of the people ) partlie for the
affection he boare to the gentilman , did promife him all affiftance,not onlie in fpeaking to
his iudges , but alfo wirh his owen prefence,
if that might bring anie thing to his right. And
fo he did in deed. For the day appointed for
that proceffe,being come, the King with princes,and all other who vfeth to affift his M. in
fic actions,repaired to the Palace,where being
arryued he fhewed to the court of parliament
that he was come there to fee them do iuftice
according to their charge & oathe, and chief-

H                              lie to

lie to that gentilman, whose action was in
hand, and who had donne him good seruice
sundry tymes wherein he yet continued. They
on the other part promist (with all submission
and reuerence) to do their duetie. Euerie man
according to his rank hauing taken place, the
aduocat, who was for the gentilman, begane
first, and with great eloquence defended his
parties cause, wherwith the King was verie
glad, not only in him self (as he shewed by
his countinance) but also vtered the same by
wordes, saying to the first president (who was
sitting vnder) *il h a gaigné, He hath vvonne.* The
president answered modestly, it wil please
your M. to heare the other partie, which the
King granted the more willinglie for that he
thought his fauorite had alredie wonne his
cause. The other aduocat hauing entred in the
matter with as great eloquence, but meakle
better right, made the King first to doubt, nixt
to incline somwhat, and last of al to approue
so his title, that before he had pleaded out the
cause, the King burste out with theis words,
*Monsieur le president, ils ont tous deux gaigné. They
haue vvonne both.* Ye know by long experience
what is to be done in sic thinges, I leaue it to
you and your companie. And so before the
last aduocat had ended, he past away. He had
bene versed in the greatest affaires of Europe
during his tyme both in peace & warres, and
had experimented both good and euill fortune
before, and in his reigne, yet not being trained
                                        vp in

vp in matters of law and iudging of processe,
he was easelie moued to both the sydes by eloquence filled vp with apparand reasones. But
as a most worthie and noble Prince he did acknowledge, his owen imperfection, leauing
the iudgement of sic affaires to the ordinarie
officers of iustice, to iudge as they thought
most reasonable, as who by long and daylie
experience had great knowledge of the law,
and by examination of manie difficill actions
which passed by their hande, were sufficientlie armed against fraudful craft of the parties, who easelie may circumuēt a new iudge.
My aduyse is (good sirs) that we imitat & follow this noble king (who being so potent a
monarche durst not rashlie iudge on earthlie
matters) in these controuersies of religion re-
ferring the iudgement to the kirk, who hath
bin theis manie hondreth yeares in possession
of that office by Gods owen commission, and
who with sick equitie hath decided so manie
intricate and difficil questions, wher doubtles,
if we had bene constituted iudges we wold
haue pronounced the sentence for both the
parties, seing that many of vs haue done wel
worse hauing condēned the kirk the spouse of
IESVS CHRIST vnhearing hir, following the
first that hath accused hir & praised him self.

This historie was pronounced with such
grace and authority that it appeased our dispute, and pleased verie well the whole companie; and (if I be not deceaued) is not vnpro-

pre to

pre to end our present discours, which is of
the same subiect. Wherefor without anie farther, I wil pray you and al good readers (if perchance any man wil bestow the tyme to read
this rude discourse of myne) to excuse my language considering my long absence out of my
natiue contry : and that the verity doth best
appeare, when it is least painted , as the scrip-
turs them selues do , vsing no eloquence, for
*simplex est veritatis oratio* . Sure I am if this subiect had fallen in an eloquent mans hand, that
it might haue ben traicted more quicklie and
more plainly and with greater contentemen-
te of the reader. I haue done what I could , &
not what I wold , except that in parte I haue
done what I wold, seing I haue written to the
simple and vnlearned as I could and according
to my possibilitie, I know not if according to
their capacitie . How soener it be I wil pray
the good reader to take my paines in good
part. Perchance some other sory to see a good
cause so vnskillfully handled by me, wil take
occasion to do it, as it should be done . Which
wilbe very easy to many learned men , of
which ther be good nôbre (thanks be to God)
in our Iland, who may take from me the vi-
ctory of eloquéce, but not the honour of good
wil, Wherin euery man may triomph without
preiudice of his compagnion. Wherefor I pray
the learned and Godlie Catholik endeauour
him self to trraict this subiect as it meriteth in
the name of God, who blisse vs all.

AMEN.

# JEAN PIERRE CAMUS

*A Discours*
*Hapned betwene*
*an Hermite called Nicephorus*
*& a Yong Lover called Tristan*
*1630*

# A
# DISCOVRS
## HAPNED.

### BETWENE AN HERMITE
called Nicephorus & a yong louer
called Triſtan, who for that his
Miſtreſſe Petronilla entred into
Religion would faine become an
Hermite.

*All faithfullie dravven out of the Hi-*
*ſtorie of Petronilla, compoſed in French*
*by the Right Reuerend Father in God*
IOHN PETER CAMVS *Biſhop*
*of Belley.*

And Tranſlated into English by P.S.P.

Printed with Permiſſion.
1 6 3 0,

58 ··· 341, 2

# TO *THE CATHOLIKES*
## *of Irland.*

ENOWNED Catholikes the Hiſtoire of Petronilla Coming to my hands, compoſed by the Right Reuerend Father in God Iohn Peter Camus Biſhop of Belley a man of knovvne learning, eminent pietie & of an Apoſtolicall life, the fancie tooke me to imploy ſome time in the reading of it, not doubting but coming from ſo famous an Authour, I ſhould find ſome thing in it worth my labour. Going then forward in the rea-

*He VVrote many bookes.*

á ij

ding therof, amongſt many other good things, I lighted vpon this Treatiſe, which when I conſidered, I ſaid thus to my ſelf: it might be thought, that this man had reuelation, or ſome notice giuen him of the emulation & variáce which is betweene the Hierarchicall Clergie and the Regulars in Irland, & that in conſequens therof he framed this Diſcours. For it is ſaid, that the Regulars there, thinking therby to magnifie and extoll themſelues (for I know no other reaſon they can haue for it) make no conſcience nor ſcrupule both in their publike ſermons, and in their priuat cóuerſations amógſt you, to ſay and affirme, that Prieſts are but meere Seculars,

that théſelues are true Paſtours,
that it belongs to them only
to be called Fathers, that they
are the choice and beſt part of
the Eccleſiaſticall Hierarchie, &
which is more abſurd, that their
Regular Superiours are more
worthy then Bishops. All which
aſſertions manifeſtly falſe, and ill
becoming men whoſe inſtitution is chiefely grounded in
humilitie and contempt of
worldly honour and reſpects,
being touched and diſcuſſed in
this Treatiſe, I thought in my
loue and naturall affection
towards you, my deere Country
men, that I was in a manner
bound, fearing theſe things
should giue you ſome erronious
impreſſions, to impart it vnto

you . Wherupon I tooke the paines to tranſlate it out of French into English & to haue it printed. And if I ſhall vnder-ſtand that it takes effect, & cauſe theDelinquéts reflect vpon their errour, herin & vpon that ſaying of S. Iames the Apoſtle: *If any* Iac.5.c.26 *man think himſelf to be Religious not bridling his tongue, but ſeducing his hart, this mans Religion is vaine,* then will I think my labour well imployed. And that which is moſt to be deſired of them is, that they doe conſider firſt, that ſuch aſſertions and compariſons doe more hurt then good, do rather deſtroy then edifie, rather peruert then conuert the people from their euill courſes, & rather breede hate & enuie, then loue or charitie: and secondly that they consider, that Priesthood, which is the fontaine and fondation of all Ecclesiasticall functions, is the same in Secular Priests (as they terme them) and in Regulars, whence Priests may iustlie say to the Regulars with saint Paul, that if they be Hebrewes so are they, if they be Israëlites soe are they, if they be the seede of Abraham so are they, if they be Ministers of CHRIST so are they; yea more, that they are their elders and haue higher offices and dignities in the Church then they haue. And for you worthy champions I shall desire you not to be scandalized to see one Catholike write against an other,

2. Cor. 11. v. 22.

beleeuing that Catholikes as Catholikes doe agree in matters of Faith, but as men that they may varie in other opinions. S. Peter and S. Paul, S. Auftin and S. Hierome difagreed in fome opinions without breach of fayth or charitie. About the obferuation of Eafter there was great debate betwixt Sainɛts & Sainɛts till the Church decided the controuerfie; yea Angels haue diffented in opinions. But this you may note in this controuerfie, that learned Doɛtours in thefe Countries, and fome of them Religious men, with whom I did cófer of the fame, do much admeere that the Regulars in Irland do cóteft with the Clergie for the faid points, wheras in no Catholike

*Gal.3.*
*Act. 15.*
*Hieron*
*ep.86.*
*Aug. ep.8*
*& fequ.*
*Euf.lib.5.*
*cap. 24.*
*& 25*
*Bedal. 3.*
*Hiftor.*
*Angl.cap.*
*24 & 25*
*lib.5.c.16.*
*Dan. 10.*

Catholike Countries do the Regulars fpeake of the like, but cótaine themfelues within the precinct of their Monafteries, and the obferuance of their Rules, which teach the quit contrarie of all that they doe in this kind And if they will alleage that hauing no Monafteries in Irlád they muft goe vp & downe amongft you, like other Priefts, me thinks they should the leffe claime any perfection or refpect ouer other Priefts, and my warrant for this is S. Hierome, who fpeaking of fuch Monks and Religious men faith: *Sicut pifcis extra aquam caret vita fic Monachus extra Monafterium.* As fish being out of the water doth want life, fo doth a Monke or Religious man being out of his Monasterie. For the life of a Religious man, as such, is to obserue his Rules, and keepe his vowes, which he cannot doe so well, if he do it at all, being couersant in the world, & not doing it, what prerogatiue can he claime ouer others? To conclude if the Regulars be true Pastours as is aboue said, how can they excuse themselues that they take no more care of their flock then some odd times like passingers to preach vnto them, God knowes with litle fruict? Who will not say but the good Priest is more like to be the true Pastour: *Who giueth his life for his sheepe*, seruing them, not by starts but all the yeere long, by day and by night, in heate and in cold, in raine and in tempeſt, with much miſerie & litle profit? Laſtly who can beleeue that the Regulars are true or proper Paſtours whenas they cannot take any ſuch chardge vpon them if firſt they be not diſpenſed with all in their vowves. Add that in Catholike Countries, where all Clergie men get their due, they cannot preach nor Miniſter any Sacrament out of their owne Conuents without the expreſſe leaue of the Biſhop of the Dioceſe, and of the Paſtour of the place, conformable to the Coun- Seſſ.24. cell of Trent? Howſoeuer they will anſwere to all theſe things, I make no doubt but after their accuſtomed manner, ſome of them vvill ſay (for I knovv that many good men amongst them doe not approue such things) that he is no frend of Religious men that doth propound them. But God is my vvitnesse, I do honour & respect all Religious men, and vvish all others to do the same, as long as they containe themselues vvithin the limits of their Rules, & that they do not prefer the honour of their order, as many seeme to doe, to the honour and seruice of God, to vvhose diuine protection I commit you, and pray him, to giue vs all the Spirit of vnion and charitie, & so rest

Your deuoted seruant
in Christ Iesvs
P. S. P.

# A
# DISCOVRS
## HAPNED.

*Betvveene an Hermite called Ni-*
*cephorus and a yong louer called*
*Tristan, who for that his Mistres-*
*se Petronilla entred into Religion*
*vvould faine become an Her-*
*mite.*

Mitting the historie of all
that past betweene Tristan
and petronilla, and the tra-
gicall end which came of
their loue, I will only rehearse the discours past betweene Tristan & Nicephorus, contayning many points
much disputed of in these our dayes.
Tristan a proper and wel bredd yong
gentilman much grieued that his mi-

A

streffe petronilla whom he purfued
fo long time ( of difpleafure that shee
could not obtaine her parents confent
to marrie him ) went into Religion,
refolued alfo to retire himfelf from
the world in fome religious Monasterie; but after communicating his refo-
lution therin to feuerall Religious
men of diuers orders and getting
their opinions therof, at length he
follovved his owne fancie & inclination, which was to goe to the wil-
derneffe and leade an Heremiticall life ; and the Perinean mountaines
vvhich feparate France from Spaigne
being the neereft vnto him, he went
thither, taking with him a good purfe
of mony and his lute, at which he
was very skilfull. But neither his lute nor his folitarineffe did any thing
affwage his paffion, or make him forget the creature which brought him
to that anxietie of minde, but rather
inflamed him more, efpeciallie the lute conformable to the old prouerb,
which faith, that mufick is an impor-

tunat geſt to a hart afflicted. Being
then in this perplexitie he was told
that not farr from him there was a deuote and wel built Hermitage wherin dwelt a venerable Hermite whoſe ſainctitie of life gaue a good odoure to all the Country about, and who
by long experience did learne how
to guide himſelfe to perfection by the
way of ſolitarineſſe in that wilder-
neſſe. His good Angell made Triſtan
draw towards this ſainctly old man,
vvho receiued him with the ſame
charitie wherwith he was accuſtomed
to receiue and intertaine other paſſing
Pilgrimes (for he was in pilgrimes
weede) who ſtraying from their way
in thoſe dreadfull deſerts, fell ſometimes vpon the litle path which leade
to his ſell. Triſtan beholding him did
take him for an Angell of God, and
beleeued that he was the Raphaël
which would conduct him to Rages,
I would ſay, to the perfection of the
contemplatiue life. Hauing then brieflie declared his intent to the good

Hermite, he gaue him for answeare,
that to loue a thing it is necessarie to
know it before, and that the Heremiticall life as well as the Monasticall
doth require a good approbation of a
man before he be admitted to it. Tristan hauing submitted himselfe to him
in all things. My child, quoth father
Nicephorus, for so they called this religious man , it is nothing for a man to
vndertake such a life if he be not called to it by God, & amongst many that
are called , few are choosen. I know
wel that it doth not appertaine but to
God, to know perfectlie and waigh
iustlie the hearts of men, yet his will is
that his seruants do see and trie whether they be of true or false coine: the
touchstone of such as are called to the
seruice of God is , the renunciation of
all things, and of themselues also. Father, quoth Tristan, if that be the marke of the elect I haue it ; for I do freelie quitt the world, the subiect which
retayned me in it being separated
from me, & it will be easie likewise for

me to forsake my selfe seing I haue relinquished an obiect of which I did esteeme much more then of my selfe.

My child, quoth Nicephorus, the warrs seeme sweet, according the prouerb, to such as did not trie it, do not triumph before the victorie, and do not proclaime victorie before the battle; none shall be crowned, saith the word of veritie, that will not reasonablie and valorouslie fight, and the battle which wee haue with our selfe loue doth last as long as our verie liues: for that errour is so deepely ingrauen in our nature, as it doth subsist after wee renounce our selues; wee may mortifie it, but not make it die, contrarywise it seemes like the fabulous Gyant, to take new forces from it prostration and ouerthrow, and like great trees, the more they be shaked, the faster the fix their rootes. It may be assaulted but rarely ouercommed, & neuer rooted out: the walls of that rebellious Hiëricho, although

*Selfe loue ingrauen in our nature.*

A iij

they be vndermined and sometimes
razed to the ground, yet do they get
vp againe of themselues. I do not say
this to discourage you, nor to imitat
those timorous spies, which would faine disswade the children of Israël
from vndertaking the conquest of the
land of promis; I know there be difficulties in it, but I tell you with Iosüe
and Caleb, that you may boldlie enter in the power of our lord, who, if
he be for you, nothing can preuaile
against you, for who can resist the will
of the highest power, of this Lord of
armies, who is terrible ouer all powers, if he vndertake to fight with
you? But you must not hope that he
wil put himself of your side, if you
do not put all your trust and confidence in him, by a perfect distrust of
your self, which may not consist with
those loftie termes, which promis mer-
uailes, and carrying you vpon the
wings of the wind make you aspire to
great matters, which surpasse the reach
of a man that is not yet a Nouice. It is

not, that I do lightlie iudge of your foule, which I beleeue is more perfect then my owne, who serues God so negligently and loue him so coldlie, not that I am ignorant but in the confusion of the Babylon of the world, God hath seruants and secret disciples, which do not bow their knees to Baal, and that keepe their hearts pure amongst the impuritie of the world, of which number you may be; add that the extraordinarie effects of grace do produce in an instant admirable conuersions, which puts those that are replenished with it, in a state of great perfection, conformable to that which is written, that the workes of God are perfect and without repentance, that is to say, without defect.

Tristan, who beleeued that this discours of the Hermite did tend to deferr and put of his reception, esteeming (as he was full of worldly maximes) that the Hermite did feare that chardging himself with him, his almes would be too short to furnish him a

portion said, Father the time will make knowne whether I be touched with
true or fained charitie, & the triall will
make manifest the force or the weaknesse of my vocation. but to the end
that you may not think that I come hither to incommodat, or importune
you, I will shew vnto you that it is rather to occommodat you, & to draw
you from the paine of going here and
there to searche your liuing, which
must bring much interruption to your
contemplation, which require repose
& silence, and may not be had but in
the wildernesse. Know then that being
left an orphan without father and mother I was emancipated by publick authoritie a litle before the terme of my
maioritie & consequently put in the
possession of my goods which are not
so small but they are sufficient to nourish twentie Hermits as you are, &
I beleeue that not making the vow of
pouertie in any Religious order, that
I may keepe them and dispose of
them as God shall inspire me. We
shall

shall then liue together & what reuer-
sion wee shall haue we will bestow it
in almes, & in such other pious works
as you shall think good, without trou-
bling our selues to begg for our maintenance. And to shew that it is true,
that I came not hither with emptie
hands, or vnfurnished of things necessarie to nourishe and cloathe my
selfe, behold a scantlet of the matter.

Then did he shew the Hermite a
great purse full of pistolls, and also some pretious stones more worth then
gold, and yet did occupie lesse place.
Good Nicephorus, who did not see
while he kept in this wildernesse such
great quantitie of this yealoue mettall,
whose luster doth dazle the eyes of
many men in the world, did firmely
beleeue in his minde that he was the
Tentator, who vnder a humaine shape
came to diuert him from the way of
perfection, which is that of holy pouertie, which he traced for many yeeres within his litle caue. Wherupon ar-
ming himselfe with the marke of our

B

saluation and vttering the name of our
Sauiour with a low voice, seing that
Tristan did not vanish away, to cleare
himselfe of his doubt, he tooke him
softlie by the arme and said to him ; If
I had not knowne that spirits haue neither fleshe nor bones, as I do feele
you to haue, I would say that it is the
Diuell that came to sollicit me to my
ruine, offring me richesse, as he did to
the sonne of God when he assaulted
him in the wildernesse. But I feare that
not taking vpon him the forme of
man he doth possesse your hearr to
produce in myne the same effect, & to
slide into it the death of grace by the
venime of auarice. I will then say vnto
you the same that the Apostle said to
Simon Magus, away with your gold &
siluer from me, which I know are the
I dolls of the world, to which they are
like, that do adore them, and that put
their confidence in them : that man is
abondantly riche that is poore in
IESVS CHRIST. I loue my begging,
by which I cóquer heauen for my selfe

( & make others to conquer it for them, making them to merit euerla-sting goods when they giue me of their earthly goods ) better then all your treasure: It is long since I haue put of that shirt of earthly possession, and how should I putt it on againe? I haue washed my feete & chased from my minde those grose affections, and how should I contaminat them of the new? I will neuer call back againe what I haue once quitted and renounced with a good will for the loue of my Maister; he hath nourished me so many yeeres in these deserts, both with the dew of heauen, which is the Manna of his consolations, and with the fatt of the earth, which is the daylie bread of the necessitie of the body, as I haue all subiect to blesse his prouidence, & to confirme my selfe in this truth that such as seeke for God and his kingdome can neuer want any thing. For my part, I will promis you no gold nor siluer, but that only which God will send me by the hands of such as he

shall inspire to do me charitie, I will
impart it to you. In the meane time I will tell you, that if you will do
as Iacob did, quitt the house of the
traitour Laban, which is the world,
to inioye the embracing of Lia and
Rachell, to witt, Action and Contemplation, it is necessarie that you
burie those Idolls at the foote of
the Terebinthe of the crosse, and
that glorifying in nothing but in
I E S V S  C H R I S T crucified, you will
imitat him in his nuditie, gloriously
ignominious, by depriuing your selfe of the care of temporall richesse,
according the Counsell, which he
gaue to that yong gentilman, who
*Matt.*19. was like to you, to quitt all, that
*v.*21.    he might be perfect, not admitting
him of his traine if first he vvould
not distribut to the poore all that
he possessed. But my sonne quoth
the good Hermitte, I feare you re-
semble too much this yong man, &
that like vnto him you will retire
your selfe with à heauie heart, not

being able to digeſt the bitterneſſe
of this drugg, which make men for-
ſake all the goods of the earthe,
that they may aſpire to heauenly
goods, and that you will not ſo ea-
ſely diſpoſſeſſe your ſelfe of them
as Iacob did putt of the skins which
couered his hands, & good Ioſeph
his cloake.

That I may not lie vnto you,
quoth Triſtan, I could neuer beleeue
that for being an Hermite a man
muſt haue renounced the inheritance of his forefathers, but well I knew
it to be neceſſarie for to be admitted of thoſe religious orders, in which
is made the ſolemne Vow of pouertie; a thing not only neceſſarie,
but alſo very eaſie in thoſe great
Communalties whether they be ri- *The Voſſ*
che or begging Communalties be- *of pouer-*
cauſe the Religion doth oblige it *tie Very*
ſelfe to intertaine the Religious *eaſie in*
as they do conſecrat themſelues to *Commu-*
the obſeruance of the rules of the *naltieſ*
Religion. But an Hermitte that li-

ues alone without support is oftentimes trusting to a badd dynner
while he exspects Manna or larks
to fall from heauen to him; as they
did to the Israëlites; for God doth
not shew such fauours to all nations
nor worke such miracles vpon all
occasions. Such as putt their trust
in God, quoth the Hermite, are not
shaked no more then is Mount Sion:
He that dwells in Hierusalem, which
is in the protection of the God of
heauen, & whose very gates he doth
loue, is no more moued when he is
in want, then when he hath plentie
of all things, being assured that the
hand of God is not shortned, nor
his power diminished. He that hath
care of the croes litle ones being
abandonned by their Dames, and of
the least sparrow; yea, of the least
flie, will neuer abandon him that liues iust before him all his life time.
The sunne will sooner faile to lighten
the world, then his prouidence to
shine vpon such as he loues; he that

spreds his beames and pouers his raine equally vpon the iuſt and the vniuſt, that giues nourishment to all fleſh, and that neede do no more but open his hand to replenish all creatures with benediction.

All that may be good, quoth Triſtan, in the pulpet but the practiſe is quitt otherwiſe. For my parr, I would make no difficultie to renounce to the inheritance of my forefathers, nor to make a vow of pouertie in a good Conuent, which should be well rented, or being of a begging order, that should be ſituated in a good cittie, where they eate the ſinnes of the people, where all men labour for you while you pray for all men, where they find the bread ready baked, the wine all pure, the meat ready dreſſed, where they haue no care of any thing, nor think of tomorrow, practiſing, ſimplie & in good earneſt theſe words of the Scripture: *Aske and thou shalt* Matth.7. *haue, feeke and thou shalt find* ; But vers.7.

without, that, to renounce my owne,
it is a thing that all the eloquence of
men and of the Angels may not
perswade me to do, for I do see but
too much euery day how sottish and
ridiculous it is, to be a poore priest.

*It is a glorious thing before God to be a poore priest.*
So it is without doubt according
the world, said the Hermite, but before God it is a glorious thing, yea,
before that great God, who makes but
follie of the wisdome of the world,
& of the follie of the crosse wisdome,
and who doth confound the fast and
pompe of richesse by humble pouertie, before him that came to
euangelize the poore, who doth
heare their prayers, who calls himself their father and tutour, who doth
extoll them in his iudgment as much
as they are vilipended and held ab-
iect in the iudgments of worldlings.
But those that are instructed in the
schoole of the crosse, which is follie to the Gentils, and scandall to
the Iewes, but the vertue and sa-
pience of God to the faithfull are
                              of an

of an other beliefe, they hold the
poore to be very happie, according
the sentence pronounced by the
proper mouth of the sonne of God:
but the children of the word do not
vnderstand that probleme of strong
Samson, becaufe they do not glorie
but in the multitude of their richesse.
I must for all that graunt vnto you, *Mona-*
that the pouertie of Monasticall per *sticall po-*
*uertie vo-*
fons hath this aduantage of the po- *ry easie.*
uertie of Hermites and secular
priests (as they call them) that it is
well shrouded from all pressing necessities within a well gouerned có-
monaltie. You know I speake of begging orders, for to speake of Conuentuall friars which liue by their
reuenewes, they are not poore but
in particular, in common they are
riche, and they are poore inough
in as much as they haue no proprietie of any thing; in this fashion
then may they be said to be poore
in the middest of their richesse, and
riche in the middest of their pouertie.

But the others albeit they be poore
not only in particular but alfo in common, yet their pouertie is alwaies
fupported, fuccoured and applauded,
or at leaftwife honored and efteemed,
in fort that their fufferances are
regarded, and their wants glorious;
they are riche in honnour, yea, in
the middeft of their fufferances. In
fteade that a poore Hermite is def-
pifed by euery body, his complain-
tes are reieƈted, his wants vnknowne,
his neceffities do not appeere to any
but to God: He is all alone, he is fore-
faken, and abandoned, hauing no
body to comfort him, nor to take cõ-
paffion of his miferies, none to caft
him into the pond wherin he might
fish fome reliefe.

The fame, I fay of a prieft that is
in neceffitie, euery body doth laugh
at him, and in fteade of fuccouring
him they vpbraid and floud him, they
chardge him with falfe reprocheffe
and calumnies, fo that he may well
fay with the Pfalmift: O lord the re-

prochesse of those that Disdayne
your deare Vertue of pouertie, with
which you haue beene borne, you
liued and died, making your self needie and poore to replenish vs with
the inestimable richesse and treasures
of your merits; these reprochesse ô
Lord are fallen vpon me, and confusion hath couered my face: *I am* *Psal.68.*
*made a stranger to my owne brothers;*
and a vacabond to the children of my
owne mother.

Father, quoth Tristan, that is the
thing which I find least supportable
of the infinit euells, which accōpanie
pouertie: for honour of all the goods
which doth inuirō vs being most pretious, I would sooner suffer that they
should touch theball of myne eye,
then ingage me in that point. And.
I do graunt vnto you that I am not
yet come to that point of mortification, that I may suffer and indure
iests and contumelies no more then
did the Prophet Eliseus, much more holy and more patient then I am.

C ij

that could not indure the litle children to reproach vnto him that he
was bald, an imperfection very light
and naturall. and which as it should
feeme he should acknowledg, and
mocke the weaknesse of those litle
foules, rather then destroie them by
the imprecation and curses wihich he
fulminated against them.

My fonne, quoth Nicephorus,
you take this example by a bad bias,
& handle the brone where it burnes.
The Prophet did not regard the outrage which those children did vnto
him, as an iniurie done to his owne
perfonne, he was too humble to take
it in that fort: but he did it to magnifie his office, for he would be estee-
med of men as the Minister of God,
and the difpencer of his Mysteries;
and becaufe he carried the ambaffade
of God, and that an affront or dif-
grace done to an Ambaffadour doth
hurt the honour of his Maifter, and
returne to the preiudice of his glorie that fent him, according that

which is written: *He that heares you
heares me, and he that despiseth you de-*
*spiseth me.* For this reason the Prophet prayed God that he would cha-
stise those insolent boyes with exemplar punishment, to teach great men
what the fire of Gods choler would
do being once kindled in drie wood,
if it did consume the greene wood
with so great ardour; and what do
you know but the corporall euell
which he procured to them boyes
was cause of their spirituall good, and
of the Saluation of their soules, making them to tast of death in an age
more capable of innocencie then of
malice, and consequentlie more sus-
ceptible of Gods grace then of his
wrathe? in stead that had they in an
age more reepe filled vp the measure of their sinnes, and gone forward
in their vice, they might perchance
acquire their damnation. In this sort
did S. Paule deliuer to Sathan the
body of that fornicatour, who made
the liuing temple of God the mem-

*Luca* 10.
v. 16.

bers of a lecher to faue his foule from
euerlasting damnation.  O my child
how yong thou art yet in the warfare of the crosse, which in it self is no
more dolorous then ignominious &
shamefull, yea, execrable, according
that saying: *Cursed is euery one that hag-
eth on a tree.* How farr you straie from
the standard of him who for vs was
loaden with reprochesse, who did not
turne his face from those that spett
vpon it, nor his cheekes from those
that did buffet them, nor his chinne
from those that pulled of his beard;
how farr, I say, you goe from him
who was made a spectacle before his
eternall father, before the Angels
and before men, who was exposed to
be a mocking stock to those that sawe him nayled vpon the crosse, to
be iested by them & to nodd and
shake their heads on him? How
badd a disciple wouldest thou be to
those great Apostles, those high
montaignes whereon is laid the fundation of the cittie of God, who de-

*Gal. 3.*

parted frolike and ioyfull from the great assemblies where they were flouted and contumeliously handled, for the publicatiō of the sacred name and holy doctrine of IESVS CHRIST? Verely you must chāge your stile and language, and also your thoughts and maximes, if you perseuere in that holy desire of a religious life, especiallie that which regard the mortification of honour: for as I haue alreadie told you, the Conuentuall pouertie is respected and reuerenced, but our pouertie is mocked and flouted.

So I beleeue, quoth Tristan, that you Hermites are not poore but of necessitie; and not of free will, by reason of which your pouertie may not haue the glorie of the voluntarie which the Euangelicall pouertie doth deserue. This is the cause why men putt you not in the ranke of regular but of secular beggers, who are reduced to necessitie by the desaster of fortune, which if they support with patience, I beleeue they shall haue

honour befote God who fees their
hearts, but not before men. And that
I do not lye vnto you, I would not
esteeme it an act of prudence of him
that hath à patrimonie and makes
himself an Hermite, to renounce to
that which he doth possesse, to make
himlelf afterwards by begging odious
and importune to the cõmon wealth,
perswading my felf that a man
should drinck of the water of his
owne cesterne, and draw the last
drop of it, before he would goe to
the well or fontaine of his neighbour,
being that it is reasonable that euery
man liue of the goods which God
gaue him, or at leastwise, that he eate
his bread by the sweat of his browes.

Deare sir, quoth the Hermite, the
holy Apostle doth say, that being a
litle one he spoake according his age
but comming to be more great, he
had thoughts and discourses of a higher kind. I know well by your song
that you are yet in a spirituall infan-
cie,

eie, but when you shall be more aduanced in it, you will change those
humaine maximes into Euangelicall
axiomes, which are of a higher note,
and of a more excellent accent; if
thou haddest beene a Religious man
thou wouldest learne to speake according the precepts of Religion,
which consist in the practise of the
Euangelicall counsells.

That is good, quoth Tristan, for
those Religious men which oblige
themselues by vowes, but not for
you Hermites, who do nothing but
what you please, who liue after your
owne fancie, and who are your owne
maisters. I will replie ynto you, quoth
the Hermite, that which an ancient
painture said to a great lord, who *The*
tooke vpon himself within his shopp *saying of*
*an anciet*
to discours of the art of painting, as *painteur.*
many words as you speake are so
many solecismes against my art, hold
your peace or els my apprentices
will mock your ignorance. It is true
that your ignorance is pardonable,

D

considering that being a soildiour
(for Tristan had a swerd at his side)
you speake of Religious affaires,
euen as a Churchman would
speake of matters of warrs. But if
thou wilt inrolle thy self in the holy and spirituall warfare of Religion
you will discours more netely and
more correctly of these things. Father, quoth Tristan, I told you already that I desire much to be an Hermite, but not a Religious man. And
I, quoth Nicephorus, do answere vnto you, that that is as if you would
say, I would faine be a reasonable
creature but not a man, or otherwise,
I would faine be a Monke and no
Religious man; or thus, I would be
a Religious man and no Monke, considering that a Monke & a Religious
man is the same thing, as is a man
and a reasonable creature. But many,
saith Tristan, do not vnderstand it
so, for I haue seene many Religious
men which would take it for an iniurie, & for a kind of disgrace to be

*A Monke*
*& a Re-*
*ligious*
*man is*
*the same*
*thing.*

called Monks, and such as confesse themselues to be Monks and are so named in their rules are glad to be called Religious men, so much this holy mame of Monke, so venerable *The name Monke now out of request* in ancient time is become disagreable to the eares of this our age, and that without doubt, through the fault of those that did profane and dishonour it by their badd liues.

You say true, quoth the Hermite, and this imaginarie distinction hath beene inuented of late yeeres, and that only in France, because of the heresie which defamed that holy name of Monke, as she did open her vnpure mouthe against the church, corrupting that which shee knew, and blaspeming that which shee knew not, or was ignorant of, and lancing out quippes & tants (in which she putts all the force of her arguments) against the most sacred mysteries of our holy faith. And when I say that this distinction of a Monke and a Religious man is of a new

D ij

impreſſion, and came lately out of
the braines of ſome which ground
themſelues vpon imaginations diſtil-
led. I know not how, I do not ſay it
of any contempt of their ſubtilitie,
but to maintaine the truthe, of which
I haue for witneſſes all thoſe that are
beyond the Alps & the Perinean
montaignes, as the Italians and Spaniards, among which the word Religious is not knowne, albeit thoſe
Countries do abound more with
Monks, then doth our Countrie of
France. The Italians do call Religious men 1. *Monachi,* or 1. *Fratti,* the
Spaniards call then *Los Monyes,* or *los
Frayles,* which is as much to ſay, as
the Monks or Friars of ſuch an order. As for the name Father, which
the vulgar ſort do giue to the Regulars, who are honored with the Sacerdotall character, and with the dignitie of prieſthood, it was not attributed in the begining of Monaſti-
call inſtitution but to the Superiours
of euery Monaſterie, who as ſuch, we-

*The VVord re-ligious is not Vſed in Spaine nor in Italie.*

re called Abbotts, which is as much
to say as father, and all the rest that
were their children and subiects
were called brothers. And to
speake as I think, if those that are
married folke haue not the qualitie
or title of Fathers and mothers but
when they haue issue, and that the
heauens do fauour, them with the
benediction to haue children ; so this
appellation of spirituall Fathers doth
not seeme to appertaine but to Pastours only, be they Prelats or inferiour priests, who haue chardge of
soules, aud watch ouer them, as being
bound to render an account of them
to God. who is the Prince of Pastours,
the Bishop of our soules, and the
grand Maister of the vinuersall flock
of the world. Which appellation of
Father, if it be appropriated to simple priests, principallie in the administration of the Sacraments, it is because that in the dispensation of the
Diuine mysteries they hold the pla-
çe of the Pastours, who can not do

*Pastours only are to be called Fathers*

all things by their owne proper hāds
and in proper person; and to speake
with the Canons, who do administer
the Sacraments by the allowance
and permissiō of the proper Pastour,
leauing to our Doctours to decide
who that is properlie speaking, for
there is a controuersie of it, which
should not be decided by a poore
Hermite as I am. Neuerthelesse
such as I am, in my youth, I made
some voyages, and principallie into
Italie, and made some staye & seiour
in the Court of Rome, following a
great Cardinal, I say great in ranke,
as they are all, and greater in bloud
and sanctitie, as they are not all. You
know the eminencie of the qualitie
which those famous Seigneurs haue,
and to which the sea Apostolick hath
raised them: Yet when the Popes do
draw them out of Cloisters, taking
their lamps from vnder the bushell,
and putting it vpon the candlestick,
to the end that the light of their merits do lighten all the house of God,

which is the church, they neuer forfake the qualitie of brothers, or
Friars, as the marke of their regularitie, no more then they forfake the
colour of the habit of the order wherin they made their profeffion. Their
titles are moft renowned lord and
right reuerend father in God, if he
be a Bishop, brother fuch a one, Cardinal of the holy church of Rome,
Bishop of fuch a place, or prieft or
Deacon of fuch a title.

As for Bishops, when out of Religious Orders they are affumpted to
Epifcopall dignities, for a marke of
their ancient regularitie, from the
obferuance of which they are exēp-
ted paffing to an other obedience
& difcipline, they carrie alwaies the
colour, and in fome fort, the forme
of their habit, albeit they paffe from
the ftate of perfection to be acqui-
red, to the ftate of perfection acqui- *Bishops*
red, as the fucceffours of the Apo- *the fuc-*
ftles, yet be it of humilitie, or of af- *ceffours*
fection to their oder, to the title of *of the*
*Apoft.*

Right Reuerend father in God, they
add that of brother or Friar such a
Bishop, of such a church: in which
is seene that they take the name Father as they are Pastours, and the
name brother as they are Monks or
Friars. Whence it may be concluded

*Of what should Friars be called fathers.* that the name Father doth not properly belong to Friars or Monks as
such, but to Pastours and Priests who
haue Chardg of soules. Add that the
vulgar sort speaking of a Bishop that
hath beene a Religious man do say;
that Bishop is a Friar or Monke, and
those Prelats do not take it to scorne
to be called Monks or Friars, as do
in those parts some simple Conuentuall Friars; otherwise called Religious men.

I confesse vnto you, quoth Tristan, that I haue as litle skill in those Monasticall matters, as I haue experience in that kind of life, which
is sequestred from the world; Wherfore I went still with the common
opinion, which as I perceiue is a popular

pular errour. Yet cannot I well yeld
or affent to what you propofe, when
I cõfider that this word Monke doth
fignifie a man who of deuotion doth
leade a folitarie life, which Conuentuall friars do not, liuing in Com-
munitie, and if I may fo terme it, in
troups within their Cõuents, hauing
all their exercifes in common, &
being almoft ftill together, be it in
the quire, or in the Refectorie, at
their Chapter, or at their corporall
labours, at their leffons and at their
conferences, and alfo at their con-
uerfations with the neighbours, in
fort that me thinks they haue reafon
to call themfelues Religious men, as
it were men tyed together by a fo- *Reafon*
cietie of an vniforme life, which ma- *Sshythey*
kes, that albeit their companies con- *may be*
*called Re-*
fift of diuers members, they are ne- *ligiousmē*
uertheleffe conducted by one & the *drasŝen*
*out of the*
fame fpirit and mind, which is the *freuche*
plafter and mortar by which they are *Sŝordre-*
tyed and ioyned in God the one to *liē.*
the other, according to that which

E

is written of the firſt Chiſtians, that
they had not amongſt, them but one
hart and one ſoule. And the moſt
preſſing knots which bind them together, beſids the knot of charitie,
which bind the moſt perfect of them,
and is the great tye of perfection, are
the ſolemne vowes, by which thoſe
that be profeſt do oblige themſelues
to the order in which they are incor-
porated, & the order in like manner
doth oblige it ſelf to ſuch as it recei-
ueth. And the are thoſe vowes, as
farr as I could learne of learned &
*Their ſo-* deuote Religious men, that put them
*lemne* in the ſtate of perfection: in which
*voſſes* are not the Anacorits who make not
*putts the* are not the Anacorits who make not
*in the ſta-* theſe vowes; at leaſtwiſe ſolemne,
*te of per-* but lead a priuat aud particular life,
*fection.* without hauing any other ſocietie
with their neighbours, but that which
tye all Chriſtians one to an other, as
children of the ſame church.

In the time of our Sauiour, ſaith the
Hermite, Martha murmured againſt
Marie. I ſee well that you haue

learned all thofe things out of the
mouth of fome Conuentuall friar
animated by a kind of zeale, which
if it be not indifcrite and without
fcience, at leaftwife, it is sharp, and
bitter againft vs poore Monks, the
outcaft and fweeping of the world,
and who are nothing els but voices,
which by their grones and fighes do
make the Ecchos of thefe deferts ring
and found. But bleffed by God,
who in this qualitie made vs, at leaftwife imitatours and followers of that
great fore-runner of the Meffias declared to haue beene the greateft
amongft the children of men by the
proper mouth of the fonne of God,
& placed vs vpon Maries portion,
which he faid to be the beft, notwithftanding the complaints and
going about of Martha. There is *Friars*
nothing more iniuft then thofe kind *approue*
*nothing*
of people which approue nothing but *but their*
their owne actions, and find nothing *owne*
*actions.*
good but what they do themfelues.
Happie is he that can efcape their
E ij

censures. In the meane time there is no charitie in these reprehensions, for that vertue is not iealous, and in those kind of people nothing is seene but emulation, not of the best grace, as the Apostle saith, but such as tend to certaine particularities, which breede partialities and these partialities ingendreth false imaginations of deuotion, which hath but the barke and not the true pith of pietie : for true pietie is good for all things, and all these cótentions are good for nothing. Charitie doth no idle nor euell thing, and the effects which are ingendred of those subtile questions, of those states of perfection, of these comparisons of liues, and of the diuersities of rules and Orders, are good for nothing, but very hurtfull some times to the reputation of many. Charitie is not puffe vp with pride, nor ambition, but humble and respectiue of all men, neuer preferring herselfe to any. The hart which she doth possesse is neuer puffed vp

*Compa-*
*risons of*
*liues &*
*orders are*
*good for*
*nothing.*

with prefumption, neuer lifts vp it
browes with fcorne of any body, nor
make it afpire to great things; albeit
shee be herfelfe very perfect , yet
doth she apprehend this great word
of perfection. She neuer feekes her
owne proper intreft nor profit; but
that of I ᴇ ꜱ ᴠ ꜱ C ʜ ʀ ɪ ꜱ ᴛ, & in him
that of the neighbour. Notwithftanding it is a difeafe common inough within Cloifters, and I dare fay,
in a manner contagious(not to defpife thofe of other orders; for that had
beene manifeft follie) but fo to efteeme of the order wherin they are thẽ-
felues inrolled, as if there were none
but it worthy of confideration in the
church of God. It is a Pharifaicall
fpeech to fay, I am not like other mẽ,
efpecially like this Publican. I do not
fay but a Monke or Friar may, yea
ought, as he is tyed in body & habit
to his Order, fo ought he to haue a
particular inclination to it, & to loue
it with a loue of preference, and
fingular preferẽce : But this efteeme

should remaine with in his owne
breast, without suffring it to passe out
of his mouthe, in sort that the account
which he makes of it may not obfu-
scat the merits of other Regular cō-
panies.    For euen as all particular
men, so all societies haue receiued of
God diuers graces and fauours, some
this way, & some that way, as they
receiued so many liniaments of their
visages, as do distinguith them one
from an other, and so many allurements to call them from the world
that would giue themselues to pietie
with more perfection. But, that they
should thinke to exclude, either from
the state of perfection, or from pre-
tending to perfection (which is most
desirable) such as do not make profession of that kind of Conuentuall and
Monasticall life, it would not be only
to offend our faith, but also to swar-
ue from the common opinion, and
fall into absurdities which may not
be admitted by any of solide iudgment.    For if the state of perfection

by tyed to certaine obseruations without which men may not be perfect; or depend of an habit made after a certaine fashion, and of vowes, yea solemne, more then of the practise of those heroicall vertues, which are counselled in the Ghospell, who doth not see that it must be concluded that our Sauiour himself, the patterne of the mountaine, and not the modell only of perfection, but perfection it selfe, hath not beene in this state, considering that we do not read that euer he made those vowes in which they put the essence of the state of perfection? The same may be said of his holy mother, who by the imitation of her sonne hauing perfectly obserued obedience, pouertie and chastitie, ought necessarilie to be held very perfect, albeit wee do not reade in expresse termes, that by vowes solemnely made, she promised to practise these Counsells. But if the church doth piously beleeue with S. Hierosme, that by these

*Our Sauiour did not make the vowes of Religion.*

words, which she said to the Angell
who saluted her, how shall that be
which thou saiest, that I shall be a
mother whenas, I know no man?
Shee doth witnesse that shee resol-
ued in her heart to keepe her integritie, and promised to God perpetuall virginitie; it is certaine that
this interpretation is not yet proposed to the faithfull, as an article of
faith, no more then is to this present
her immaculate Conception, but well
is proposed, that shee was a Virgin
before, during, & after her child-
birth, and in somme, that shee remayned alwaies a Virgin vntill her death.
*Apostles and Patriaches did not make the vowes of Religion.* It would follow also that the Apostles, and if wee please to ascend
higher, the Patriaches and Prophets,
and he that participated of the graces and qualities of the one and the
other, S. Iohn Baptist the greatest
amongst the children of men, should
not haue beene in the state of perfection, because we do not reade that
euer they made these vowes in which
                              they

they put the essence of the Regular life, albeit they had the practise of those vertues in an eminent & high degree. It would follow moreouer that so many millions of Monks which peopled the deserts, and whose actions almost inimitable wee cānot reade without admiration, should not haue beene in this blessed state, being that they were many yeeres before these two great law-makers of Regularitie, S. Basile in the Orient, *S. Basile, & S. Benet the.* and S. Benet in the Occident, who *net the.* first established lawes & rules, for the *first authors of Regular* gouernement of those whom the desire of perfecting themselues in the *cemmonaltes.* Monasticall discipline made to liue *naltes.* together in common. And then the vowes of these two rules were but simple vowes, dispensable according *Solemne* the will of the Superiours, the solem- *Vowes introduced but of* ne vowes being not introduced in *ced but of* the church, but in those later ages, *late dayus,* for a more sure bond and tye of Regular Orders. Euen so did the Popes decide in our dayes in consideration

F

of the regular Clarks of the focietie
of I E S V S, that fimple vowes are fufficient to put him that makes them
in the ftate of perfection which Regularitie doth promis, to the end that
the yong Nouices of this holy focietie, who make but the firft vowes
should haue the confolation to beleeue that they are in this honorall
ftate. But to diue more deeplie into
the matter, if the vowes which giue
precepts to fuch as obferue the Euã-
gelicall counfells put them in the ftate of perfection, how shall the Mon-

*The*
*vowes of*
*Benedi-*
*ctins, Ber-*
*nardins*
*& Car-*
*thufians.*

kes of S. Benet, S. Bernard and the
Carthufians, which make but vowes
of ftabilitie, & of correcting their
manners, without fpecifying the
vowes of chaftitie, pouertie or obedience, be in this ftate of perfection?
I know that the schoole Doctours
do anfwere, that the promifes of thefe three Counfells are implicitè, as
they fpeake, contayned in the two
vowes aforefaid. But if fo be, that
in a contract there is no more force,

according the prouerb, then such as
men put in it, and that words are
worth no more then as they sound,
how shall the state of perfection be
amongst the Benedictins, the Car-
thusians and the Bernardins? We
may say, that properly speaking, that
happie state is not descended from
heauen but since the Conuentuall
Friars are deuided into more branches then euer Xerxes deuided the
riuer Gindes, & that as many as will
not put themselues within their Arke shall remaine in the Deluge of imperfection. I know well they will replie, that for calling theselues Regulars they do not hold that all other
Christians are irregular, that for calling themselues brothers, they do not
separat themselues from the Frater-
nitie of Christianitie, nor do not take
from the laitie that title which the *In the*
firft Christiãs in the primitiue Church *primitiue*
gaue to themselues, that for calling *Church*
themselues Religious they do not *all Chri-*
hold other men to be irreligious & *stiãs we-*
*re called*
*brothers.*

F ij

impious, that for being inrolled in particular Orders, they do not hold that other children of the Church doe liue in diforder; but that their vowes putting them in a ftate which doth oblige them to tend to a higher perfe&ion, then that of the common fort, they haue reafon to think that they are in the ftate of perfe&io. To which I anfwere, that the ftate of perfe&ion is that, which approche neereft to the imitation of the fonne of God, of his moft holy mother, & of the holy Apoftles, and that this imitation cofifting rather in the pra-&ife of the Euangelicall Counfells then in the vowes of them, that fuch as are moft aduaunced in thofe vertues are moft perfe&, & in a more perfe& eftate then thofe that only make vowes of them, and not pra&ife them. And if they will fay that a vow doth oblige him that makes it, to imbrace alfo the pra&ife of it, & to run in that fort, as the Apoftle faith, that he may arriue to the butt of perfection; I will replie that oftentimes it had beene better not to haue vowed, then after vowing to performe so ill their promise, as many doe, for they may not mock God, but in the end they shall be punished for it: and the punishmēt which he takes is so much the more seuere that it comes but slow. But they will say, that a vow added to the practise of the Counsells hath the same aduantage that faire apparrell, and pretious stones haue being added to an excellent beautie, which is neuer so excessiue in it owne nature but the art of garments doth alwaies bring it more luster; so a vow besids the grace which it giues to a man, giues him also a certaine stablenesse & firmenesse, when he sees himselfe ingaged by these holy bōds to the seruice of God, from which he may not withdraw himselfe without incurring, or as S. Paule saith, without acquiring his damnation. And I confesse so much, that a vow

is a moſt holy and Religious action;
& that it is a ſtrong motiue, and a
preſſing ſting to make a man run the
race of perfection: but for a man to
denie alſo that many men did as perfectlie practiſe theſe vertues without
vowes, it would be to draw vpon his
owne back the examples, which we
haue already produced of our Sauiour, of his holy mother, of the
Apoſtles, Patriarches, Prophets, and
of the firſt Chriſtians, who were ſo
perfect without that vow being before the fundation of Monachiſme
and Conuentuall life. Witneſſe that
ancient Monke, who hauing conſu-
med many yeeres to perfect himſelfe in the exerciſe of the Euangelicall
Counſells, had reuelation that the
Emperour Theodoſius was equall to
him in merit, albeit according the
Rule of Regulars he was not in the
ſtate of their perfection: but he was
a good Prince in the perfection of
his owne eſtat, and whoſoeuer is ſo,
according my ſimple iudgment may

*Many did practiſe the Euangelicall vertues as well without vowes as with vowes.*

*Theodoſius perfect without vow.*

be said to be in the state of perfection. And that which doth fortifie
me in this thought is, that I do not
find that the Scripture doth attribute perfection but to the practise of
pouertie where it saith: *If thou vvilt* Matt.19.
*be perfect, goe, sell the things that thou* v. 21.
*hast, & giue to the poore, and come, fol-*
*lovv me.* And S. Peter saying to our
Sauiour that he had executed the
counsell which he gaue to him and
to his Condisciples, doth not speake
of any vow, but of the effect of it
by these words: *Behold vve haue left*
*all things, and haue follovved thee:*
*Vvhat therefore shall vve haue?* To
whom for reward our Sauiour did
promis a hundred fold in this world,
& euerlasting glorie in the other.
I know well that a vow doth oblige
a man to the practise of it, and also
that it doth depriue a man of all
proprietie, leauing him nothing but
the simple vse of things necessarie,
according the saying of the Apostle:
*Hauing foode, and vvhervvith to be* 1.Tim. 6.

*couered*, *VVith these VVe are content.*
And also I graunt that practise made in vertue of a vow, is like vnto
trees graffed, whose fruict are more
sweet, & sauorous, then that of other
trees, but I know also, that as he that
vow and effect it, shall be much rewarded, so he that doth not execute
what he promiseth shall be doublie
punished for hauing ingaged himselfe in a combat which did not succeede with him, or to speake with the
Apostle, for hauing broken his word.
And he that followes the Counselles
without obligation, if he be but simplie rewarded, he is not at all punished when he failes, in sort that it
is written: *Let him take it that can, he
that imbraceth it doth VVell, & he that
doth not, doth not ill*, in which consisteth the difference betweene Counselles and precepts. And meditating
with my self vpon this subiect, I did
often admeere, how it hapned that
perfection was attributed in expresse
termes to pouertie, and not to chastitie,

tie, nor to obedience, confidering
that thefe two laft vertues feeme to
be fo much the more excellent, by
how much their fubiect and obiect
doth excell that of pouertie:for there
is no doubt among men of iudgment, but that corporall goods,
which are the pleafures, to which
men renounce by chaftitie, and the
goods of the foule, to which men
bidd farewell by renouncing themfelues and their proper wills, are of
farr greater efteemation and worth
then are the goods of fortune,wher-
of men depriue themfelues by pouertie: for who will denie that the
foule is more pretious then meate,
and the body more worth then it
apparrell without he contradict, not
only the Scripture but alfo common
fens ? But if perfection confift in following our Sauiour, doth not he fay?
*He that vvill fallovv me let him re-* Luca 9,
*nounce himfelf, take vp his croffe and* v.23.
*follovv me?* And who is he that would
not eafier quitt what he doth poffeffe

G

then himself? toothe for toothe, and
eye for eye, saith Iob, will man giue
in counterchange of his soule, whose
Sacrifice is made by obedience,
obedience, which is better then
all the Sacrifices of body and goods?
That the practise of chastitie is a
most perfect thing, it is very euident
by that which the wisman saith: *That*
*there is no price VVhich can equall a cha-*
*ste and continent soule. O VVhat a faire*
*& excellent thing is, a generation full of*
*puritie!* And he that is more then Sa-
lomon, speaking of those voluntarie Eunuches who gelded themselues
that they might the easier aspire to
heauen, doth not he say: *That feVV*
*doth vnderstand, and feVVer doth exer-*
*cise this VVord*, shewing by the raritie
of the practise the excellence of this
vertue? In like manner, if I durst say
so, it seemeth that the vow and exercise of pouertie which is made out
of a Commonaltie ( which otherwise
hath great merit, because of the obedience which double the goodnesse

*Sap. 4.*

*Matth.*19
*v.11.*

*A vovv of*
*pouertie*
*made out*
*of a Com.*

of the action by the force of her in- *monaltie*
fluence) is more compleat, as shee is *What*
*it.*
more difficile and hard, then that
which is made within a societie, where
the one carrieth the burthen of the
other, where they incourage & comfort one an other, and to speake
with the Scripure, where the one
doth heate the other in deuotion,
and succour his brother in his necef-
sitie by a mutuall ayde; in steade that
a solitarie Monke, who sells all that
he hath, & distribute it in almes, &
renounce all that he had, or might
pretend in the world, to follow our
Sauiour in that nakedneffe, remayning with this proppe without any
other proppe but the eternall prouidence, doth exercise more according the letter (I cannot tell what he
doth according the Spirit) the Counsell of pouertie after the manner that
it is laid downe in the Ghospell, then
the other, where it is said, that a man
must quitt all that he hath and follow
the sonne of God in this absolute

G ij

nuditie, which hath no proppe in
earth, and makes a man caft all his
thoughts on God. And who doth
not fee that he who renounceth his
patrimonie, and puts himfelf into a
Monafterie well rented, or to a
Conuent of begging friars, which
probablie hath her maintenance at
the gate for demaunding it; doth
not often times paffe from a litle and
poore fecular familie into a riche and
well fupported regular Monafterie,
where he is more affured that he
shall want nothing that is neceffarie
for his maintenance, then if he had
remayned in the world, where fuch
as are moft fauoured by fortune,
*The ftate* and that are moft aduaunced in ho-
*of fauo-* nours and richeffe are fubiect to
*rits.* ouerthrowes, to great falls, and to
ftrange defafters, and are like vnto
thofe falfe ftarrs which fall and neuer
get vp againe? In one word, it is very cleere to fuch as haue eyes, that
as Conuentuall pouertie hath a lufter
and an aduantage becaufe of the

vow of it, so is shee also well
rampared against the assaults of all
misfortune, well refresched by the
help of many assistances, though those many times may be more cerimo-
nious then compassionat. True pouertie is that which indure with patience the want of things necessarie;
and to desire to haue the glorie of
this vertue without feeling the other
points of necessitie, it is to desire
triumph and victorie without combat, laurell and palme crownes without putting himself to any hazard.
Euerie body knowes that Ananias
and Saphira for hauing ambitiouslie
desired the honour to seeme poore
like other Christians, who did cast all
their goods without reseruing any
thing, at the feete of the Apostles,
were strucken with the anatheme of
death by the Spirit of God passing
out of the mouthe of the Prince of
the      tles. I know that the subti-
litie      hoole diuinitie, where the
vertu.  are refined as within a cruset,

*True po-
uertie
What is
it.*

hath found out a number of faire reasons to colour with a liuely, and pretious enamel the Conuentuall pouertie, which, when all is said, doth consist in disappropriating a man of the possession of the goods wherof he retaines the vsage: but it happēs often that these determinations so distilled, do ressemble those quintessens which turne into vapours as *No man* soone as they see the aire. For in *in this* fine who in this world can say that *World* *hath but* he is proprietaire of any thing, con- *the Vse of* sidering that life it self, without which *things.* all other goods, mouable and immouable are vnprofitable, is not giuē to vs but in vsufruict, and not in proprietie? And to say that a man doth renounce to his life, but keeps onely the vse of it, is it not to say that he quits that which he keepes, seing that life as well as richesse doth not consist but in vsage?

By this reconing Princes' ːeat lords who are inglutted in ꞏꞏꞏures and wealth ouer head and shꞏulders

should be without vow in the state
of pouertie, seeing that like vnto the
Conuentuall friars they haue but the
vse of their treasures, & that they do
not handle it but by the hands of
their treasoriers, and such other officers; and the greatest kings of the
earth what haue they but their liuing
in this world, and the vse of the same
sunne and the same elements which
the simplest Countryma doth parti-
cipat equallie with them? Yet for all
that the regular Doctours do not
graunt vnto them to be in the state
of perfection, albeit that in the Scripture the soueraigne powers of the
earth are putt in a state of sublimi-
tie. O how the first Monks proceeded
after an other fashion, if not in vow,
at leastwise in the practise of pouertie, for after hauing sold & distributed
to the poore their patrimonie, they
did cast themselues into the deserts,
flying from the world as well in body as in hart and minde, and there
afflicted, necessitous and miserable,

to vfe Apoftolik termes, they retired
thēfelues into caues and holes within
the earth, imitating our Sauiour, who
during his life had not a place to put
in his head, hauing no houfe of his
owne, no Cloifter, no cell, no Conuent nor any other thing, which he
might call his owne, but the croffe,
which he carried vpon his shoulders
to Mont Caluaire. Alas! when shall
that happie time come, in which the
Monks, Anacorites and friars will re-
fufcitat in themfelues the Spirit of
that great Apoftle, which may induce them to gaine their liuing by
the labours of their hands, and to
eate their bread with ashes, by the
*Monks &* fweate of their browes, without mo-
*friars* lefting this man or that man, fome ti-
*should* mes by begging of almes from doo-
*rather*
*Worke* re to doore, fome times importunat-
*for their* lie demaunding fundations for their
*liuing* Monafteries, and fome times taking
*then begg* dowries, as they do in Nunries; &
to fpeake in facred termes, and therfore irreprehenfible, making lucre of
pietie

pietie & busying the simpler sort to *Tits* 1.
draw profit to theselues & doing like 6.12.
the liuer, which doth not become
fatt, but by the leannesse of other
members? I haue not beene a bur- *Act.* 10.
then to any man, saith S. Paul glo- 1.*Cor.* 4.
rifying himsef in God, but teaching,
preaching and labouring, I haue by 1.*Thes.* 2.
the work of my hands prouided what 1.*Cor.* 9.
was needfull for me. So did, so liued
these ancient Anacoretes, who made
basketts & other small works which
they carried to the market to be sold,
to nourrish themselues with the price of them, & to giue the surplus to
the poore. So did also the ancient
Regulars, as may be easelie seene in *Ancient*
the Chronicles of the Orders, who *regulars*
liued in the seruice of God, and in *their*
the obseruance of their rules, tilling *labour.*
the earthe, digging and labouring
the vine-yards, gayning their daylie
wages during the haruest and the
ventage, and bringing all to the cō-
monaltie, without reseruing any
thing to themselues in particular,

H

vnder paine of excommunication,
and to be buried, if they were found
dying, poffeffours of any thing
whatfoeuer, in the fepulchers of
beafts: cutting the woods, drying
vp marrish grounds, playing the
joyners, and the carpenters, building
of houfes, keeping of cattle and doing
all other Countrie hufbandrie: the
weaker fort giuing themfelues to
thofe arts which are leffe painefull,
as to play the taylours, the paintu-
res, working, of wooll, & coppying
of books, before printing became fo
common. In this fort euerie one did
cōtribut his paine without any other
reward to himfelf, but the abondance
which is promifed in heauen. The
millions of Monks which liued in
Monafteries did infinit good to the
neighbours about them, in fteed of
incommodating & oppreffing them
as now fome do, they made themfelues by their labourious induftries the
Fathers of the poore, being themfelues poore in all refpects. I do not

intend by this to blame the reuenewes of the church ( knowing that
all extremities are vitious and incline
to errour) fo they be moderat : for if
moderation in all things is to be efteæ-
med, in this kind it is not only praife
worthy , but in fome fort neceffarie, the experience of fo many ages
making vs to fee and feele that ex-
ceffe doth carrie men to abufes and
licentioufneffe, that I fay no worfe;
and as S. Bernard faith, that if fo be
deuotion doth ingender richeffe ,
thefe bad daughters when they become great doth fuffocat & ftifle their
mother, and induce her to finne, as
Loth that was fo holy was induced
by his owne daughters. Much leffe
do I intend to blame mendicitie or
begging, confidering that my felf
doth make profeffion of it, and
knowing that it hath beene deuout-
lie permitted in the church, and that
fuch as cried againft the begging
Orders of S. Francis and S. Dominick when they were newly inftitu-

ted, were conftrained to imbrace the
filéce which was impofed to them by
the foueraigne Bifhop the Pope. But
it is to be wifhed, that this médicitie
should not be vfed but to fupplie
the default of manuel labour, when
after a diligent imploy they should
find themfelues short of meanes to
nourish the Commonaltie: for in that
cafe they might vfe the priuiledg of
the law of nature, which permit
euerie man to aske his liuing when
he cannot labour for it. But to re-
duce that to a forme or fashió, which
is ordayned by the rules of the Monafterie touching corporall labour,
towards the inclofures of gardens,
which they till rather, for the health
and pleafure of particular perfons,
then for the profit and vtilitie of
the houfe, and rather to haue flowers
to deck and adorne the altars then
to haue fruict to putt vpon the tables; is in my opinion to make a
delicat Sabath at the chardges of the
common wealth, whom it concernes

*Begging*
*is to be*
*vfed whē*
*men can-*
*not gett*
*their li-*
*uing by*
*their la-*
*bour.*

that euery body labour, and make vſe and profit of his talent, and induſtrie, in manuring the vigneyard, that is to ſay,in following the vocation which fell to his lott, according the line of diuine diſtribution. The Emperour Diocletian hauing putt of the Empire, tooke great paines to trim and dreſſe his litle garden, paſſing ſweetlie his time in the innocēt imploy of tilling the ground, and after that faſhion he ſaw himſelf as riche in his pouertie, as before being in his Emperiall dignitie, he found himſelf poore in the middeſt of his richeſſe, hauing not alwaies wherby to recompence worthelie ſuch as ſerued him well, nor to pay his armies. It is not that in this occaſion, I would iuſtifie my ſelf, conſidering that I was conceiued in iniquitie, and that I am all rotten with vitious cicatrices, and much leſſe would I preferr my ſelf to thoſe whoſe ſhooe latchets, I am not worthy to looſe. But I may aſſure you, that I do not begg

*The Emperour Diocletiā did Work*

in these quarters but in as much as
my infirmities do take from my armes the pouer to trauaile, hauing
seene my self sometimes of that force
and vigour, that I had by my owne
industrie the meanes, not only to intertaine my self without chardging
any other, but also to intertaine
others that came to visit this cell.
And if now necessitie doth constraine me to haue recours sometimes to
the charitie of those to whom, I gaine
heauen through the good which
they do vnto me, my age and my
weaknesse doth pleade my cause before their pietie, & make them harken to my petition.

Here Tristan, as in a place which
to him seemed very proper to offer
his goods to Nicephorus, breaking
the cours of his long discours; Father,
saith he, the prouidence of God hath
conducted me hither, and to speake
otherwise, hath leade me by the hãd
of his will, to draw you out of all
paine, and your old yeeres from care.

and labour. I haue by the grace of
God abondantly to maintaine you
without suffocating your Spirit by
bodely labour, and putting your self
to trouble to fearche your lyuing.
Sir, quoth the Hermite, if I had not
knowne in your face your ingenui-
tie, and the finceritie of your intention in the offer which you make vnto me, I would make you the fame
anfwere which our Sauiour made to
S. Peeter, who would faine diffwade
him from going to fuffer to Hieru-
falem wherof he heard him fpeake to
Moyfes & Elias vpon mont Thabor:
Retire from me Sathan. What? you
are then come hither to tempt me
to defcend from the croffe of holy
pouertie, in which I defire to die, in
the nuditie and nakednesse of my
Sauiour. Ha! not fo Sir, nothing
shall feparat me if I can from the
charitie of IESVS CHRIST, not
death nor life, not hunger, not cold,
not nuditie, not pouertie nor want,
not mē nor Angelles, not the powers

of the earth nor that of hell, not the
time paſt, nor the time preſent, nor
the time to come: For I am certaine
with the help of his grace to remaine conſtant in my reſolution, and
neuer to relent in any one point of
it: I meane to die poore with him
that being riche made himſelf poore
for our ſakes, to the ende to inriche
vs by his want. Labour taken for
him is no labour, for he made the
yoke of his croſſe ſo ſweet and eaſie
by the oyle of his bloude which is
baulme ſhedd for vs, that his burthen is rather a ſolagement then a
chardge, reſembling the feathers of
birds which lift them vp to the ayre
in ſteed of waighing them downe to
the earthe. There is no paine where
there is loue, or if there be any, it is
but a deare and deſirable paine; for
to labour for that which a mã loueth,
of all delices it is the ſweeteſt. And
if you think that manuel labour doth
diſſipat the Spirites (that which ſome
delicat fellowes ſaid, vnworthy mēbers

bers of a heade all torne with thornes) cōtrarywiſe, I hold that it doth
rather fortifie it, witneſſe the Apoſtle 1 *Cor.* 12.<br>9. 1 0.
ſaying, that his Spirit was then moſt
vigorours and ſtrong when his body
was ouercommed and weakned by
infirmities, or by voluntarie morti-
fications; and I feare much that ſuch
as ſay that manuel labour might cauſe
the diſſipation of their Spirit do ap-
prehēd more the diſſipation of their
bodys, and as S. Paul ſaith, the diſſipation of this machine & terreſtriall ha-
bitatiō which inuirone the ſoule. For
euē as the nobilitie which in peace time do reſerue for thēſelues ſlouth &
idleneſſe, and in warr time the exerciſe of armes. In like manner it ſee-
meth that theſe fathers more contē-
platiue then actiue do confine themſelues to the ſinging of Pſalmes, as
if it were a function very laborious to
ſing, or that it had beene the harp of
Dauid to chaſe away the Diuells of
vice by her melodie, which poſſeſſe
ſinners, or that it had the force of the

I

Sacerdotall trōpetts, at whose sound did fall the walls of Hiericho, or of the hands of Moyses which gaue victorie to the childrē of Israëll against Amalec. Certes, if by the effects we may iudge of the vigour and force of the cause, we may well say of their Congregations that which the sacred Cantique doth say of the Sulamite, what will you see in her but Quires of combattants and squadrons of Choristers? It is there they take that sweet and pleasant sleepe vpon the breast of our Sauiour, from which, no lesse then the Amant and louer of the same spouse would they be drawē or waked, vntill it please themselues to passe from the ease and content-ment of this sacred contemplation to the action, & from the sweet attentiō of Marie to the tumultuous labours of Martha; in the meane time the litle ones demaund bread, & few do breake it vnto them; the neighbours do grone and waile, & few do succour them: many are wounded vpon the

way of Hiëricho and there are but
few Samaritans that would solace *Ioan.4.*
and comfort them. The Countries *v.34.*
are white to harueſt, and there are
but few harueſt-men : the vigne-yard
is deſert and vntilled, and there are
but few venteners, much worke and
few workmen.

*The three principall functions of an Ecclesiastiall perſonne.*

   Of the three principall functiōs of
the Eccleſiaſticall ſtate, which are to
preach, to adminiſter the Sacramēts,
and to pray, be it in particular men-
tally, or vocally ; be it in publick by
ſinging of the publike office, the
greateſt part of the friars toke this
laſt, which is the moſt ſpecioufe and
leſſe profitable, for the lott of their
inheritance, and for their imploymēt
ſaying with the Pſalmiſt : *I vvill ſing
your iuſtices o lord , in this ſejour of my
pilgrimage.* And in effect, when all
shall be well counted, for three or
foure which announce to the people
the word of God, which is the breade
of life and vnderſtanding, for the ad-
miniſtration of which the Apoſtles
              I ij

themselues did cease from distribu-
ting the sacred communion, which
the holy text doth call to serue to
the tables, there are fiftie or three
scoare in great Conuents deputed
only for the Quire, and fifteene or
twētie lay brothers tyed to the dome-
sticall functions. But perchance they
will say that they imploy the Friars
according the talents which they receiued from God, it being very reasonable that in the Church which is
a terrestriall Paradis, the trees do
beare fruict according their kind, &
that men do worke according their
qualities, and that the tallent of preaching or of helping soules, which require great science and prudence in
discerning of Spirits, being giuen but
to a few, there are many more that
are capable of the Quire then of the
chaire. To which I answere that such
as are proper for the Quire cānot be
vnproper for manuel labour, and that
perchāce the weale publique would
be as much content and solaged by

their labour as by their finging. It
is not that I call in doubt the excellencie of prayer, and that I do not
know that men may fay of her what
that anciēt painteur faid of his owne
worke, that shee labours for the eter-
nitie, and that shee hath this aduantage ouer mechanicall things, that
thefe being vifible are confequentlie
tēporall as the Apoftle faith, & that
the other which is inuifible, as that
of prayer; is eternall. But if in this
age men esteeme more of finfible
thē of fpiritual things, none being in
it which doth not preferr almefdeeds
to prayer, & alfo to fasting; it may
be faid that manuell labour which
doth neceffarily nourishe a poore
man, as he is, that worke of neceffitie, shall not be lesse eftimable then
prayer, and that the worke of thofe
hands wherof the great Apoftle did
glorifie himfelf, shall not be lesse efti-
med then was his rauishment to the
third heauen, a fauour which ferued
him rather for recompence then for

merit. Hence is it, that he doth name
himfelf in the one and not in the
other, as hauing fome part in the
one and none in the other, which
arriued to him by a gratuit grace,
fuch as reuelation is, and the gift of
Prophecie. By reafon of which the
Pfalmift doth call happie, not thofe
that are euerie day in extafie, but
thofe that maintaine themfelues by
the fweate of their browes.

*The par-*
*ticular*
*office of a*
*Monke.*

Peraduenture fome will fay that
the particular office of Monks, according S. Hierome, is to weepe &
to pray, and that the functions to
preach and to adminifter the Sacraments are not for them but in way of
fupererogation, that they might not
fall into the reproche which is made in the Ghofpell to the prieft and
Leuite, who did not fuccour him that
was left for deade by the theeues
that thought to murther him in the
high way. But feeing that the difference which men put betweene
Monks & Religious men, is drawne

from that, that Monks do not applie
themselues, or ought not to applie
themselues by their inftitution but
to the folitarie and pure contemplatiue life, and that the Religious do
not applie themfelues to prayer only, but alfo to côtemplation, making
as our Sauiour and the Apoftles did,
a kind of life called a mixt life, of
action and contemplation, by which,
as by Iacobs ladder, fome times they
lift themfelues vp to God by prayer,
fometimes they defcend towards the
neighbour by the works of mercie;
a life which the fcholafticall diuinitie,
grounded vpon great reafons, eftee-
meth the moft perfect; it should
follow that fuch as call themfelues
Religious men, and that obtayned
of the foueraigne Bishop fo many
exemptiôs and priuiledges, that they
might exercife Clericall or Ecclefiafticall functions for the feruice of
foules, should attend more to fowe
the facred word, & to adminifter
the Sacraments, then to the exercife

of the Quire, which is more conue-
nient for Monks then for them.
And seeing that none doth enter
their Orders, but by the choice and
trial which they make of such as present themselues to them, they should
not receiue any but such as should
haue the talents necessarie for the
functions of the mixt life, which they
say, as the most perfect, to be conformable to their institutiõ, and to their
state of perfection. In this manner
the commonwealth should be more
solaged by their labours then by their
clamours; for to tell no lye, it seemeth, as said great S. Charles of his
owne time, that as the Church of
this our age tormented by Libertins
and Hereticks, hath more neede of
goodPastours then of goodReligious
men, so hath shee more neede amõg
Religious men of those that are people of action, then of singers & con-
templatiues, and of Champions then
of Choristers: for albeit Marie choosed the best part for her, it is not for
all that

*The church hath more neede of good Pastours then of good Re-ligious men.*

all that the beſt alwaies for the neighbour, & albeit it is the moſt eminent part, yet is it not the moſt profitable. And if they ſhould alleage
Moyſes praying, and Ioſūé with ſo
many thouſands Iſraëlites fighting,
the obiection will carrie it owne anſwere with it ſelf, ſeing that for one
that lift vp his hands praying, thouſands of others do exerciſe their hãds
againſt the enemies. Which is contrarie with the Regulars, who for a
hundred that ſing in the Quire
haue not two that take paines to
deſcend to the ſuccour of the neighbour and of the church, forſaking the
mountaine of prayer, a fatt mountaine, a mountaine of creame, a mountaine all of honny, where it pleaſeth
them to remaine with God in peace,
rather then in warr among the in-
combrances which are found in the *Regulars*
tabernacles of ſeculars and Paſtours. *ſhould*
Euen ſo ſome ſinners who cannot *not take*
draw themſelues from their badd ha- *the pai-*
bitudes, and who deferr their con- *nes that*
*Paſtours*
*do.*

K

uersion till the time of their death
do make a badd buckler of the exãple of the good theefe, who conuer-
ted himself vpon the crosse, and the
very same day entred into Paradis
according the promis of our Sauiour:
because, that for that one man that
was saued in that point, thousands
and thousands are lost and damned,
it being very reasonable saith S. Au-
stin, that he doth forget himself
dying, who lyuing did not remēber
to returne to God. Euen so the Spaniards in their Solemnities, because
that Dauid danced once before the
Arke by an excesse of pietie, and by
an extraordinarie motion of the holy
Ghost, would not think to make a
good procession if there were not
dancers in it.

That is the same thing, quoth
Tristan, which some Religious men
said to me, to whom I did communicat the dessigne which I had to retire
my self to an Hermitage; that Monks
were not good but for themselues,

but Religious men are neceſſarie for
the Chriſtian common wealth, which
is the church. To which Nicephorus
replied, if by Monks they vnderſtãd
the Hermites which applie themſelues ſoly & ſimplie to contemplation,
and of which men call Anacorites,
they haue ſome apparance of reaſon,
but if to preach, to catechiſe, to viſit
the ſick, to attend to the conuerſion
of the ſtrayed, to adminiſter the Sacraments of pennance and the Eu-
chariſt, & to do all things according
the commaund of the Ordinarie, and
vnder the imploy of the Paſtours,
do make a Religious man, many
Hermites will be found, which will
be no more Monks, but Religious
men, and many Conuentuall Friars,
which do nothing of all theſe things,
ſhall be no Religious men but Mõks.
And to ſhew vnto you that it is not
in that point that this bleſſed diſtinction of a Monke & a Religious man
doth conſiſt; But in I know not what
imagination, which I conceiue as litle

K ij

as I do the Ideas of Plato, and the
atomes of Dimocrites; The Benedictins, the Bernardins, the Celestins,
the Fueillantins, and those of the
Order of S. Basile, to whom they
giue the name of Monks, as being attributed to them by their rules, do not
they liue in Conuents, do not they
preach, do not they teach the Christian doctrine, do not they administer the Sacraments in vertue of so
many indults and so many immuni-
ties, and Bulls as they haue from the
Sea Apostolique? in sort as I do not
*Monks do*　see, neither in their liues, nor in their
*not differ*　functions in what they differ from
*fromCon-*　the Conuentuall Friars who call thē-
*uentuall*　selues Religious men. The differen-
*Friars.*　ce is not in mendicitie for there are
Conuentuall Friars which call themselues Religious men who are not
beggers: it is not in abstinence from
meate, for in that the Minimes are
more austere then the Benedictins
or Celestins, yea, or the Carthusiās
themselues: it is not in mendicitie &

abstinence together, for in that the
Reformed Dominicans and the bare
footed Carmelits are admirable in
abstayning fró the vse of flesche,they
liuing but by almes. And to say what
1 think, I see so litle difference, betweene those whom they call Monks
aboue named, and the Conuentuall
Friars be they beggers, or not beggers,shodd or not shodd,that I think
men may call Monks Religious men
by as iust a title,as they call Religious
men Monks; and I must graunt vnto
you that, I am not so subtile nor so
penetratiue as he that found seuen-
teene essentiall differences betweene
the habit of the Capucins and that
of the Tertiarians which men call
Regular Penitens of the third order
of S. Francis of strict Obseruance.
To say that the differéce doth consist
in the vowes, I see no apparance of it,
becausethe three essentiall vowes of
Religion, which are the three Euangelicall consells, are common to all
orders as well Monks as Religious

*The Re-
formed
Domini-
cãs differ
much frõ
the Mitti-
gate.*

*Seuẽtine
essen-
tiall dif-
ferences
found
betvvee-
ne the ha-
bit of the
Capucins
& that of
the Tier-
tiarians.*

men. In this fort I do not fee that the name Monke may be properly attributed to any but to the Carthufians, to the Friars of the Cógregation of Camaldoli, and to fome shutt vp Anacoretes, becaufe of their filence, of their inclofure, and of their folitarineffe, which interdi-&ing them the commerce of men, doth alfo take from them all Clericall fun&ions, for which the Conuentuall Friars called themfelues Religious men. And for the word Regular, it is certaine that as many as make profeffion of any rule do affume it to thefelues, as do thefe new Congregations of Clearkes which are called Regulars to the imitation of the Chanon Regulars which liue vnder the rule of S. Auftin, Wherof I remember being in Rome, which is the nurcerie of all thefe Orders as being the matrice of the Church, to haue obferued feuen fortes, without

*Seuē forts of Clekes Regulars* counting the priefts of the Oratorie, called of our ladie of the white-well,

or of Vallicelles, inftituted by fainct
Philip Nerio Florentin, and the
Oblats of S. Ambrofe, founded by
S. Charles, and the priefts of the
Oratorie of I ɛ s v s, whofe Congregation fprong vp in France are
almoft all Frenchmen, powre out a
fweet odoure of fainctitie and vertue
throught all the French Church, &
begins to extend it branches, like a
vigne planted neere the Oliues of
grace, to forraine Countries.

Is it poffible, quoth Triftan, that
there are fo many forts of Regular
Clearks, wheras there are but foure
forts of begging Orders? I told you
that I obferued feuen feuerall infti-
tutions of them while I was in Italie,
and I know not but fince there is
fome other new fashion fprong vp.
If my memorie doth not faile me, I
beleeue I shall name them well yet.
The Theatins are the firft for the
date of the time, inftituted by the
right Reuerend Father in God
Iohn Peeter Carraffe Bishop of

Thiette, who renounced his Bi-
shoprick, to lead a kind of life
truely Apostolicall, with some priests
which did associate themselues to
him, renouncing all things as well in
common as in particular, adding this
point to the strict pouertie of begging
Orders, that albeit they liue onely
*A strange* by almes, yet do they neuer begg
*institutiō* neither by themselues nor by any in-
*of the*
*Theatins.* terposed persons, casting all their
thoughts vpon the paternall care of
the prouidence of God concerning
their maintenance, and putting in
practise according the litterall sens
this Euangelicall Counsell, not to
think of to morrow, nor of that
which is necessarie for foode or cloa-
thing, imitating therin the Lyllis of
the fields, and the birds of the aire,
which God doth cloathe and feede
without that they spinne or labour
themselues for it. This Bishop, in-
stitutour of this holy Congregation,
after hauing illuminated & seasoned
all the Court of Rome with the light
and

and falt of his Doctrine, and of his
good life, was eleuated from the
preambular dignitie of Cardinall to
that of the foueraigne Bishop, pof-
feffing the Sea Apoftolique vnder
the name of Paul the third. The
vulgar fort named thefe Regular
Clerkes Theatins, in fteed of calling
them Thietins, as who would fay, the
Clerkes of the Inftitution of the
Bishop of Thiette. They haue many
houfes in Italie, and I know not if
they exted themfelues elfwhere, this
much I know, that as yet wee haue
not feene of them in France, where
it is to be thought they should be ill
addreffed if they would not aske or
begg, cofidering that fuch as do begg
do often find their almes very short,
fuch is the humour of our Nation,
which haue their hands open for
vaine expenfes and prodigalities, and
shutt vp to iuft and holy liberalities,
by which doth appeere that the end
of the world will come by that way
feing charitie is growen fo cold

L

in it. Which is not in Italy, where men beleeue more firmely then we do, that sinne is redeemed by almesdeeds, and that by this lauor or font all their filth & ordure are clensed. The second institution of Regular Clearkes is that of the priests of the societie of I E S V S, of which, as that ancient writer said of the magnificēce of Rome, it is better say nothing then say litle, being sufficiēt that this holy societie is praised by the mouthe of the holy Counsell of Trent, which is that of the holy Ghost, saying that their institution is praise worthie. The Barnabites doth make the third institution; this Order tooke it origine in Millan, the ordinarie residēce of their Generall, and they are so called, becaufe that the first Church where they did assemble together was called of sainct Barnabe, euen as the Friars Preachers of the Order of sainct Dominick are called Iacobins in Paris, becaufe of a Chappell of S. Iake, otherwise

Iames where they firſt loadged. The
Clerkes Mineurs, which are of the
inſtitution of PopeSixtus V. who was
of the Order of the Friars Mineurs,
do make the fourthe ſort. The fift
is of the Sommaſques, a name ſome-
what ſtrange to ſuch as do not know
the origine of it, which is, that this
Congregation of Regular Clearkes
was inſtituted by a gentilman of
Veniſe in the marche of Treuiſane,
in a bourg called Sommaſcha. So
that as the Chartreux or Carthu-
ſians were ſo called of the place
called Chartreuſe , where they
made their firſt aboade , and
where is the Capitall houſe of their
Order, as the Cluniacenſes were
called of the towne Clugny, the
Ciſtercienſes of Ciſteaux, Camaldu-
lenſes of Camaldoli, euen ſo did the
Sommaſques receiue their nomina-
tion from the place where they were
firſt eſtabliſhed. Theſe do extend
theſelues in Italy & in France vnder
the title of Fathers of the Chri-

stian Doctrine whose houses are
renowned in Prouance, Languedoc
and Guenne. The Sixt institution is
of Regular Clearks surnamed the
Infirmes, because their chardg is, to
serue the sick, be it within the publick
Hospitalls or in priuat houses, & also
to succour such as are most miserable
and forsaken. The seuenth is that of
the Regular Clerks of the mother
of God, called the Congregation of
the priests of Lucques, wherof Father
Franciotti, who wrote so deuotely,
hath beene one of the principall
pillars.

And that which is admirable in
this varietie of institutions is, that
they are all particular rules, which
leuell at some particular marke; the
Theatins do applie themselues to
study and to leade a retired life;
the Iesuits to instruct youthe; the
Barnabites to the Quire and to heare
Confessions; the Clearks Mineurs
to the rigour and austeritie of morti-
fications; the Sómasques to keepe S.

and maintaine forsaken Children, &
Orphans, and to teache the Christiã
Doctrine; The Clearks of the infirme to looke to the sick, and the
Clearkes of the mother of God, to
direct deuote people to spirituall
things. This notwithstanding they
haue all but the self same habit, which
is that wee see the Iesuits carrie. All
of them make professiõ of a certaine
rule with the solemne vowes, and
call themselues Religious men, diffe-
ring in this from the Conuentuall
Friars, that these vnder different habits do make but the self same thing,
and the other do make differẽt functions vnder a like habit. In sort that
the one and the other coming to the
succour of the Pastours do exercise *All those*
Clericall functions, which heretofore *Regular Orders*
was not affected or ordayned but *came to*
for the priests of the Ecclesiasticall *succour*
Cleargie, some of them may be *the Pastours.*
called Religious Clearks, others
Clearks Religious, and all of them
are comprehended vnder the Name

of Regulars. Befids, all the Chanons, which liue vnder the rule of
fainct Auguftin, who are very many, do call themfelues Clearkes Regulars, as thofe of the Order of fainct Anthonie, of fainct Ruf, of Val de Choux, of Val des Efcoliers, the Trinitarians, the Friars de la Mercy, the Hieromites, the Dominicans, and fo many other Militarie Orders which haue this rule for the line of their direction and obferuance.

Why do you put the Dominicans, faith Triftan, among the Chanons, or Regular Clearks, wheras they are one of the foure begging Orders? If you number, quoth the Hermit, the begging Orders according their rules there are but three forts of them, for the Dominicans and the Auftin Friars haue but the felf fame rule, albeit their habits and conftitutions do differ; the Friars Mineurs haue the rule of S. Francis, and the Carmelits that of fainct Bafile, or of the Patriarche Albertus.

But if you take them according their
Congregations, the begging Orders
do farr exceede the number of foure;
the only rule of sainɛt Francis doth
fournish ten forts of them : The
Cordeliers called Obferuantins; the
Conuentualls called the great Friars,
which begg almoſt euery where,
albeit they may haue rents; the Re-
colects of ſtriɛt Obferuance, the Capucins, the Becquins, the Tertiarians;
the Religious women of S. Clare,
who hath a particular rule framed
by S. Francis, which are fubdiuided
into Damianiſts & Vrbaniſts, befids
the Capucin womē and the Hofpita-
liſts of faint Francis, in fort that men
may fay the ten begging Orders of
Francis. Add to this the Dominicans, as well the Mitigated as the
Reformed; the Friars Hermites of
faint Auſtins Order as well the Mitigated as the Reformed, the shodd
as the vnshodd : In like manner the
Carmelits as well the Mitigated, and
the vnshodd of the reformation of

*Of the
rule of S.
Francis
there are
ten forts.*

S. Terefa, as the Reformed shodd; the Friars Hofpitalifts of the Charitie inftituted by S. Iohn de Diτu; the Iefuates inftituted by fainct Iohn Colomban; the Minimes, which are put among the begging Orders, as are alfo the profeffed Iefuits of the laft vow, the Theatins, the Clearks Mineurs, the Clearks of the Infirme, the Friars de la Mort, and the moft part of the Hermites; befids many others which are feene in Italy begging after diuers manners, as thofe that are called *Fate ben Fratelli*, and thofe that crie asking almes: *Faciamo bene mentre che hauemo tempo*, and fuch like, in fort that according the count which we haue now made, not fpeaking of that wherof we are ignorãt, wee should not fay the foure but the nyne and twentie Mendicant Orders. To which if you will add fuch as liue by rents and fundations, you shall find a litle armie of Regulars, of which men may fay what Iacob faid of the Angels, thefe are the fqua-
drons

drons of the God of battles. Now
to know among fo many people,
who are they whom wee may call
Monks without offending them, and
who are to be called Religious men,
it is no fmall matter, and to do it
without danger of miftaking, a man
muft know many particularities and
many hiftories, which is caufe that
men, to efchew all thofe formalities,
do call all Regulars Religious men,
& that the rather that all true Mōks
are very glad to be fo called, and that
fuch as hold themfelues to be Religious men, do take it for an outrage
and inciuilitie, when men call them
Mōks. Which make me call to mind
our gentilwomen who are very glad
when men through errour do call
them Dames, and our grand-Dames
who could not indure that men
should call them Gentilwomen, no
more then thofe priefts who will not
haue themfelues called Clearks. In
what then, replied Triftan, doth cōfift
this ftate of perfection of which
M

all Monasticall and Conuentuall persons, Monks or Religious men, call them as you please, do make so great account, and from which they say you Hermites are so farr, as you can neuer pretend it?

For my part, quoth Nicephorus, I beleeue they are as well grounded in the possession of the state of perfection, as they are in the title of Religious men. Those that are called in the Acts of the Apostles, Religious men, were deuote persons in the primitiue Chutch, which were neither Monks nor Regulars; and all Christians which liue according the precepts of the Ghospell, and of the Catholike Religion, established by I ESVS CHRIST seemeth to me to haue right to call themselues Religious men, though they be lay and married men, and what other trade they be of. And that it is so, who doth not know that S. Francis wrote a third Rule of pennance, in which all faithfull people of what sex or

*All good Christiās may be called Religious men.*

condition foeuer they be may be en-
rolled, and carrie the qualitie of Religious men of the third Order of this
Seraphicall Father? Yea but, replied
Triftan, thofe Religious men are not
in the ftate of perfectió, as the others
are which make the three vowes
conformable to the Euangelicall
Counfells: for me thinks the faid Fathers faid to me, that it is in that that
this ftate of perfection doth confift,
from which the Hermits are excluded. At this word excluded, the bloud
mounted to the Hermits face, & coloured it, if not for fpite and cholar,
at leaftwife for confufion and emo-
tion. This then made him replie in
this fort: if wee be excluded, it is with
good companie, for befids that we do
not read, as I faid alreadie, that our
Sauiour, his holy mother, and the
Apoftles euer made the faid vowes,
well wee reade that they practifed the
holy vertus counfelled in the Ghofpell; and by this practife they arriued
both to the perfection of their eftate,

and to te state of an eminent perfection; they must exclude with vs all
the Chanons of the Cathedrall and
Collegiall Churches, all the Pastours
& venerable Priests which are in the
Church and haue no other rule but
the rule of rules which is the holy
Ghospell, to the line and square of
which all other rules should be framed to be made right. Behold then
wee are in good companie, the Pastours, Doctours, and Preachers, if
they do not vow vnder a certaine
rule, they shall not be in the state of
perfection, they that are the salt
of the earthe, & the light of the
world. And a lay Brother that
beggs vp and downe, that playes
the Cooke, and the gardener in a
Conuent, shall be in a more eminent
state in the Church of God then all
those people. A man without doubt
must be well versed in the' subtilities
of the schole to comprehend this
Diuinitie, very hard to be inculcated
to ignorant men. Let vs mount our

*A hard censure.*

ẽ

ſtring to a higher note, and ſay that
the Biſhops, the Cardinalles and the
Pope himſelf ſhall not be in this ſtate
of perfeɛtion, hauing not vowed the
obſeruance of any of theſe rules approued by the Church, vnder which
the Regulars are inrolled.

To this the Regulars do replie,
quoth Triſtan, that thoſe Paſtours are
in a ſtate of perfeɛtion more eminent
then that of theReligious, in ſo much
as they call it the ſtate of perfeɛtion *Biſhops*
acquired, and the other but a ſtate of *are in the*
perfeɛtion to be acquired. So that *ſtate of*
they are the ſunne which comprend *acquired.*
in their light all the light of the leſſer
ſtarrs: and the firmamēts of the earth
lifted vp ouer the topp of the mon·
taignes of perfeɛtion, whoſe fruiɛt do
extend it ſelf farr ouer mount Liban,
where theſe puiſſant Gods of the
earth are ſtronglie placed, becauſe
they are the children of the higheſt,
and his arrowes in the hand of the
Omnipotent, which flee out with im-
petuoſitie. This is the eſtate which is

called the supreme amongst men in the militant Church, which corres-

*They cor-respõd to the Sera-phins in the Hie-rarchie.*

pond to that of the Seraphins in the first Hierarchie of the Angelles. In sort that as the rodd of Moyses did swallow vp the rodd of the Magitiãs, euen so in the estate of Prelatship & Pontificat are contayned all the per-fections of all the Regular Orders, in the same manner that Priesthood doth containe in it self the inferiour Orders. But my difficultie is to know in what doth consist this distinction betweene perfection acquired, and perfection to be acquired; for I be-leeue that the greatest part of the world are in the last, and but very few in the other. For to say a perfect man, is to say a man without sinne, and he that saith he hath no sinne, is a lyer and hath no truth in him, ac-cording the holy Scripture : *Vvho thinks to be vvithout sinne doth seduce himself, for vvee are all conceiued in iniquitie.* To say also with that Bishop of the Apocalyps lo : *I am full of*

grace, and haue no neede of any thing, is to say, I am in the topp of perfe-
ction, and consequently to get this reproche: *Thou art naked, poore & miserble, & foolishlie you esteeme your self riche.* For I hold that man to be very imperfect that thinks himself to be perfect; it is in a manner to say as said the father of the proud: *I Will lift vp my throne of the North side, and I shall be like to the highest.* Behold so much for the perfection acquired, & for the perfection to be acquired, it is a condition wherin are those that are most imperfect, seeing that at the most it suffiseth them to haue the will to arriue some time to it when they shall be purged of their faults, and for men to vant themselues to be riche, either by the goods, which they desire to haue, or pretend to gather, is expresse vanitie. And by this estate to think to draw themselues from all paritie, and to be se- *Friars in*
parated from the rest of the lay or *their*
secular people, it is in some sort to *estimatiõ*
*oßne*

sing that song blamed in te Ghospell: *I am not like other men.*

Sir, quoth the Hermite, I see well that neither you nor my self are too well versed in these scholasticall subtilities, this is a wrangling point which is not good but to intertaine disputations vpon the stooles; it is properly according the prouerb to contest with the Bishop for his crosiers staffe. But as I heard say heretofore, they put great difference betwene the state of perfection acquired, or to be acquired, & perfection it selfe, be it acquired or to be acquired. I know that this distinction will astonish you at the first sight, as it did terrifie me the first time that it sounded in my eares: but our maisters the Doctours haue farr more subtile distinctions which would deuide the very atomes. They say that he may be in perfection or perfect, that is not in the state of perfection, and that some are in the state of perfection which are farr from being in perfection or perfect.

And

And that it is fo, wee fee but too
many Monks, Religious men, & Paftours of very fcandalous and badd
liues who are neuertheleffe in the
ftate of perfection, and many lay
men of very holy conuerfation, and
moft compleat in their owne profeffion, & as it were perfect in their
œconomie, who are not for all that
in the ftate of perfection; yet our
Doctours after many debats do conclude, that it is farr better to be in
perfection without the ftate, then in
the ftate without perfection: Which
do much comfort the fimpler fort
who goe more round to worke, and
preferr their faluation to their reputation; in fort that it is much better
at all aduentures to be in the perfection of his eftate, then in the ftate of
perfectió, hauing nothing more fure
in all that matter then to fearche
his perfection in his owne profeffion, and to liue in peace according
the Counfell of the Apoftle. This
makes me think of thofe Polititians,

N

who seing themselues balanced
betwixt reasons of state, and the
consideratiōs of Religion, as it were
betweene the tree and the barke, do
leaue sometimes to support Religiō,
& run to succour the state; or els they
let the state perish to conserue Religion, whenas they should maintaine the one and the other if it were
possible, as being the two poles, &
the two hinges of all well ordered
common wealthes, giuing to Cesar
what belongs to Cesar, and to God
what belongs to God. Euen so amōg
these cōtestations, sometimes a man
doth quit the perfection of his estate
to run to the state of perfectiō, sometimes he doth not care for the state
of perfection to aspire to the perfection of his estate: but it happens
often to such bad Polititians, desi-
ring to conserue the state at the cost
& chardges of Religion, that they
loose the one & the other, as it doth
happen to vnskilfull Pilotes vvho,
to preserue their shipp and mar-

*Pollicie*
*& Reli-*
*gion are*
*the two*
*poles of*
*all well*
*gouerned*
*common*
*Wealthes*

chandife do make shipwrake of both
together: thofe that omitt to perfect
themfelues in a laicall ftate thinking
to aduaunce themfelues more in fpi-
rituall things in a Religious ftate, dif-
fipating their attētions, do not prof-
per in the one nor in the other, like *Romain*
vnto that Romain Senatour, who *Senatour*
being a very good man in his chardge
of Senatour, did beleeue that in making himfelf à Monke he would become an Angell, but he had fuch bad
fucceffe in the Monafticall exercifes,
that his Abbot one day faid vnto him:
My frend you left of to be a good Se- *Many*
natour to make a badd Monke. An *that are*
example which makes me remember *good in the*
an other very remarkable which is *World*
rehearfed in the life of faint Philipp *may be badd in*
Nerio fundator of the Oratorians of *Religion.*
Rome; he brought vp a yong Polo-
nian Prieft, called Francis Baffus, who
remayning for certaine yeeres vnder
his difcipline became a great prea-
cher, and full of rare qualities; at
length a temptation furprifed his

N ij

thought, perswading him that being but of the Oratorie, which is a Congregation of reformed Priests, who haue no other vowes, but such as the Church annexed to Priesthoode, that he was not in a state of so great perfection, as if he had made himself a Monke in one of the begging Orders. Notwithstanding any exhortation that S. Philipp made vnto him he yealded so much to this impression, that he neuer ceased to pursue his pourpose till such time as he was admitted to the Dominicans. Sainct Philipp did assist at his reception, & at his profession, & albeit the Friars did think to haue purchased a great deale of honour to their Order, by the organe of a subiect which seemed to them so worthy of consideration, yet the good Father, who loued him tenderlie, did nothing els but weepe during the solemnitie of these actiõs; and wheras the Dominicãs thought that it was because he lost one of the most famous worke men of his vigne-

yard: Ha! faith he, it is not that, for
charitie is not iealous, nor fubiect to
it owne proper intreft, I deplore only
the euident loffe of fo many vertus.
He was a Prophet, for he that was
fo prudent, & of fo good edification
in a Cógregation, in which he did not
beleeue to be in the ftate of perfectió
to be acquired, much leffe acquired,
did committ fo many fcandalls after
in the Regularitie, that he gaue much
paine and difcontent to his Order. It
is not alwaies the beft to afpire to
the fublimeft degrees, the moft dangerous trades are thofe that are exercifed in eminent places; the higher
the afcenfion be the heauier is the
fall. You muft not looke to be eminent wife, faith the holy word, but
keepe your felf in an humble feare;
*Do not affect fublimitie*, faith the
Apoftle, *but accommodate your felf to
the litle ones.* Let vs remember Iacob,
who whould not haften to goe with
Efaü, nor goe with a great pace
towards his Fathers houfe, but

choosed rather to goe soft & faire
after his children & his lambs,
meanely, but surely.

I do not intend by this discours
to diuert any man from embracing
the Regular life, contrarywise I do
counsell it as much as I may, as did
the great Apostle counsell chastitie,
wishing that all had beene Virgins
like himself. I know with what ana-
themes they are threatned that
diuert faithfull people from these
pathes of peace, & from the way of
the crosse, and that it is in this point
most of any other. that the Talion
law should be executed with rigour,
rendring to God in himself seruant
for seruant, & soule for soule. Also
I know it is of this state of life that it
is said, whosoeuer can embrace it let
him take it; yea, that it is good to
presse sweetly, without constraint,
such as be doubtfull and staggring
to put themselues in it, to see & tast
how sweet our Lord is. It is good I say
to giue them courage to lift them-

*It is not lawfull to disswade any from Religion.*

felues vp vpon this facred Palme, to
gather of it fruict: for no man can
denie without offending our holy
faith, & the difcipline of the Church,
that which S. Ambroife faid heretofore of voiled Virgins, fuch as
are now our Nuns, but it should and
may be alfo faid of the Regulars, that
they are a famous portiō of the flocke
of IESVS CHRIST. That which is
to be defired in all this matter, according my iudgment, (which is but
a fmall thing) is, that fuch as are in
this ftate of perfection, either to be
acquired as are the Regulars, or acquired, as are the Paftours, do not
looke difdainefullie, and as it were
ouer the shoulders on thofe that are
at their feete, no more then doth
the horfe troups of an armie defpife
the foote companies, becaufe that
thefe foote men, I would fay thefe
whofe fecular condition doth not
oblige them to fo great points of
perfection, may make themfelues
perfect and agreeable to God in

*Euery
mã in his
oVVne
profeffion
may
VVork his
faluation*

their owne profeſſion. And recipro-
cally, it is not fitt that ſuch as are not
in the ſtate of perfection do inſolent-
ly looſe the reſpect which is due to
thoſe that dedicated themſelues to
God by holy motions, and by the
profeſſion of a life ſequeſtred from
the world. This is neere the opinion
of that great Apoſtle, who would not
haue him that faſtes to deſpiſe him
that eates nor tax him of gluttony,
much leſſe would he haue him that
eates mock him that faſtes, and
reproach him of hypocriſie. And
albeit thoſe that lead a chaſte life are
in an eminent condition, as ſaith the
holy word, that continence cannot
be duely prized: Yet is the ſtate of
marriage holy & bleſſed by God,&
therfore ought to be reſpected, by
Virgins themſelues. It is good for a
man to humble himſelf in all things,
ſaith the holy Ghoſt, and not to aſpire to things which are too great,
or too ſublime. They muſt be honored that are in the ſtate of perfection,

fection, but thofe that are in the perfection of their eftate, do merit farr
greater commendation , according
that which the Apoftle faith , that
thofe who in the Paftorall chardge
haue learning ioyned to good life ,
are worthie of double honour: for to
that honour which is due to their
qualitie fhould be ioyned that which
is due to their proper merit.

*Good Pa-
ftours are
worthy
of double
honour.*

All thofe faire confiderations ,
faith Triftan, do not fatiffie my defire, which is to know in what doth
confift properlie this ftate of perfection acquired, or to be acquired.
That I may not lye vnto you, quoth
the Hermite, I am fo badd a fcholafticall Diuine, that thofe very termes,
which are not fo well knowne to me
as they are to fuch as haue them
euery day in their mouthes, and dif-
pute hard of thē vpon the Bench, do
feeme very fauage & ftrange to me.
This word of perfection attributed
to men doth aftonifh me, confidering
that the very Angels, which are in

the ſtate of ſubſiſtēce do not attribute
it to themſelues but turne their wings
ouer their eyes before the throne of
God, who is only good and perfect,
without euell and without fault. But
that I do not blame, or it may be
blaſpheme that which I do not well
vnderſtãd, without cenſuring the Authours, or authoriſing the cenſurers
of a Doctrine wherof I vnderſtãd ſo
litle, that the ſame litle is nothing; (if
none vpon earthe be without ſpott,
not a child of one day, ſaith the
ſacred Texte; if the ſtarrs be not nete
before him, who found diſorder
amongſt his Angels) who can iuſtly
alleage that he is in the ſtate of perfection, conſidering that to be perfect
& to be iuſt is the ſame thing, and
that no man liuing can iuſtifie himſelf before God? There is a certaine
*Prou.* 30. generation, ſaith the holy Ghoſt
*v.12.* which ſeeme to it ſelf, cleane & yet
is not waſhed from their fithlyneſſe:
I know not which it is, but whatſoeuer it be, we may compare it to the

Peacocke which attēd fo much to the looking glaffe of her round taile, that shee forgetts the deformitie of her feete. Thofe kind of people putts me in minde of that anciēt Hermite who imagined that he was an Angell, & fo threw himfelf into a well wherin he had died miferablie if his fellowes had not drawen him out, and cured him of his follie. Notwithftāding, that I may not take the firebrand where it burnes, I will tell you my opinion with the fimplicitie of a poore Mōke, who knowes better how to make Images then to decide a point of Diuinitie: I do think that the Regulars do fay they are in the ftate of perfeðion to be acquired, in as much as they haue choofen the Euangelicall Counfells as the fhorteft way to arriue to perfeðion, or els, becaufe that there ftate doth oblige thē to fearche for that perfeðion which is propofed vnto them by their Rules, which is, as it were, the creame of the Euangelicall Doðrine: in fort that

*The imaginatiō of an anciēt Hermite.*

*Vvhy are Regulars faid to be in the ftate of perfeðion to be acquired and*

Q ij

*Prelats in the sta te of per fectiō ac quired.*

their life should be nothing els but a perpetuall combat, a studie & exercise that aime at the acquisition of perfection. And they say that the Prelats & Pastours are in the state of perfection acquired, becaufe they are in eminent cōditions, whervnto none should be called but men confummated in Vertue & fciēce: Or els becaufe they are the fucceffours of the Apostles whom wee may not doubt to haue beene both very perfect, as being confirmed in grace, and alfo in the state of perfectiō: or otherwife becaufe they are obliged by the greatneffe of their dignitie, to be a patterne to the flock which are committed to them, by their good exāple: or alfo becaufe they ought in this state, to exercife not fimple & cōmon vertus, but heroicall and important vertus, wherof the greateft according the iudgment of the Gofpell, is to giue his owne foule for the faluatiō of his flock. This was alfo the Rule by which our Sauiour meafured the cha-

*Prelats the fucceffours of the Apostles.*

ritie of sainct Peter, before making him his Lieutenant in earthe, when he demaunded of him three times if he did loue him more then the rest, & that to his affirmatiue answeares CHRIST replied; *feede then my sheepe,* finding no greater proofe of loue then the exercise of this Pastorall charge.

If Monastical and Conuentuall persons, quoth Tristan be not in the state of perfection to be acquired but in respect of the obligation which they haue to make themselues perfect, & that the Prelats are not in the state of perfection acquired, but because they are obliged to be exemplar, me thinks the state of all Christians in generall is such, considering that our Sauiour in the Ghospell said vnto vs: *Be perfect as your Celestiall father is, Who doth make his sunne shine equallie Ypon the good and Ypon the bad, and povVre his raine VVithout distinction Ypon the land of the iust and the iniust.* And what? Kings & Potetastes, who as Conſtantin the great ſaid, are the exterior Biſhops, Magiſtrats, Good-men of houſes, and all thoſe that are in ſublimitie and Superioritie, are not they bound to giue good example to their inferiours, and to be a good odour to all men in I E S V S C H R I S T? After this manner they shall be in the ſtate of the perfection of Prelats, who are the Princes within the Church. And all Chriſtians that pre-tend to come to the perfection of their eſtate shall not they, by this deſire, as well as by vowes be in the ſtate of perfection to be acquired, as well as the Regulars?

I would be neere of your opinion in that, quoth the Hermite, if I did not feare to offend our Maiſters the Doctours, who haue in their hands the kees of the doctrine, who doe open that which no man durſt shut, who doe shutt that which no man durſt open, and who haue, the Em-pire of ſcience. But the reſpect which I beare to their opinions, which to

me are Oracles, to which I submitt my
owne iudgment , do make me renounce to my owne particular reason,
and follow the most common opiniō,
considering that the Apostle doe for-
bidd vs all contentions. But yet when
I consider with my selfe that the *The An-*
Angels of heauen were at variance *gels were*
*at varia-*
betweene themselues for the posses- *ce for the*
sion of the body of Moyses, I doe be- *body of*
*Moyses.*
leeue that men consecrated to God ,
either by the Sacerdotall character, or
by the Monasticall habit, who are
called in the Scripture the Angells of
the God of armies, may a litle contest
about the state of perfection, euery
one being glad , without preiudice to
humilitie and charitie, to magnifie his
owne ministerie, according the counsell of the diuine Apostle.

Passe for magnifying their ministerie , but to despise others and to pull
from those who according God &
man do both appeere, and are in effect more worthy then they ; that is
the thing which I cannot approuue,

quoth Tristan, for had you knowne
how the Conuentuall Friars did des-
chiffer vnto me the Ecclesiasticall
Clergie whom they call Seculars; how
they did depresse this condition, &
reprefent it vnto me not only to be
bafe but alfoe dangerous, and aboue
all the reft, how they did teare in pie-
ces the condition of you Hermites, I
beleeue that had you had the patiéce
of Iob you would breake out in choler againft them.

   For why should they take from
the Paftours, Priefts, Preachers, Doctours, Confeffours, Vicars, Chanós,
Deanes, Abbots, and Priours called
Commendataries, & from you Hermites the pretention to the ftate of
perfection to be acquired? Sir, quoth
Nicephorus, I did wind my felfe ex-
prefly about this fubiect without entring into it, to shun this rock againft
which you force me now to ftrick, all
that I can doe is, to fay with S. Paul,
that you conftraine me to paffe
through this danger and exceede a
                                    litle

litle the limits of moderation : *Be an-grie,* quoth the Pfalmiſt or according an other verſion : *Stirr and frett a litle, but do not ſinne.* Vnder this permiſſion *Pſal. 4.* I vvill ſay to God : *Lord put a ſentinell to my mouth, and a doore of circumſtances to my lipps, to the end that my tongue may not ʋtter VVords of precipitation , or of mallice.* I know it is vvritten, *thou ſhalt not ſpeake ill of the Gods:* That is to ſay, of eminent perſons, either in qualitie or ſanctitie, becauſe that greatnes and pietie doe make men approche to the Diuinitie. But albeit Socrates and Plato are my frends , and that I doe perfectlie honour the Regular Com-panies , yet the zeale of the truthe hath more power ouer me then all that. I will then ſay this word of li-bertie , not for my ſelf who am the meaneſt of all men, & the moſt con-temptible ( a title which one of the Prophets gaue to our Sauiour) but for ſoe many graue and venerable Eccle-ſiaſticall perſons which are in the ranke of the Clergie, and compoſe

P

the true Hierarchie of the Church inftituted by IESVS CHRIST, and whofe miffion & vocation is altogether diuine, that it is to pull away the faireft rofe of the crowne of foe many facred Priefts, to take from them the honour to be in the ftate of perfection, at leaftwife to be acquired, in which the Regulars doe not ftick to put their feruants, & the verie Nuns, as well thofe that fing in the Quire, as their maids feruants that looke to the bufineffe of the Conuent. Ah! where fhall Prieftly vnctiõ be placed, which make thofe that are adorned with it a holy and Royall people, if they make the ftate of it inferiour to the ftate of a fimple girle, who hath commaund to hold her peace, and no right to fpeake within the Church, or to fome porter or gardener of the Conuent? Thofe that approche to the Altar, to whofe words God doth make himfelf obedient,

who haue the kees of the kingdome of heauen, who doe bind and loofe,

who are the Magiſtrats of the Church,
who ſitt vpon the ſeate of iudgment
in the houſe of Dauid, and iudge the
twelue tribs of Iſraël, that is to ſay,
all the world; whoſe ſentences giuen
vpon earth are confirmed and ratified in heauen, whoſe hands bleſſed
and conſecrated doe handle the moſt
dreadfull myſteries of our Religion,
and who do that thing which the
Angells do adore; who haue power
ouer the Diuels, who diſpence the
Sacraments, and confer the grace of
God to all mortall men; thoſe Diuine men which S. Francis preferred
to the Angels, becauſe that one only
man of them doth make euery day
that which all the Angels in heauen
cannot doe. For to whom of the Angels was it euer ſaid, conſecrate my
body, and what thou ſhalt looſe on
earth ſhall be looſed in heauen? thoſe
men that are almoſt to be adored, &
that the Angells do reuerence and
call their fellow ſeruants to God,
ſhall they be the vnderlings of thoſe

P ij

which doe not merit (in consideration of their dignitie) to loose the
lachets of their shooes? Ah! Regulars, pardon me, it is the zeale
of the house of God which doth
gnaw me, it is the desire of his glorie and of his beautie which I see
dried vp in his principall members,
which doth transport me to tell
you, that you vse very discourteously
your elders the Ecclesiasticall Cleargie, whom (forsooth) you call Seculars, notwithstanding that by their
Clericall habit they haue deposed
the ignominie of the secular habit, &
that by the reception of their holy
Orders they haue renounced to the
desires of the world, and to all that is
profane in it. It seemes that you
would imitate Iacob, and supplant
them as if they were all Esaüs, but
know, that if you be Hebrewes, so are
they; if you be Israëlites, so are they;
if you be the seede of Abraham,
so are they; and I will say more for
them, that they are both more an-

*Secular is no fitt Epitetho for a priest.*

cient in the Church, and of a greater
ranke (witnesse the processions) & of
a higher dignitie, & of more eminēt
functions, I will say so much ( for it
is no time for a man to hold himself
vp when he is shaked and falling
downe) that their imployments are
more vtile and more necessarie then
yours, for the Church hath beene &
may be without Mōks, but it cannot
be without Pastours, without Vicars,
without Priests, without Doctours,
without Preachers : for if the salt be
moltē with what shall men salt? if the
candle be quinched how shall men
haue light? Perchance you will say
that you doe the same actiōs which
the Pastours doe, but in you it is but
in way of accessarie, in them principally; in you it is pleasure, in them
paine; in you it is of free will, in them
of necessitie; in you by way of recreation, and as passingers, in them
it is of dutie and office; in you it is
without chardge of soules, in them
with chardge, which make them to

*The Church may be without Monks but not without Pastours.*

*It doth not properly belong to Regulars to administer the Sacraments.*

be anfwerable for the foules, and fo
farr anfwerable that they shall giue
foule for foule, and bloud for bloud;
in you it is but in fome things, in
them in all things; in thē at all times,
in you when you pleafe, & that your
commoditie doth permit it; in you
fo that the feruice of your commonaltie doth marche before that of the
neighbour, in thē there is no exception; in you it is at certaine houres,
in them at all moments; you fight
as voluntaries, they as neceffaries;
you marche but in the wings of the
battle, they make the body of the
armie; they carrie the waight of the
heate of the day, and the cold of the
dew of the night, in fummer and in
winter, in fpring time and in harueſt,
without rule in their dyet, without
affurance in their fleepe. Of feuen
Sacraments you adminifter but two,
and the one of them which is the Eu-
chariſt, but at your eafe, within your
houfes, without carrying it to the
fick in the heate of the funne, in

froſt, in ſnow, in raine and in *Th life*
tempeſt, at all houres of the day & *and exer-*
of the night, and all dayes of the *ciſe of*
yeere through the dirt & incōbraces *poore Pa-*
of the cities and townes, through *ſtour exa-*
the woods and the meere, through *cribed.*
the mountaines and the vallees,
through the ſtones and the moores
of the fields. And the other Sacrament which is that of pennance you
adminiſter, when you are prayed, &
particularly called vpon, and as
pleaſeth your Superiours, who haue
as great care of the conſeruation of
their owne ſubiects, as they haue of
the ſick, for whom they are not an-
ſwerable. But the Paſtours by obligation ought to keepe ſtill neere the
ſick, to preſſe them to enter in fauour
with God by the Sacrament of recō-
ciliation, to preache vnto them in
ſeaſon and out of ſeaſon, to the end
to make them think of their ſaluation, which is part of their owne ſaluation, as being bound to giue
account to the Prince of Paſtours

the Bishop of our soules I E S V S
C H R I S T, of his sheepe committed
to their Vigilance. As for Marriage,
Baptisme & Extreme-Vnction, they
are things which you do not medle
with all ( they are for the gleaners )
no more then you medle with Con-
firmatiõ and Order which you leaue
for the Bishops. This you shew your
prudéce,& declare that you haue eatē
both butter and honny,which make
you reiect the least and choose the
best , & that you know how to make
vse hansomely of the fanne which se-
parate the corne from the chaffe,and
pretious things from vile and base
things. You doe not snuff your lamps
but with golden snuffers, & you doe
not take the coales as the Seraphim
of the Prophet, but with gilt tongs.
The rodd of Moyses doth not please
you, becaufe sometimes it is turned
to a serpent and deuoure, or doth
worke dreadfull and rude effects :
The rodd of Aaron fitts you best,
becaufe it ingenders nothing but
flowres

*Isaia* 7.
*V.* 15.

flowres & fruict. Euen so you know
how to pull the rose without touching the thornes, to gather the hony
without feeling the sting of the bee,
to eate the kernell of the nutt & cast
away the shell, & to doe as children
doe when they gett bread & butter,
licke away the butter and leaue the
breade. To cooperate to the saluatiō
of soules without taking chardge of
them, is properly to take away the
creame and leaue the curd. It is an
admirable thing to see that such as
gouerne the people will not take
chardge of them, and such as haue
chardge of them and are answerable
for them, cannot haue the gouernement of them. And with all these delicatnesse & spirituall allurements,
they are in the state of perfection,
and those who like Gyants do grone
vnder the waters, that is to say, vnder
the chardge of the people, who are
the waters of the sea of the world,
shall be out of perfection? Truely I
am faithfull, and beleeue all that the

*Friars ta-
ke the
profit &
leaue the
paine for
the priests*

Q

Church doth beleeue, and if the Church beleeue that, I beleeue it alfo, but not without captiuating my vnderftanding to the obedience of faith.

Would not you thinke that thofe good people vould faine add a cubite more to their ftature, or to fpeake otherwife, would faine extoll their owne eftate putting betwixt thē & the Paftours inferours to Prelats, their lay brothers? For if thofe be in the ftate of perfection, and not the Chanons, Paftours and other Ecclefiafticall perfons of the Clergie, to what height do they raife themfelues, placing their feruants and their cookes before thofe that are the Maifters, the Fathers, and the Doctours of the people? What? and if they preferr to them fimple vailed girles, yea the lay fifters, is it not to deftroy the law of nature, and the gouernement of the Church, which in all kind of fashion hath declared women kind inferiour to men? If the iniquitie of a man is

preferred to the well doing of a
woman, what good can a woman do,
suppose shee made miracles, which
may be compared to the greatnesse
of Priesthoode? Would not men
laugh at the impertinèce of him that
would giue the title of Excellence to
a poore man that asketh almes from
doore to doore, & would but thou
a gètle man of note, or a Magistrate.
The Regulars, and principally the
begging Orders haue baggs which
speake dayly for them asking almes,
and yet they must haue so many Pa-
ternities and so many Reuerences
giuen them; and the Pastours and
Priests shall be without honour, and
vnworthelie treated so farr forth as *Great in-*
to be putt in a ranke and state in the *equa-*
Church, more low then that of the *lities.*
Friar seruants of the ¡Reüerend Fathers. But yet amongst themselues
they know well how to keep the best
place for Priesthoode, and keepe the
Conuers or lay Brothers in the humilitie and basenesse of seruitude, di-

Q ij

stinguishing themselues by these termes Fathers and Brothers, albeit all
of them are Brothers and children of
one Order & of one habit, making
profession of one and the self same
rule, liuing vnder the same obseruance and the same vowes, & all of them
as well priests as others not permitted
heretofore to take any other title but
that of Brother, which is well obserued by the most humble and most
moderate of them. And I pray you,
is priesthoode an other thing in the
Regulars thē it is in the Clergie? Is it
an other charracter, an other Order,
an other power, for being vnder a Ca-
puce, vnder sandales, vnder a scapu-
lar, or vnder a claspe? Is it more eminent so then vnder a surplice, vnder a
sutane, and vnder a corner capp? Certes we are now come to the time
wherin the last are the first, and the
first are put in the last ranke. In your
opinion to plant cabbage, to washe
disheste, to carrie a bag, to keepe a
doore, to snuff lamps, to patch, ha-

*Friars he-
retofore
had no
other de-
nomina-
tion but
that of
Brother.*

bits, the ordinarie exercife of the lay brothers of the Conuents, are they employments comparable to that of the Paftours, who do confecrate the body of the fonne of God, who difpence the merits of his bloud in the Sacrament of pennance, who do baptife, who do annoinct the fick, who do marrie thofe that are called to that holy yoake, and do fuch other Paftorall functions?

*The functions of Paftours.*

Verely, quoth Triftan, you reftore them well what they lent you, and their bill of exchange is well payed in the fame coyne. If I had not knowne that you are well verfed in thefe matthers in controuerfie, I would fay that you are a Prophet, and that you haue heard part of that which they faid to me, to diuert me from being an Hermite, or of the fecular Clergie, fo well you rehearfe the particularities of that which they infinuated to me. For me thought I heard them fay, that all deuotions cōpared to Religious deuotion is but orpin cōpared to gold, &

glasse compared to a diamant, & that they are like to those Romā scarlets, which seemed all stayned and decolored, when they were put neere that piece of purple of Tyr and Sidon, *The functions of Regulars inferiour to that of Priests & Pastours.* which for the excellencie of it was sent to the Emperour. For ought I see then their state of perfection doth not proceede from their functions, which are inferiour in greatnesse, in eminencie, in vtilitie, in necessitie to that of Priests and Pastours, but from their vowes; it is so held commonly *Schoole diuinitie disputes of all matters, & moues as many questions as it doth decide.* in the schooles, quoth the Hermite, but seing this sort of Theologie doth maintaine as much dispute and controuersie as it doth decide,& stirrr vp as much as it doth resolue, no point of faith so sacred on which she doth not moue questions and frame difficulties; of this point which is but of gouernemēt, I think that without offending Religion, wee may speake problematically, submitting alwaies most humblie & most absolutely our particular reason & iudgment to the

iudgmēt of the vniuerfall Church, &
to the holy fea Apoftolike, the firme
& fundamentall ftone, againft which
errours, which are the gates of hell,
may not preuaile. I fay then after
this proteftation, which may ferue
me as a buckler againft the plotts of
calumnie, that if the ftate of perfection to be acquired doth confift in
vowes, the Priefts of the Clergie, who
are in the Hierarchie of the Church,
ought to be admitted to it: For they
make two folemne and indifpenfable *Priefts*
vowes of chaftitie and obedience, an- *make*
nexed to their holy Orders. And if *two folo-*
*lemne*
they do not make the vow of poo- *vowes.*
uertie, it is becaufe that being not in
Commonaltie, as the Regulars are,
but as the Apoftles were, difperfed *Priefts*
amongft the people as the falt of the *difperfed*
*amongft*
earth, it would be impoffible for *the people*
them to obferue it in that manner *do imit-*
that the Conuentualls do. But if it *tat the*
*Apoftles.*
pleafed them to goe to the Countrie,
and to fee in the villages to what ex-
tremitie of neceffitie are the poore

Paſtours brought, they would haue
occaſió to ſay that it is much eaſier to
vow pouertie , as the Regulars doe,
then to practiſe it as the Paſtours do.
The Regulars cannot ſing but in very
*The plea-* cloſe Quires, they cannot ſay Maſſe
*ſat life of* but with ſiluer challices , with nete
*Regulars*
*in theſe* veſtments & with parfums, they can-
*Countries* not ſleepe but in hoate celles , they
cannot eate but very nete meate, pro-
per & well ſeaſoned, in gilt and painted Refectories , accompanied with
pleaſant lecture , hauing after euery
refection a full houre of recreation,
they cannot walke but in faire gar-
dēs all laced with flowers & arrouſed
with fontaines, they cannot goe but
vnder Cloiſters & well couered from
ſunne & raine , they cánot make their
aſſemblies but in Chapters well po-
liſhed and very lightſome, they cannot ſtudy but in faire and ample Bi-
bliothekes , in ſomme he that would
learne a thouſand litle ſecrets for the
commoditie of mans liuing, let him
take the paines to conſider the Mo-
naſticall

nasticall & Conuẽtuall life. In steede
that the Pastours of the Countrey *The life of a Country Pastour.*
(for those of the citie are a litle better
prouided, but yet are they also in
trouble ouer head & shoulders) are
loged in cabanes, like the grott of
Bethleem, exposed at all times to the
iniurie of the aire, they lie vpon the
straw and vpon the ground, they are
nourished like clownes, without con-
uersation, without consolation, they
haue much paine and litle Vnction,
they are ill loged, ill attired, ill payed,
ill assisted, miserable in their Churches, in their ornamẽts, in their load-
gins, in their houshould-stuffs, & in
all other things. And for all this, the
Regulars amiddest all commodities *Priests held to be riche though otherwise more poore thẽ Friars.*
haue the glorie of the state of pouer-
tie, and the Pastours in all necessities
and want are held for riche, & to be
dispossessed of the state of perfection,
which properlie doth not consist so
much in the vow of pouertie, as wee
said before, as it doth in the practise
of voluntarie, & Euangelicall pouer-

tie, which is when a man felling all
that he hath doth giue it to the
poore, without affurance of any prop
or the help of any commonaltie, of
which wee fee very few exãples. For,
to forfake thirtie or fiftie pound rent
to caft himfelf into a Monafterie that
hath a thoufand pound rent, and to
haue his part of the fame with thirtie or fortie other Monks, I do not
fee that fuch a leape is any thing
dangerous: but to leaue great reuenewes in the world & diftribute them
to the needie to put himfelf all alone,
& without aydein a naked mẽdicitie,
as did the Apoftles, who referued
nothing of all the goods which the
firft Chriftiãs brought & laid at their
feete, is a practife that is as rare as it
is excellent, & fome Regulars might
be found which would call it temeri-
tie, although it be the true manner of
the pouertie counfelled in the Ghofpell, in which our Sauiour, who did
counfell it, did place perfection. But
let vs make this matter agree, a Reli-

gious man that is proprietaire shall be
deepelie in imperfection, becaufe he
doth contrarie to his vow, and yet in
vertue of the fame vow, he shall be
faid to be in the ftate of perfection : *It is not*
and a fecular mã who doth diftribute *all one
to be in*
all his goods in almes to follow our *the ftate*
Sauiour, by this renouncement of his *of perfection &*
goods shall be without doubt well *to be per-*
aduanced in perfection, and yet shall *fect.*
not he be in the ftate of perfection?
For my part I muft acknowledge at
one time both my ignorance, and
the grofeneffe of my vnderftanding,
that cannot get out the connection,
of this admirable diftinction, which
me thinks cannot fubfift but by this,
*effe rationale*, wherof there is fuch
great debate betweene the Philofo-
phers, and by feparating by the
thought the ftate of perfection, as
they feparate in man, the animal part
from the reafonnable. But perchance
I shall expound my felf better by this
example.

A good Paftour of a village, who *An exãple.*

*of a poore Pastour.* was (as almoſt all of them be) in the perfection of pouertie in his owne eſtat, receiued to his poore cabane a Conuentuall Friar, that should be a foote by his rule, but in effect was well mounted he entertayned him according the short extētion of his power & of his meanes. Wodden & earthen disheſſe were his beſt mouables, new ſtraw was his beſt bedd, the ground was his moſt aſſured bedſtead, two brones made his fire, and the middeſt of the place was his cheminie, a block was his chaire, his table was two plāks ill ioinct together, held vp by ſome ſticks made in forme of a treſtle, ill faſtned ; for the reſt he was ſo auſtere that ſcarce he did weare any lynnen: he found neuertheleſſe ſome napkin; for the vſe of table-cloathes were as much vnknowne to him, as they are to the Capucins. The Religious mā who had occaſiō to eſteeme more of his good reception then of his good cheere, and of the Paſtours goodwill then of the effects of it, drew

a purſe out of his ſleeue, well furniſhed with a kind of mettall which
is the rule and meaſure of all things,
yet forbidden in the rule of Conuentuall Friars; With this he thought
to entertaine himſelf in all places: but
this village was as ill furniſhed with
things neceſſarie, as was the houſe of
the good Paſtour. He was therfore
conſtrayned to content himſelf with
a kind of pottage and ſome pulſe, but
to take this leane refeation he vſed
many faſhions, & diſpoſed himſelfe
with much delicatneſſe and proprieties; he drew from his pocket a caſe
wherin there was a ſiluer ſpoone, a
forke of the ſame mettall, & a knife
with a haft alſo of ſiluer. The good
Paſtour who had a pleaſant witt, and
knew a litle more then his Proſne or
ſonday Sermons ſeing this Regular
ſumptuoſitie ſaid to the friar, Father,
you and I would make one good
Mõke, for you would make the vow
of pouertie, and I would keepe it.
This blow of the beck or mouth did

not hinder the good Friars teeth, who did not loose a whitt of his appetit for it. Now tell me, I pray you, who before God had the merit of pouertie, he that was really poore, and vsed hospitalitie, or he that was not poore but in vow, with so much delicatnesse? For my part, quoth Tristan, I beleeue that as he is much commended in the Scripture that might transgresse, and do euell, & did it not: Euen so he, that putting himself in the state of perfection, & doth not tend to it, but lett himself fall into imperfections, shall be whipt with many stripes. And as the merits of Regulars, are very great whē they do their dutie well, so are their faults very notable when they faile therin. They are like the figgs of the Prophet, either all good, or all badd, which makes me remember an other example.

*An exāple of a man of qxality & of his seruant.* A man of qualitie that liued very dissolute, being touched with repentence of his sinnes did cast himselfe

into a Monasterie: and a seruant of
his much fearing God following him
in that retrait of the world, was receiued in the same Monasterie in qualitie of a lay brother. What hapned?
the Maister that knew his owne iniquitie, and that saw without cease his
sinnes before his eyes, became so
humble by that consideration, that
he became a good Religious man,&
the seruant contrarywise seing himself entred into the portion of Saints
in a good riche Monasterie, became
so insolent & so delicate that nothing
could content his vanitie and delicatnesse: He that was his Maister in the
world seruing him with all sort of
charitie and cordialitie he did checke
and rebuke him like a slaue; which
the other did indure with incredible
patience, by which he gayned heaue,
and the seruant became so arrogant
and so presumptuous, that in the end
his sottisnesse and disorder did oblige
the Comonaltie to take the habit frō
his back and chase him away ignomi-

niouflie like a knawe, that became as
infupportable as he was incorrigible.
Euen fo the fame funne which melt
wax, doth harden dirt, & Regularitie
which is inftituted as a holy Acade-
mie, to guide thofe that put themfelues in it, as becommeth, to perfectiő,
was caufe of the imperfection of this
feruāt, who had done far better if he
had remayned in his firft ftate of life.
And indeede folitude, which the
Scripture and experience doth teach
vs to be fo proper to draw to it the
Spirit of God, is often caufe of the
ruine of fuch as caft themfelues in-
toit without iudgment. Loth, that
was fo wife and fo chafte in an infa-
mous citie infected with the moft
horrible diforder that fenfualitie
could commit, became diffolute and
inceftuous in the defert. And fome
Regulars do fay that they find none
fo tractable nor fo humble as thofe
that were before eminent in dignitie
in the world, nor none fo arrogant &
harder to be gouerned then thofe
that

that coming from bafe defcent, do fee
themfelues as the Affe of Ifis in the
Embleme, honored becaufe of the
reputation of fainctitie which there *The Friars*
habit doth gett vnto them, and that *much ho-*
without it, neither by their birth, *nored by their ha-*
nor by their merits should they be *bits.*
any thing efteemed. It is to thofe that
it belongs to fay with the Pfalmift, my
cordes or knots, that is to fay, my
vowes do me great honour, & they
are the moft excellent portion of my
inheritance. And if eafe & commoditie doe carrie them to immodera-
tion, then may they fay that their iniquitie doth proceed frō their fatneffe
and from the abondance of their
breade, being no more fubiect to the
labour & trauaile of other men. And
if proprietie do flide amongft them,
then is all loft, for that is the finne
of Achan which draw malediction,
vpon their heads.

For ought I can gather out of your
difcours, quoth Triftan, the ftate of
perfection acquired in which are all

S

Prelats doth confift in the eminencie
of their dignitie & character: and the
ftate of perfection to be acquired,
wherin are the Regulars, doth confift
in their three vowes, in which they
put the effence of Regularitie. That
is the opinion of fome Doctours, faith
Nicephorus, but in this fubiect all are
not of the fame opinion. And that
it is fo, the Regulars themfelues do
make diftinctions of the ftate of perfection amongft them, and although
their Prouincialls and Generalls who
with the do hold the place of Bishops
and Archbishops in their particular
Hierarchie, are but fimple Priefts for
their character, & for thefe dignities
vnknowne in the Church foure hundred yeeres agoe, neuerthelesse do
they repute them to be in the ftate of
perfection acquired as Prelats are, &
they giue them alfo the name of Prelats, which doth paffe to the Abbots
by they Titulars or Comendataries,
and to many others in the Court of
Rome, which haue no Prelatship but

*Supe-*
*riours of*
*Regulars*
*are but*
*fimple*
*Priefts.*

by name only, hauing no chardge of
foules nor any functiō in the Church.
Some Regulars do make this ſtate of
perfection acquired to deſcend yet
more low, to their Priours, Gardiens,
Miniſters, Correctours, Rectours &
other Superiours of particular Conuents, although they denie it to Cu-
rats & Paſtours of Pariſheſſe, it may
be with as litle reaſon as they do attribute it to themſelues. For I do not
think that I ſhould ſwarue much frō
the iudgment of the truthe and of the *Paſtours*
Church, if I ſhould ſay that the Pa- *as great*
ſtours are at the leaſt as great & grea- *as the Su-*
ter then the Superiours of Regular *periours*
houſes, as hauing many more ſoules *of Regu-*
vnder their gouernement then they *lar hou-*
haue; for where is that Monaſterie *ſes.*
which hath fortie or fiftie thouſand *S. Euſtaſe*
Friars in it, as there is a Parish that *in Paris*
hath ſo many Pariſioners within it *for one.*
precinct, and which is more, holding *The Hie-*
the ſame rāke in the firſt, principall & *rarchie of*
moſt anciēt Hierarchie of the church, *the Cler-*
which is that of the Cleargie, that *gie is the*
                                    *principall*
                                    *& moſt*

S ij

the Clauſtrall Priors and Superiours
do hold in the ſecond and new Hierarchie, of Regulars? There do not
want alſo ſome famous Doctours
which haue placed the Paſtours in the
ſtate of perfection acquired; as the
Prelats are, becauſe they haue the
ſame obligation which they haue ( &
in ſome ſort more ſtrict then they, becauſe they are the immediat Paſtours
of the people that put their liues in
hazard for the ſaluatiō of their flock.
For it is in that that the high point
of perfect charitie doth conſiſt, and
conſequentlie the topp of acquired
perfection . Wherfore then ſaith
Triſtan, do they caſt you ſo farr of (I
ſpeake of you Hermites) from the
ſtate of perfection to be acquired? It
is without doubt, becauſe you do not
make the vowes nor the profeſſion
of any rule. Sir, ſaid Nicephorus, I did
alwaies diuert my ſelf from that blow,
deſiring rather to ſpeake of thoſe that
are of ſome worth in the Church thē
of vs poore ſolitarie people, who liue

*Marginal notes:*

*Ancient of the Church.*

*The Regulars make a neẅ Hierarchie by thēſelues.*

*Perfect charitie in the Paſtorall chardge.*

in obscuritie, among the dead men of
the world, of which there is no mention in the Catalogue of the liuing:
but seing you, by your inquiries do
present them vpon the stage, who by
the profession of their life ought to
hide theselues, to imitate our Sauiour
in his hidden life, it is requisit that I
speake vnto you of a thing that is
not, as of a thing that is. Know then
that as there are Conuentuall friars
and Conuentuall friars, so are there
Hermites and Hermites. There
is not almost any Order of Regulars
wherof there is not a Reformation, in
sort that such as liue according the
strict obseruance of their rule are called the Reformed, and the others the
Mitigate, a name truely too milde,
which doth iniustly flatter their disorder and relaxation. For mitigation
doth presuppose some temperature
of austeritie in the rule by Apostolicall authoritie: But not so manifest
infraction of the vowes of obedience and pouertie, as that which is

*Good &
bad friars
as there
be good
and bad
Hermites*

knowne to be, and which the holy
sea did neuer authorize. In like manner there are Hermites vacabonds &
voluntaries, who haue neither house
nor home, children of Belial, who
will haue no yoke nor subiection,
who liue after their owne fancie, and
as the Psalmist saith, who do walke in
their owne desires, & passe their liues
according the inconstant affection of
their harts: *Cloudes vvithout vvater* &c. Iuda.
*carried about of vvindes*; and for whom
the tempest of darknesse is reserued,
& perpetuall vnquietnesse in punishment of their instabilitie. These kind
of people are Hermites only by habit,
& not by life, by apparence and not
by effect, people without approbatió,
slaues to their proper wills, and not
only farr from the state of perfectió,
but also from the perfection of their
estate, if a condition so vncertaine &
so irregular may be called an estate.
But there are other Hermites, who
are in the stabilitie of a setled life,
true followers and children of those

firſt Anacorites, who like shining
ſtarrs lightned the heauen of the primitiue Church by the liuely beames
of their holy vertues, whoſe memorie
shall neuer perish, but will be ſtill cō-
ſerued freshe, in the very decline of
time, and in the old age of the world
They are men that ſtick like Iuie to
the ſtock & wall of the Eccleſiaſticall
Hierarchie and like the vigne that
ioyne faſt to the elme tree. Thoſe mē
do ſequeſter themſelues from the
world by a locall ſolitude, to the end
to harken more attentiuely in the
mentall ſolitude that, which God
shall ſpeake to their harts. They
haue choſen the beſt part with Marie, but in that ſort that when the neceſſitie of the neighbour or the ſer-
uice of the Church doth call them,
they imitate theſe wiſe maydens, as
ſaid that ancient Hermite, who neuer
departed their fathers houſe, but to
carrie water when their neighbours
houſe was ſurpriſed with fier. Charitie
& neceſſitie being the only two cau-

ses which might and ought iustly in-
terrupt the sweet repose of their
silence. These Hermites are ab-
solutelie and entirelie subiect to the
Ordinaries, who are the Bishops,
they may be iudged by their Offi-
cialls, they are subiect to the visits of
their Generall Vicars and Archdea-
cons, and they acknowledge also for
their Superiours & Pastours, the Pastours in whose Parishesse are situated
their Hermitages. These do receiue
their holy habit at the hands of the
Prelats, or of such as are deputed by them to cloath them with
the Ecclesiasticall benedictions & ceremonies, they goe not out of the
Diocese without leaue, they establish
themselues in their dwellings with
the permissiō & leaue of the Bishops
*A good*      and Pastours, & also with the cōsent
*example*     of the neighbouring people, they
*for Regu-*   do not begg but with the licence of
*lars.*       the Pastours; in somme they depend
in all things of their wills. If they be
Priests, they make the two solemne
                              vowes

vowes annexed to holy orders, betwene the hands of the moſt Reuerend Bishop who doth confecrat them, which are the vowes of chaſtitie and obedience, and that they may not loofe alfo the merit of the vow of pouertie, befids the practife which they make of it by begging, many of them do vow it betwene the hands of the Prelats or of their Officers, bereauing themfelues of all proprietie, and referuing but the fimple vfe of the almes which are giuen them, readie to quitt the fame at the firſt command of thofe whom the heauēs hath giuen them for Superiours. What think, you Sir, are thofe men in the ſtate of perfeƈtion to be acquired as are the Conuentuall friars? I would think they are, quoth Triſtan, but the Conuentualls do not think it, who do not put the ſtate of perfeƈtion in the vowes only, but do require befids that they be made vnder fome of the Rules approued by the Church.

T

Truely, quoth the Hermite, that
is extreme rigour; but I pray you,
what better rule can wee haue then
that of the Scripture, then the examples of the Patriarches & Prophets,
who liued in the wildernesse, then
that of our Sauiour fasting in the de-
sert, transfiguring himselfe vpon mõt
Thabor, and passing a great part of
his life vpon the most retired mountaines; then that of his fore-runner
saint Iohn Baptist, then that of saint
Paul the first Hermite, of great saint
Anthonie, of saint Hilarion; in somme, of so many thousand Anacoretes, whose names writtē in the booke
of life are glorious in heauen, and
blessed on earthe? Can any man
doubt but these excellent Anacoretes were in the state of perfection
although they did not make the
three vowes vnder any rule? In good
sooth, a man must haue extraordinarie patience to indure these inequali-
ties; and to speake with the sacred
Amante; *The children of my mother*

*fought againſt me,* & *put me, in the gard of the* ✝*ignes.* It did not appertaine but to S. Paul to diuulge his owne proper praiſes with good grace, becauſe he did know how to referr all very properly to God, when he ſaid: *Not I, but the grace of God in me, by* ✝✝*hich I am that which I am: but I did menage it well,* & *in ſuch ſort as it was not inutile in my hands.* I dare neuertheleſſe praiſe my ſoule in God as ſaith the Pſalmiſt, to the end to reioice the curteous, and tell you, that if ſo be the Regulars do ſay they are themſelues in the ſtate of perfection, for hauing made the three vowes vnder a certaine Rule betwene the hāds of their Superiours, who are but ſimple Prieſts, I think to haue right to ſay the ſame, hauing receiued my habit by the hands of a Bishop, made profeſſion of the ſame vowes betwene his hands, vnder ſuch rules & Conſtitutions as pleaſed his charitie to preſcribe vnto me, and hauing ſo ſubmitted my will to his, that I haue no other deſire but to obey

*The Supe-riours of Regulars are but ſimple Prieſts.*

him : When he bids me goe, I goe,
when he bids me come, I come,
shuning no occasion by his com-
maundement to do seruice according
my power to the sheepe of his folde,
with the permission of the Reuerend
Pastours; In this sort I do visite the
sick in these quarters , I confesse
those that come to me , being for

*Regulars should haue the approba- tion of the Bisshops.* that purpose approued by the Ordinarie, I do administer to them the
holy Eucharist when they, come to
the Oratorie of this house; I goe from
village to village teaching the Christian doctrine to children, Catechi-
sing the rude, Euagelizing the poore,
instructing the great ones, & making
exhortations to them according the
tallent which God gaue me. If in con-
sequës of this they do me some good,
it is according the Apostle, to reepe
temporall things hauing sowen spirituall things; and what I get ouer and
aboue what is necessarie, I giue it to
the poore. Loe how I passe ouer this
life, caring litle if I be in the state of

perfection or no, so that I correct my
selfe of the imperfections which are
vnworthie of my estate, litle curious
of those titles which the Cenobiticall
friars do attribute to themselues, to
be the Coadiutours of the Bishops, *Specious*
to be Apostolicall men, to leade the *titles*
*which*
Apostolicall life, to be men sent by *the Regu-*
the sea Apostolike to supplie the de-*lars giue*
*to them-*
fects of the ordinarie Pastours, to be *selues.*
troupes of succour, to be the props
of the Church, to be the pillars and
firme colomnes of her which is herselfe the colome and fundation of
truthe, knowing that all these qualities
are annexed to Priesthoode, sith that
Prelats ordering Priests do call them
their cooperators & fellow workers,
the supporters of their Pastorall Order, and many other very honorable
names. The condition of a Monke is
truely very venerable, so is that of
Conuentuall friars, of Religious men;
let them call them as they will, and
as they please, or in one word, that
of Regulars or of Friars, (albeit the

Regular Clerkes do apprehend as much to be called this laſt name, as they would to handle a burning cole without tongs. ) But for my part, I beleeue that all men of good vnder-standing will alwaies eſteeme as much *The con-* and more the condition of a Prieſt as *dition of* any of thoſe.  Notwithſtanding to *a Prieſt is* *ſo be eſti-* shun the obſtinat contention which *med as* the Apoſtle doth ſo expreſly forbid, *much or* *more, as* it is better leaue them in the arbitra-*any other* ble poſſeſſion of the ſtate of perfe-*ſtate in* *the* ctiõ, ſeing that by their tongues as by *Church.* the tongue of Hercules Gaulois the Deſtinies do ſpinne the reputation of men, nothing being well done, according the Caſtilian prouerb, but that which proceedeth out of a Monke or friars head.

# *THE RESPECT*
*and honour vvhich is due to the Order & dignitie of Priesthood declared and proued by the authoritie both of holy Scripture and of the ancient Fathers of the Church.*

YOV haue feene gentle Reader in the precedent Difcours how the Regulars to extoll themfelues are not content by their rigorous cenfures to giue a fentence of exclufion againft Hermites and Secular Priefts (as they terme them) from the ftate of perfection in which they place the meaneft of themfelues, in vertue of their three vowes of pouertie, obedience and chaftitie, but alfo proclaime them to be bafe and of no

confideration. And that you may
iudge whether that be conformable
to the holy Scripture & to the Doctrine of the ancient Fathers of the
primatiue Church, I thought good
to produce here a few authorities of
the one & of the other, prouing the
dignitie and authoritie of Priefts.

God inftructing the children of
Ifraël how to decide all controuerfies
that should arife amongft them, faid:
*Thou shalt come to the Priefts of the Le-*
*uiticall ftock, and to the iudge, that*
*shall be at that time: and thou shalt aske*
*of them, vvho shall shew thee the truth*
*of the iudgment. And thou shalt do*
*vvhatfoeuer they, that are prefidentes of*
*the place, vvhich our Lord shall choofe,*
*shall fay and teach thee according to his*
*lavv; and thou shalt follovv their*
*fentence: neither shalt thou decline to the*
*right hand nor to the left hand. But he*
*that shall be proude, refufing to obey the*
*commandement of the Prieft, vvhich at*
*that time miniftreth to our Lord thy God,*
*& the decree of the iudge, that man shall die.*
                                          What

*Deut.*17.

*The high*
*Priefts*
*chiefe*
*iudge of*
*all con-*
*trouerfies*

What could be said more to shew the dignitie and authoritie of Priests then whofoeuer would not obey them, nor ftand to their iudgment should die; but that is not all.

The Prophet Malachias fpeaking of the couenant which God made with the tribe of Leui faith to the fame purpofe: *The lipps of the Prieft* Mala.2. *shall keepe knowledge, and the law they shall require of his mouth: becaufe he is the Angell of God.*

The Ecclefiafticus teaching à man how to carrie himfelf firft tovvards God,& after towards the Priefts faith Ecclef.7. thus: *In all thy foule feare our Lord, & sā-*
*ctifie his Priefts.* And after; *Honour God withall thy foule, & honour the Priefts.*

Saint Peter vvho vvas a Prieft himfelf fpeakes thus to Priefts: *You* Pet. 2. *are an elect generation, a kingly Prieft-*
*hood, a holy Nation a people of purchaffe.*

Was it not to Priefts that our Sauiour himfelf faid: *Whatfoeuer you* Matt. 18, *shall binde vpon earth, shall be bound alfo* v.18. *in heauen: and vvhatfoeuer you shall loofe*

V.

*vpon earth, shall be loosed also in heauen.*

Many other passages might be produced out of holy Scripture to proue
the dignitie of Priests, & the respect
which is due to them, but these shall
suffice at this time so you consider
them well: for you see that to Priests
God gaue power to iudge and decide
all controuersies, and that he gaue
sentence of death vpon any that
would not obey them. You see moreouer that they are called the Angells of God, that all men were commanded to honour and respect them,
that they are called an elect generation, a holy nation, and that their
Priesthood is a Royall dignitie. And
which is more then all that, you see
how CHRIST gaue them the power
to loose and bind vpon earth, and
that their act therin is ratified in heauen.

Now rests to shew what the ancient Fathers of the primitiue Church
do say of Priesthood, and in what

efteeme Priefts were in their time, in
which there was no fpeech neither of
Benedictins which are the Anciēteſt
in our Latin Church, and began the
yeere 529. nor of Dominicans, nor
Francifcans, which began the yeere
1209. nor yet of Auguftins, nor Car-
melites as they are approued by the
Church, no nor of Bernardins, much
leffe of the reſt which now, flourish
in the Church vnder feuerall names,
but all was ruled and gouerned by
Priefts.

    Sainct Ignatius Martyr and the
third Bishop of Antiochia after S.
Peter commaunding all lay perfons
to be fubiect vnto, and reuerence *Epiſt. ad*
Priefts and Diacons faieth thus: *Dia-* *Smyrn.*
*cónos reuereamini Vt ex Dei præcepto mi-*
*niſtrantes*: Honour yea the Deacons
as miniſtring by the precept of God. *Epiſt. ad*
And after: *Enitimini chariſsimi fubiecti* *Epheſ.*
*eſſe Epifcopo & Presbyteris & Diaconis.*
*Qui enim his obedit, obedit Chriſto.* My
deareſt doe your beſt to be fubiect
to the Bishop, and Priefts, and Dea-

cons, for he that obeyeth thefe
obeyeth CHRIST.

*Epift. ad*
*Philip.*

Sainct Policarp difciple to faint
Iohn the Apoftle faieth: *SubieEtieftote*
*Presbyteris, & Diaconis, ficut Deo, &*
CHRISTO. Be yea fubiect vnto the
Priefts and Deacons, as to God and
CHRIST.

*Conft.*
*Apoft.l.2.*
*c.8.*

*c.35.*

*c.38.*

*Priefts*
*are fpiri-*
*tuall Fa-*
*thers.*

Sainct Clement difciple to faint
Peter, faith: *Presbyteris fi affiduè in ftu-*
*dio docendi verbum Dei laborauerint, fe-*
*ponatur dupla etiam portio in gratiam*
*Apoftolorum Chrifti, quorum locum te-*
*nent, tanquam Confiliarij Epifcopi & Se-*
*natus Ecclefiæ. Si de parentibus fecundum*
*carnem ait diuina Scriptura: Honora pa-*
*trem & matrem vt benè tibi fit. Et qui*
*maledicit patri aut matri, morte mo-*
*riatur: Quanto magis de Patribus Spiri-*
*tualibus verbis Dei moneamur, honore &*
*charitate eos profequi, vt beneficos & ad*
*Deum Legatos. Quanto anima corpore*
*præftantior eft, tanto eft Sacerdotium re-*
*gno excellentius.* Let there be a double
portion, referued for the Priefts in
honour of the Apoftles of CHRIST,

which shall haue laboured in teaching
of the word of God diligently,
whose places they enioye, as Coun-
sellours of the Bishop, and the
crowne of the Church. They are the
Councell & Senat of the Church.
If the holy Scripture saith of carnall
parents: Honour thy Father and thy
mother, that it may be well with thee.
And whosoeuer doth curse his father
or his mother, shall die : how much
more shall we be admonished by the *Priests*
words of God, of our Spirituall Fa- *are spiri-*
thers, to respect them with honour *tuall*
and charitie, as beneficiall to vs and
Legats to God? How much more noble the soule is then the bodie, so
much more excellent is Priesthood
before à kingdome. And S. Ignatius *Epist. ad*
addeth: *Sacerdotium est omnium bono-* *Smyrn.*
*rum, quæ in hominibus sunt apex; qui*
*aduersus illud furit, non hominem igno-*
*minia afficit, sed Deum & Christum Ie-*
*sum primogenitum, qui naturâ solus est*
*summus Sacerdos Patris.* Priesthood is
the ornament of all things, vvhich

are in men; whosoeuer doth rage against it, he doth not dishonour a man, but God & Christ Iesus the first begotten, who by nature is the only high Priest of his Father. The Apostles write by saint Clements penne: *Si Reges inuadens supplicio dignus iudicatur, quamuis filius vel amicus sit, quanto magis. qui Sacerdotibus insultat: quanto enim Sacerdotium regno est excellentius, cum regendarum animarum officio præsit, tanto grauiori supplicio punitur, qui aduersus id aliquid temere fecerit, quam qui aduersus regnum*: If he that setteth on a king is iudged worthy of punishement, although he be his sonne or his frend, how much more should he be blame worthy that insulteth ouer Priests. For by how much more Priesthod excelleth a kingdome, when it doth by office gouerne soules, by so much more greater punishment is he to be afflicted, who shall rashly doe any thing against it, then he who hath offended a kingdome.

*Const. l. 2. cap. 2.*

*The prerogatiue of Pastours.*

*Presbyteri sunt* ( saith saint Ignatius ) *Epist. ad Trallen.* *conceſſus quidam & coniunctus Apostolorum Chorus, ſine his Eccleſia electa non eſt:nulla ſine his Sanctorum Congregatio, nulla Sanctorum electio. Quid Sacerdotium aliud eſt, quam ſacer cætus, Conſiliarij & aſſeſſores Epiſcopi.* Priests are indeede a certaine Aſſemblie, and vnited quier of the Apoſtles. Without *The Church cannot be without priests.* theſe the Church is not choſen, without theſe there is no Congregation of Saincts,nor electiō of Saincts. What elſe is Prieſthood, then an holy Aſſemblie Conſellours and Aſſiſtants of the Biſhops?

Saint Anacletus Pope liuing in this *Epiſt. 2.* age & made Prieſt by S. Peter, ſaith: *Iniuria Sacerdotum pertinet ad Chriſtum, cuius vice funguntur.* The iniurie done vnto Prieſts, appertaine to Chriſt, whoſe place they ſupplieth.

Sainct Chryſoſtome treating of *Homil. 5. de verb. Iſaia: Vidi Dominum.* the ſame matter and comparing a Prieſt to a king, ſaith : *Ne mihi narres purpuram neque Diadema, neque veſtes aureas, vmbræ ſunt iſthæc omnia, verniſ-*

*que flosculis leuiora. Ne inquam mihi nar-*
*res ista, sed si vis videre discrimen quan-*
*tum absit Rex à Sacerdote, expende mo-*
*dum potestatis vtrique traditæ, videbis Sa-*
*cerdotem multo sublimius Rege sedentem.*
*Regius thronus rerum terrenarum admi-*
*nistrationem sortitus est, nec vltra pote-*
*statem hanc præterea quicquam habet au-*
*thoritatis : Verum Sacerdoti thronus in*
*cælis collocatus est, & de cælestibus negotijs*
*pronũtiandi habet authoritatem. Quis hæc*
*dicit? ipse cælorum Rex: Quæcũque ligaue-*
*ritis super terrã, erunt ligata & in cælis, &*
*quæcunq; solueritis super terrã, erũt soluta*
*& in cælis. Deus ipsum Regale caput Sacer-*
*dotis manibus subiecit, nos erudiens, quod*
*hic princeps est illo maior.* Speake not
to me of these things, but if thou wilt
see the power giuen to them both,
thou shalt see the Priest sitting much
higher in dignitie then the king. The
throne of a king is chosen of the ad-
ministratiõ of earthlie things: neither
hath he any other authoritie besides
this : but to a Priest a throne is placed
in heauen, & he hath authoritie to
iudge

iudge of heauenly businesse. Who saieth this? The king of heauen him-selfe. Whatsoeuer yee shall bind vpon earth shall be bound also in the heauens: and whatsoeuer yee shall loose on earth, shall be loosed in the heauens. God hath subiected to the hands of the Priests the Regall head, teaching vs, that this Prince is grea-ter then that. The same Authour speaking further of this matter saith:

*Sacerdotibus datum est, vt potestatem ha-* *Chryf. l.3.* *beant, quam Deus neque Angelis neque* *deSacerd.* *Archangelis datam esse voluit. Neque enim ad illos dictum est: Quæcunque alli-gaueritis in terrâ, erunt alligata & in cæ-lo, Et quæcunque solueritis in terrâ erunt soluta & in cælo.* It is giuen to Priests, that they shall haue power, which God would haue giuen neither to Angels nor Archangels. For it is not said to them: whatsoeuer you shall bind vpon earth shall be bound also in heauen: and whatsoeuer you shall loose on earth, shall be loosed in hea-uen. The power of binding which is

X

in Princes, is only ouer bodies, that of Priests ouer soules, and extendeth to heauen.

*Chrysost.*
*ibidem.* A continuation of the same Au-thour: *Habent & terrestres Principes vin-culi potestatem verum corporum solum: id autem quod dico Sacerdotum vinculum ipsam etiam animam contingit atque ad cælos vsque peruadit.* Terrene Princes also haue the power of fetters, but of the body only; but that which I say, the bonds of Priests toucheth the sou-le it self, and passeth vnto the heaues. This is the doctrine deliuered by CHRIST, so expounded both by the Greeke and Latine Church.

*Chrysost.*
*Homil.2.*
*super 2.*
*adTimot.* Item, In an other place he saith: *An ignoras quid sit Sacerdos? Angelus vtique Domini est, non ex se ipso loquitur, si de-spicis, non illum despicis sed Deum qui illū ordinauit.* Art thou ignorant what is a Priest? he is verily the Angell of our Lord, he doth not speake of himself, if you despise, it is not him that you despise, but God who ordayned him.

And in an other place: *Monachorum*

*certamen ingens & labor multus est: Ve-* *Chrys.lib.*
*rum si conferre quis volet instituti illius fu-* *de Sacerd.*
*dores cum rectè administrato Sacerdotio,*
*certè tantu esse inter duo illa discrimen com-*
*periet, quantu est inter priuatu & Regem.*
The conflict and labour of Monks is
great: but if any would confer the paines & labour of that institution with
priesthood duely administred; truely
he shall find as much difference betwene them both as betwene a king
and a priuat man. Loe how farr he
putts à Priest beyond a Monke or
Religious man.

Saint Hierome who was himself a *S. Hier.in*
Religious man saith: *Sacerdotibus ac* *Malac.3.*
*Leuitis honorem debitum deferamus: quod*
*qui non fecerit, Deum fraudare & sup-*
*plantare conuincitur.* Let vs giue due
honour to Priests & Leuites: which,
who will not do is manifestly proued
to defraude and supplant God.

The same Authour in an other place *Epist.ad*
saith: *Mihi ante Presbyterum sedere non* *Heliod.*
*licet, illi si peccauero licet tradere me Sa-*
*thanę in interitu carnis.* It is not lawfull

X ij

for me to sitt before the Priest, for
him it is lawfall if I sinne, to deliuer
me vp to Sathan, to the destruction
of the flesh.

Saint Ambrose in his learned trea-
tise of the dignitie of Priests salutes
them with those venerable Epitets:
*Audite me, beatissimi Patres, etsi dignum
ducitis, sanctissimi Fratres, audite me
stirps Leuitica, germen Sacerdotale, pro-
pago sanctificata, Duces & Rectores
gregis Christi. Et paulò post. Honor &
sublimitas Sacerdotalis, nullis poterit com-
parationibus adæquari, si Regum fulgori
compares, & Principum diademati, longe
erit inferius, quam si plumbi metallũ, auri
fulgorem cõpares: quippe cum videas Regum & Principum colla submitti genibus
Sacerdotum, & exosculatis eorum dextris
orationibus eorum credunt se communiri.*

Heare me, most blessed Fathers, &
if you take it in good part, most holy
Brothers, heare me you Leuiticall
stock, you Sacerdotall branch, you
sanctified race, you leaders and gouernours of Christs flock. *And a litle*

*Lib. de dig.Sacer.*

*It is due to Priests to be called Fathers.*

*after*; The honour and fublimitie of
priefthood cannot be equalized by
any comparifons, if you compare it
to the fplendor of kings, & to Princes crownes, that will be farr more
vnequall to it, then if you did compare the mettall of lead to the
fplendor of gold : for you fee the
neckes of kings and Princes bowed
downe to the knees of Priefts, and
hauing kiffed their right hands they
beleeue that they are fortified and
ftrengthned by theirprayers.

S. Chryfoftome wrote fix bookes
of the dignitie and power of Priefts
putting it aboue all kings, Princes
& Potentats of the earth, and in his
third booke he faith thus : *Sacerdo-*
*tium ipfum in terra quidem peragitur,*
*fed in rerum cæleftium claffem, ordinem-*
*que referendum eft, atque id quidem me-*
*rito; quippe non mortalis quifpiam, non*
*Angelus, non alia quæuis creata potentia,*
*fed Deus ipfe ordinem huiufmodi difponit.*
Priefthood truely is exercifed in
earth, but it is to be referred to the

ranke and order of celeftiall things,
and that truely very worthely; becaufe it is no mortall man, nor Angell nor any other created power,
but God himfef that doth difpofe &
appoint this order.

*Sacerdotibus ficut Epifcopis*, inquit
fanctus Ifidorus, *difpenfatio Myfterio-*
*rum Dei commiffa eft : præfunt enim*
*Ecclefiæ, & in confectione diuina cor-*
*poris & fanguinis confortes cum Epif-*
*copo funt, fimiliter in doctrina populorum*
*& in officio prædicationis*. To Priefts
as to Bishops the difpenfation of the
myfteries of God is committed : for
that they beare the rule in the
Church and in the diuine confecra-
tion of the body and bloud of Chrift,
they are conforts with the Bishops
likewife in teaching the people, and
in the office of preaching.

Philippus de Hareing a Religious
and a moft learned Abbot in his
worke which he wrote foure hundred
and fiftie yeeres agoe : *De dignitate,*
*fcientia & iuftitia & continentia Cleri-*

*Lib. 2. de*
*Diu. Off.*
*cap. 7.*

*torum,*doth highly commend the Regulars, but in euery chapter he preferreth the Clergie before all Regulars, though himfelf was one : In his 17. chapter he faith thus: *Noſtrum eſt nouiſsimum locum eligere nec ad altiora volatu præſumptuoſo nos ipſos erigere.* It is our partes(that is to ſay,the part of Religious men) to chooſe the laſt place, and not by a preſumptuous flight to eleuat our ſelues to higher things. And in his 17.epiſtle he ſaieth, that from all the bounds and limits of the earth, all antiquitie did euer extoll the Clericall order, and euer gaue it amongſt the other Orders the principall ranke and degree, and though by diuine diſpoſition a Soildiour or Ruſtique do excell in ſanctitie, yet the Clergie man in excellencie of Eccleſiaſticall dignitie; and although the Clergie man as we do ſometimes, decline to worldly things, and to the weake & poore elements, yet their Order declineth not in authoritie. Thus he: To which I muſt

add this other paſſage of ſaint Iero-
me which doth occur vnto me :
*S. Hier in* *Communi Presbyterorum Concilio Ec-*
*ep.adTıt.* *cleſiæ gubernabantur* :   The Churches
were gouerned by the common
councell of Prieſts ; And I muſt not
forget this paſſage of Bellarmin
who was a Ieſuit and a Cardinall :
*Belar.l.2.* *Tria ſunt Eccleſiæ membra præcıpua, pri-*
*cap. 5. de* *mum eorum eſt, qui in ſtatu perfectionis*
*Gemitu* *adeptæ eſſe dicuntur, qui ſunt Epiſcopi*
*Columbæ.* *Ecclesiarum Principes, & Magiſtri, qui-*
*bus adiungimus Presbyteros qui ſunt mi-*
*nores Sacerdotes,atque eorum adminiſtros.*
There are three chiefe members of
the church;the firſt of them are thoſe
that are ſaid to be in the ſtate of perfection acquired, which are the Bishops the Princes and maiſters of the
churches, to which we ioyne the
Prieſts, who are the inferior Prieſts,
and their aſſiſtants.   And the ſame
Authour in the preface of his ſecond
booke, *De Monachis* ſaith: *Diſſeruimus,*
*libro ſuperiori de Epiſcopis &   Clericıs, id*
*eſt,de prima & nobilıſsima parte corporis*
*Eccleſiaſtici:*

*Eclesiastici*: We haue difcourfed in the former booke of Bishops and Clergie-men that is to fay, of the chiefe & noblest part of the Ecclefiafticall body.

The Councell of Trent fpeaking of the Hierarchie of the Church faith thus: *Si quis dixerit in Ecclefia Catholica* <sup></sup>*non effe Hierarchiam Diuina ordinatione inftitutam quę conftat ex Epifcopis, Presbyteris & miniftris anathemafit.* *Can. 6:* Whofoeuer will fay that in the Catholike Church there is not a Hierarchie inftituted by diuine ordinance, which confifteth of Bishops, Priefts & Minifters, let him be curfed. Loe, You fee that the Councell makes no mention here of Regulars, which by all likelihoode it would haue done, if they had bene of this Hierarchie.

To be briefe in all thefe paffages, both out of Scripture & out of the Fathers which are not the tieth of the paffages which might be produced for this matter, the Reader will fee but litle or no mention of Re-

Y

gulars; and in the litle mention that
is made of them by late writers, he
shall find that Priests, both for dignitie & office are still preferred to
them, and are put in a farr higher
ranke then they; which confidered,
he may conclude with him felf that
the propofitions fpecified in the De-
dicatorie Epiftle of this Tretife, are
of a new ftamp forged by the Regulars themfelues: For had there bene
any fuch prerogatiue graunted to
them by God or by his Church, who
can imagine that all ancient writers,
fpeaking of all the members & dignities of the Church would omitt to
fpeake of them, & of thefe preroga-
tiues which now they challenge to
themfelues? Notwithftáding I do not
wish Priefts(but counfell the côtrarie)
to take any pride of this, nor fett the
leffe by Regulars, but acknowledge
them to be a noble & profitable
portion of Gods Church, and as fuch
to embrace & cherish them; and rather receiue iniuries patiently of

them , then offer them any, remem-
bring that saying of the Apostle:
*If you bite and eate one an other : take* Gal.5.
*heede you be not consumed one of an* 5.15
*other.*

FINIS.